*Portraits of the Eighteenth Century*

BERNARDIN DE SAINT-PIERRE
*An engraving after the painting by Lafitte*

# PORTRAITS
# OF THE
# EIGHTEENTH CENTURY

*Historic and Literary*

## VOLUME II

*by*

C. A. SAINTE-BEUVE

*With an Introduction by Ruth Mulhauser*

ILLUSTRATED

FREDERICK UNGAR PUBLISHING CO.
*NEW YORK*

Translated by Katharine P. Wormeley

14015

# CONTENTS

# ILLUSTRATIONS

# Abbé Prévost.

## 1697–1763.

## Abbé Prévost.

THE depressing effect produced upon us by great libraries, wherein are gathered the works of so many dead and gone generations, has often been likened to the effect of a cemetery peopled with tombs. It seems to us that the similitude is never more marked than when one enters such a library, not with a vague curiosity or a too zealous desire to be at work, but impelled by a special purpose to do homage to some chosen name, and to fulfil a vow of studious respect to a memory. If, however, the object of our study, and in a certain sense of our devotion, on that day, happens to be one of the few illustrious dead whose words fill the ages, the effect cannot be the same; in such case the altar appears too luminous; it constantly gives forth a powerful glamour which dispels the listless sense of regret and suggests thoughts of duration and life alone. Nor is mere mediocrity calculated to give birth to a sentiment so subtle; the impression that it causes is altogether sterile, and resembles weariness or pity.

But we are more especially impelled to ponder, and innumerable thoughts that go to the root of all moral

3

science suggest themselves to our minds, when we have to do with one of those men, half famous and half forgotten, in our memory of whom the light and the shadow blend, so to speak,—some one of whose works still lives and stands in a bright light which seems to illuminate the dust and obscurity of all the rest,—when we approach one of those meritorious and once brilliant celebrities, of whom there have been so many in the world, beautiful to-day in their silence, with the beauty of a ruined cloister, half-dismantled, deserted, and falling in decay. Now, apart from a very small number of resplendent and fortunate names, which, by the opportuneness of their coming into the world, by the constant favour of their stars, and also by the immensity of the things human and divine which they were the first to reproduce with matchless splendour, retain the immortal privilege of never growing old—apart from these, this dismal but inevitable fate is common to all those in the ranks of men of letters who bear the title of talent and even of genius.

The most unanimous and most fully deserved contemporary admiration can do nothing to forestall it; neither the most humble resignation, nor the most obstinate resistance, hastens or delays the inevitable moment when the great writer, the great poet, enters the shadow of posterity; that is to say, when the generations whose soul and joy he was have abandoned the stage to others, and he himself falls from the fervent

ABBÉ PRÉVOST

*From the copper engraving by G. F. Schmidt*

and confused laudation of his fellow-men to the indifference, not ungrateful but respectful, which is in most
cases the final consecration of the completed monument. Doubtless some pilgrims of genius, as Byron
calls them, continue to visit it and take one another's
places about it until the end; but society as a whole
has turned its attention elsewhere and frequents
other scenes. A very large part of the renown of
Walter Scott and Chateaubriand is already buried in
darkness.

These reflections have occurred to us in connection
with Abbé Prévost, and we believe them to be among
those which, at the present day, would most naturally
occur to him, if he could view himself in the past.
Not that, during his long and laborious career, he
ever actually obtained that something which is called
glory; rather than glory he had a widely diffused
celebrity, and obtained the honours due to talent,
without rising to true genius. He was, however, if
we converse for a moment with him in the vaguely
affable style of Louis XIV,—he was, take him for all
in all, a happy and dexterous genius, of extensive
learning and lucid intelligence, with a boundless memory, inexhaustible in product, equally at home in serious and entertaining narrative, renowned for the charm
of his style and the liveliness of his descriptions, whose
works, the instant they appeared, were, as was said
at the time, "the joy of sensitive hearts and ardent
imaginations." In truth, his novels had a prodigious

vogue; they were imitated on all sides; sometimes
continuations of them were written under his name,
as was the case with *Cléveland.* The booksellers
called for "something by Abbé Prévost," as they had
formerly called for something by Saint-Evremond. He
did not often leave them in distress, and his works,
including *Le Pour et Contre* and the *Histoire Générale des Voyages,* go far beyond a hundred volumes.

Of all these estimable productions, among which
there is a goodly share of original creations, what is
there left that people remember and read to-day ? If,
in our younger days, we ever found ourselves within
reach of some old family library, we may have read
*Cléveland, Le Doyen de Killerine,* or the *Mémoires
d'un Homme de Qualité,* which our uncles or our
fathers recommended to us; but, failing an opportunity of this kind, people esteem them on faith and do
not read them. And if by any chance we do open
one of them, we never go on to the end, any more
than with *Astrée* or *Clélie;* the style is too antiquated
for our taste, and repels by its intricacies instead of
attracting. *Manon Lescaut* alone still triumphs by favour of its artful negligence; its unadorned freshness
and bloom are immortal. This little *chef-d'œuvre,* to
which Abbé Prévost gave birth on a day of good fortune, and without more trouble assuredly than to the
numberless episodes, half real, half imaginary, with
which his works are strewn, holds his name for ever
above the flood of the years, and gives him a sure

foothold in the ranks of the élite of writers and invent-
ors. *Manon Lescaut* exists for ever, and despite the
innumerable revolutions in taste and fashions which
eclipse her real power, she may safely maintain with
respect to her own fate that languishing and playful
indifference with which we are familiar in her. Some
people perhaps, in whispers, call the book a little
weak, and far too simple in metaphysics and in subtle
distinctions; but when the modern seasoning has
evaporated, when the tiresome garish splendour of the
present day has faded away, that incomprehensible
girl will still be the same as ever,—simply the fresher
by contrast. The writer who drew her for us will
continue to be appreciated in our calmer moments, as
one who attained the most incredible depths of passion
by means of a simple, natural tale, and who, in that
same tale, employed his pen in a way dear to certain
hearts in all ages. He is therefore of those whom
oblivion will never submerge, or, at all events, not until that time when, the taste for sound and healthy
things having altogether vanished, we need no longer
regret to die.

Abbé Prévost's open and kindly countenance, the
decorous refinement of his language, afford us glimpses, unknown to him, of a profoundly tender inward
sensitiveness, and, beneath his moral generalisations
and the multiplicity of his tales, it is easy to detect
the traces of an exceedingly painful personal experience. In truth, his life was the first of his novels, and

in some sort the material of which all the others were constructed.

He was born, near the close of the seventeenth century, in April, 1697, at Hesdin in Artois, of an honourable, even noble, family; his father was *procureur du roi* for the district. Young Prévost obtained his early education at the Jesuits' school in his native town, and later went to the Collège d'Harcourt, in Paris, to add to his knowledge of rhetoric. He received particular attention on account of the rare talents which he exhibited betimes, and the Jesuits had already lured him as far as the novitiate, when, on a certain day (he was sixteen years old), being assailed by worldly ideas, he dropped it all to enlist as a simple private. The last war of Louis XIV was drawing to a close; commissions in the army had become very hard to obtain; but he cherished the hope, common to many young men, of being promoted at the first opportunity; and as he himself said afterward, in reply to those who spoke slightingly of that part of his life, he "was not so ill-provided in the way of birth and fortune, that he might not hope to make his way successfully." However, as he grew weary of waiting, and as the war came to an end, he returned to La Flèche, to the Jesuit fathers, who welcomed him with all sorts of caresses. He was seduced thereby almost to the point of definitively entering the Order, and he composed an ode in honour of Saint François Xavier, which has not been preserved. But a new fit of restlessness seized him, and leaving the convent once more, he resumed the profession of arms, "with more distinction and enjoyment," he says; which means with a commission, a lieutenancy or something else. Details concerning this critical period of his life are lacking.[1] We have but a few words from himself, which afford sufficient food for thought, and which disclose the complexion and tendency of his sentiments during the tempests of his early youth.

"Several years passed," he says [in the profession of arms] ; "I will admit, in the words of M. de Cambrai, that, as I was of an ardent temper and keenly alive to pleasure, wisdom demanded many precautions which I overlooked. I leave my readers to judge what, from twenty to twenty-five years of age, were likely to be the passions and sentiments of a man who wrote *Cléveland* at thirty-five or thirty-six. The unfortunate end of a too tender connection led me at last to *the tomb;* that is the name that I give to the venerable Order in which I buried myself, and in which I remained for some time so truly dead that my parents and my friends had no idea what had become of me."

This "venerable Order" of which he speaks, and which he entered when he was about twenty-four, was that of the Benedictines of the Congregation of Saint-Maur; he stayed there five or six years, engaged

---

[1] In some book of *ana,* I forget the title, the story is told that Prévost having fallen in love with a lady, presumably at Hesdin, his father, who viewed the intrigue with an unfavourable eye, went to the lady's door one evening, to berate his son as he came out, and that the latter, in the sudden rush that he made to escape, jostled his father so roughly that the old gentleman died from the effects of the blow. If this is not an atrocious libel, it is a fable, and Prévost has enough catastrophes in his life without this.

in religious duties and in assiduous study; we shall
see him take his leave of it in due time.

And so that ardent nature, far too easily led by successive impulses, was unable to settle upon anything;
it was one of those flexible natures which can readily
be worked upon and swayed, but not held fast. He
had drawn from the sincerity of his own character,
and had developed, by virtue of the excellent education
he had received, a multitude of honourable, delicate,
and pious sentiments, equally adapted, it would seem,
to do him honour among men and to sanctify him in
retirement, and he was unable to decide upon either
course of life; he tried them both in turn, again and
again; remorse tended to perpetuate his vacillation;
the world, its pleasures, the diversity of its events, of
its pictures, the tender quality of its attachments,
became, after a few months' absence, irresistible
temptations for that prematurely weaned heart; and,
on the other hand, no one of those delights availed to
satisfy him at the moment of enjoyment. Then re-
pentance and a sort of ever-increasing irritation against
an always triumphant enemy drove him back at the
first onset to the other extreme, when the austerity of
the religious life speedily allayed his zeal; and after a
fresh struggle, in a contrary direction to the last, he
quitted his cell anew for a life of adventure. A
fragment of a letter has been preserved, written to
one of his brothers at the beginning of his sojourn
with the Benedictines; it relates to his life at Saint-

Ouen, about 1721. In it he describes this moral condition of his mind in pleasing, ingenuous touches which show clearly enough that he is not cured.

" I know the weakness of my heart, and I realise how essential it is for its repose that I should not apply myself to barren studies which would leave it parched and listless; if I wish to be happy in a religious life, I must retain in all its strength the impulsion of grace which has led me thither; I must be incessantly on my guard to keep at a distance whatever might weaken it; I see only too plainly every day of what I should once more become capable if I should lose sight for one moment of the great rule, or even if I should look with the slightest favour upon certain images which present themselves only too often to my mind, and which would possess only too much power to lead me astray, even though they be half-effaced. How hard it is, my dear brother, to recover a little strength when one has become accustomed to one's weakness; and how much it costs to fight for victory when one has long found delight in allowing one's self to be conquered ! "

Abbé Prévost's ideal, the dream of his youth, the model of virtuous felicity which he set before himself, and which was long postponed by his too impulsive errors, was a mixture of study and of society, of religion and decorous pleasure, the vision of which he dwelt upon with delight on many occasions. Once engaged by indissoluble bonds, he strove that every image too exciting and too favourable to desire should be carefully excluded from this somewhat chimerical scheme, in which duty was the gauge of sensual pleasure. One loves to expatiate with him, in many a passage of the *Mémoires d'un Homme de Qualité* or of *Cléveland,* upon those meditative walks, those readings in solitude, among the woods and streams, an abbey

always in the background; upon those moral conversations between friends which " Horace and Boileau,"
he tells us, "have set down as one of the most delightful elements of which they make a happy life to
consist." His Christian doctrine is mild and temper-
ate, as we see, accommodating, but unsullied; it is a
formal doctrine "which ordains at the same time the
practice of morality and belief in the mysteries"; yet
it is in nowise merciless, but founded on mercy and
on love, with a tinge of atticism; for he had passed
through the novitiate with the Jesuits, and had dis-
solved the connection with entire outspokenness, although with ever-grateful memories.

Boileau, whom I reproach myself for not having
praised warmly enough on this point as on several
others, was inspired by this spirit of steadfast piety
in his Letter to Abbé Renaudot. The admirably
drawn character of Tiberge, in *Manon Lescaut,* shows
all its enlightenment and all its virtues combined in
action. Amid the upheavals of his youth and the
material exigencies which were the result of them,
Prévost clung with a constant effort to this moral
rectitude, instinct with humility, and he deserved to
reap its fruits in his riper years. He retained throughout his life an affectionate regard for his first masters,
and the impressions that he received from them never
left him. It is possible, if the truth be told, that
philosophy, then in its infancy, fascinated him momentarily in the interval between his departure from

La Flèche and his joining the Benedictines, and that the character of Cléveland represents some personal reminiscences of that period.   But at bottom he was of a submissive disposition, not prone to argue, thirsting for light from above, inclined to spiritual things, and extremely credulous of the invisible; an intellect of the type of Malebranche in metaphysics; one of those minds which, as he says of his Cécile, "fly with amazing ardour of feeling toward an object which is uncertain; which aspire to the joy of loving boundlessly and immeasurably," and which think themselves impeded by the " darkness of the senses " and the weight of the flesh.   He obeyed an impulsion of that mystic voice when he joined the Benedictines; but he relied too much upon his strength, or perhaps, because he was exceedingly distrustful of himself, he made haste solemnly to forbid himself any second offence of backsliding.   The sacrifice once accomplished, he recovered his lucidity of mind.   "I realised," he says, "that this ardent heart of mine was still burning under the ashes.   The loss of my liberty afflicted me to tears.   It was too late.   I sought consolation for five or six years in the pleasures of study; my books were my faithful friends, *but they were dead like myself.*"

In truth, study, which, according to his own expression, has charms of its own, but charms of a melancholy sort, and always the same,—especially that kind of study, serious, interminable, monotonous

as a penance, with no admixture of original work and
of lighter themes,—might suffice for the life of a Dom
Martenne, but not for that of Dom Prévost. To be
sure, he was fitted for it, but so he was for too many
other more alluring pursuits. He was employed in
several establishments of the Order one after another:
at Saint-Ouen, in Rouen, where he had a polemical
discussion with a Jesuit named Le Brun, in which he
had the advantage; at the abbey of Le Bec, where,
while delving deep in theology, he made the acquaintance of a great nobleman, retired from Court, who
perhaps gave him the idea of his first novel; at Saint-
Germer, where he taught the humanities; at Evreux,
and at the Blancs-Manteaux in Paris, where he
preached with wonderful success; and finally at Saint-
Germain-des-Prés, a sort of capital of the Order, where
his talents were applied, last of all, to the *Gallia
Christiana,* of which almost an entire volume is said
to be by him. At this time, according to all appearances, he began to write the *Mémoires d'un Homme
de Qualité,* while, by virtue of the multitude of interesting anecdotes, which he told marvellously well, he
was the delight of the nightly vigils of the cloister.

A trivial grievance, which was simply a pretext,
was the ostensible cause, but it was in reality his
thoughts, the course of which turned him more
strongly than ever in other directions, which led him
to solicit at Rome his transfer to a less rigorous
branch of the Order; his choice fell upon Cluny. His

petition was granted; the brief was to be promulgated
by the Bishop of Amiens on a stated day; Prévost relied
upon it, and early in the morning made his escape
from the convent, leaving letters for his superiors in
which he set forth his reasons. As the result of an
intrigue of which he knew nothing down to the very
last moment, the brief was not promulgated, and his
position as a deserter became so uncomfortable that
he could see no other resource than flight to Holland.
The general of the Congregation did, to be sure, make
a friendly attempt to reopen the doors to him; but
Prévost, having already started, was not informed of it.

This momentous step once taken, he had to accept
all the consequences of it. Rich in knowledge, inured
to study, expert in languages, bursting, so to speak,
with reminiscences and adventures from his own ex-
periences or learned from others, which he had silently
stored away in his mind, he seized his ready and
flowing pen, never to lay it down again; and by his
romances, his compilations, his translations, his journals, his anecdotes, he easily opened for himself a
large place in the literary world.

His flight was in 1727 or 1728; he was thirty-one
years old, and he remained away from France at least
six years, partly in Holland and partly in England.
In the early days of his exile appeared the *Mémoires
d'un Homme de Qualité,* also a volume translated
from President De Thou's *Universal History,* [1] and a

[1] [De Thou wrote in Latin.—Tr.]

*Histoire Métallique du Royaume des Pays-Bas,* also a translation. *Cléveland* came next, then *Manon Lescaut,* and *Le Pour et Contre,* the publication of which, begun in 1733, was not finished until 1740. Prévost had returned to France when he published *Le Doyen de Killerine,* in 1735. As this is not a full inventory, nor even a general criticism of our author's numerous writings, we will touch only upon those which will help us to paint him.

The *Mémoires d'un Homme de Qualité* seems to us —apart from *Manon,* which, in truth, is simply a charming episode by way of postscript—seems to us beyond controversy the most natural, the most sincere, the best preserved of the romances of Abbé Prévost,—the one in which, being as yet unsurfeited with the romantic and the fictitious, he confines himself more to what he has felt inwardly or observed in his immediate neighbourhood. Whereas, in his later romances, he loses himself in broad expanses of territory and affects outlandish characters which he clothes with hybrid peculiarities, and whose verisimilitude, which was questioned even then, cannot sustain a glance to-day,—in these *Mémoires,* on the other hand, he sketches for us to perfection, and without fixed design, the manners and sentiments of fashionable society toward the close of the age of Louis XIV. The satirical side, which Le Sage prefers, is altogether lacking here; the vulgarity and ribaldry which constantly made themselves manifest beneath that fair exterior have no

place in Prévost's work.    I always omit *Manon* and
her Paris of the time of the "System," [1] her Paris of
vice and of filth, in which ordure of all sorts is heaped
up, although only incidentally, be it remembered, and
although strewn about with no design to make it
prominent, and illumined from end to end with the
same reflection of sincere feeling.    But the society
ordinarily pictured in Prévost's works is a decorous
and polished society, observed at a little distance by
a man who, after certainly having had a taste of it,
had regretted it bitterly in the depths of his province
and of the cloister; it is a refined, gallant society, with
high standards of honour, such as Louis XIV would
have liked to establish; society of the sort that Boileau
and Racine described as their ideal, which is within
range of the Court, but which often abstains there-
from.    Prévost freely modifies his tales, makes them
dignified, serious, or pathetic, and is easily roused to
enthusiasm.

His romance—yes, his romance, notwithstanding
the *fille de joie* and the swindler whom we know so
well—descends in an almost direct line from *Astrée,
Clélie,* and the romances of Madame de La Fayette.
There is not a suspicion of laboured composition, or
of art, in his first work, any more than in the succeeding ones; the marquis tells what has happened to him

---

[1] [The gigantic and disastrous swindle of which the Scotsman
John Law was the inventor, and which kept all Paris in a ferment for
several years (1717–1720), was known as the "Mississippi System."—
Tr.]

and what others have told him about themselves; it is
all commingled, and it goes on at random; no proportion between the parts; the light purposely equalised;
a delightful, rapid style, jumping about at haphaz-
ard, but with an imperceptible instinct of good taste;
hurrying over beaten paths, intervals, preambles,
everything that we should carefully describe to-day;
travelling through the country in a smooth-rolling
carriage, with the curtains drawn; leaping, if his
hero happens to be aboard a vessel, " over an infinitude of ropes and nautical instruments," without the
inclination or the ability to call a single one by name;
and, in his extraordinary ignorance, dilating times
without number upon a few Court scenes, which are
repeated again and again, and the most affecting of
which are without an adequate setting.   The work is
clearly divided into two parts: the author, seeing that
the first had succeeded, fastened the other to it.   In
this first part, which is the shorter, after moralising at
the outset upon grand passions, distinguishing them
from concupiscence pure and simple, and striving to
discover therein a special design of Providence to
effect unknown ends, the marquis tells of his father's
misfortunes, his own, his travels in England and Germany, his captivity in Turkey, and the death of his
dear Selima, whom he had married there, and with
whom he had come to Rome.[1]

[1] While he was imprisoned in Turkey, his master, Salem, tries to
convert him to belief in the Koran; and when the marquis, like a good

It is his inconsolable grief for that loss which leads
him to say with an accent of sincere conviction quite as
persuasive as our pompous obscurities of to-day: "If
tears and sighs may not bear the name of pleasure, it is
none the less true that they are infinitely sweet to a
person mortally afflicted." Driven by his despair to
take refuge in religion in the Abbey of ——, where he
remains three years, the marquis is taken thence, by
dint of well-meaning violence, by M. le duc de ——,
who begs him to act as his son's guide in various
journeys. They go to Spain first of all, then visit
Portugal and England, the old marquis under the name
of M. de Renoncourt, the young man under that of Marquis de Rosemont. The mentor's advice to his ward, his
constant and respectful zeal for "the glory of the amiable marquis"; the books that he recommends to him

Christian, declaims against the sensual impurity sanctioned by Ma-
homet, Salem argues with him thus: "God, as he did not choose to
manifest himself to mankind all at once, made himself known at first
by figures of speech only. The first law, which was that of the Jews, is
filled with them. It proposed to man, as the motive and reward of
virtue, naught save carnal joys and gross pleasures. The law of the
Christians, which followed the Jewish law, was much more perfect because it attributed everything to the spirit, which is unquestionably
superior to the body. That was the second state through which God
was pleased to make men pass. And now, lastly, it is no longer corporal pleasures alone, as in the law of the Jews, nor spiritual pleasures
alone, as in the gospel of the Christians, but felicity of body and spirit
alike, which the Alcoran promises to all true believers." It is an interesting fact that Salem, that is to say, our Abbé Prévost, imagined a
species of union of the Jewish and Christian laws in the Mussulman
law, by a process of reasoning very like that which has been so boldly
developed in our own day in Saint-Simonism.

and allows him to read—*Télémaque* and *La Princesse de Clèves;* why he forbids him to speak the Spanish language; his solicitude that, in a man of his rank, destined to play a part in the great affairs of the world, study should not become "a passion as in a fellow of the University"; the enlightenment that he gives him concerning the mutual inclination of the sexes and the singularities of the heart,—all these details possess, in the romance, an indescribable savour which does more, and at less cost, to place before us the manners and the tone of the society of that day, than our oceans of local colour are able to do. The marquis's love for Dona Diana, the murder of that beauty, and, above all, the death-bed marriage, have an interest which corresponds, in the category of romance, to that of *Bérénice* in tragedy.

After the journey to Spain and Portugal, and during the voyage to Holland, M. de Renoncourt unexpectedly meets on board the ship his two nephews, sons of Amulem, Selima's brother; and this attractive *turquerie,* cast in the path of our French gentlemen, causes only so much surprise as is fitting. Upon landing, the excellent tutor finds his brother-in-law in person, and we listen while they narrate their respective adventures since their separation. As for these sons of Amulem, these nephews of M. de Renoncourt, it happens that the more charming of the two is a niece, who had been disguised in that fashion for greater safety during the voyage; but the marquis,

who was so profoundly afflicted by the death of his
Diana, is not on his guard against this innocent decep-
tion, and, by dint of loving his young friend Memisces,
he unwittingly becomes unfaithful to her whom he has
mourned so bitterly.

Generally speaking, these characters are thoughtless,
changeable, guided by first impressions, and easy-
going to a degree that makes one smile at times; love
is born in them suddenly, in the twinkling of an eye,
as in idle and unoccupied minds; they have wonderful dreams; they give or receive sword-thrusts with
incredible celerity ; they are restored by mysterious
powders and oils; they swoon and recover consciousness swiftly at every shock of grief or joy.  They belong to the race of refined gentlemen of that time,
which the author has modified a little to suit himself.
Young Rosemont in the highest rank, the Chevalier des
Grieux [1] in the depths of degradation, retain the essential characteristics of that type and represent it with
equal fidelity in its most divergent aspects.  The first,
despite his outbursts of passion and two or three quite
involuntary murders, is already paving the way for all
the honours due to the virtue of a Grandison; the chevalier, after a few knaveries and a homicide of little consequence, remains incontestably the most attractive,
by virtue of his amiable bearing, and the most honourable of unfortunate wretches.

The line of demarcation between the marquises

---

[1] [The hero of *Manon Lescaut* —Tr.]

—the one who is simply a gentleman of quality and
the one who is son of a duke—is faithfully drawn;
the ducal prerogative shines in all the splendour of
prejudice. Excellent M. de Renoncourt's perplexity
when his ward wishes to marry his niece; the remonstrances that he addresses to the poor child, asking
her, with reference to the young man, "Have you
forgotten what he was born?" his appeal, in his
despair, to the marquis's father, the noble duke, who
receives the news as if the affair were altogether too
impossible, and waves it aside with an airy assumption of superiority, which in our eyes would be the
last degree of impertinence,—these touches, which
lapse of time has made interesting, cost Abbé Prévost
nothing, and, from his kindly pen, conveyed no malicious implication. As much must be said of the old
marquis's inclination for the lovely Lady R——. Prévost's only purpose was to make his hero perplexed
and interesting; the element of comedy slipped in
without design on his part; but it is comedy subtle to
detect, tempered by kindliness, dominated by respect,
and silenced by emotion,—comedy of the sort of
which there is an infusion in Goldsmith's excellent
character of Dr. Primrose.

I care much less for *Cléveland* than for the *Mémoires d'un Homme de Qualité;* in its day people
may have formed a different judgment; to-day its improbabilities and chimeras make it almost as insipid
reading as *Amadis.* We cannot go back to that

legendary geography, that *Pyramus and Thisbe* scenery, vaguely filled with cliffs, grottoes, and wild men. The only portions that are still fine are the philosophical arguments, tinged with a dignified melancholy, in which Cléveland and the Earl of Clarendon engage in several places. The quasi-psychological scrutiny to which the hero devotes his attention at the beginning of the sixth book shows us an enlightened probity and serene elevation of thought in harmony with the barrenest and most unsavoury practical consequences. The impotence of solitary philosophy when face to face with real ills is vividly laid bare, and the attempt at suicide with which Cléveland ends, sets forth for us and vividly clinches that moral doctrine—a doctrine more profound, I venture to assert, than it could have seemed at the time to its author.

As for the *Doyen de Killerine,* the last in date of Prévost's three great romances, it is a book which, although it drags sometimes and is unconscionably long, is after all infinitely pleasant reading, if one sets about it with a favourable prepossession. The worthy Dean of Killerine, a slightly ridiculous personage, after the style of Abraham Adams,[1] with his two humps, his crooked legs, and the wart on his forehead, the zealous and perplexed guardian of his brothers and his pretty sister, makes me think of a hen which has, by an oversight, hatched a brood

1 [In Fielding's *Joseph Andrews.*—Tr.]

of little ducks; he is for ever engaged in travelling
from Dublin to Paris, to bring back one or another of
them who has left his side and waded out into the
vast pond of the world. This sort of life, to which he
is not at all adapted, involves him in situations most
amusing for us, if not for him; as, for example, in the
boudoir scene where the coquette tries to seduce him;
or when, playing the part of a woman in an assigna-
tion at night, he receives against his will the passionate kisses of the lover, who does not see what he is
about. Abbé Desfontaines, in his *Observations sur
les Écrits Modernes*, among divers just criticisms of
the plan of this work and its improbabilities, bears
too severely upon the excellent dean when he calls
him a lifeless character, and a man as intolerable to
the reader as to his family. As for his family, I would
not swear that he was always entertaining to them;
but how can we, who are not lovers, be angry with
him when he tells us: "I proved to him by incontro-
vertible logic that what he called invincible love,
inviolable constancy, essential fidelity, were so many
chimeras, which religion and the order of nature did
not recognise in any such trifling signification."

Despite the dean's demonstrations, the love affairs
of all those charming couples ran their course and became insanely complicated. The amiable Rose, in
her heart logic, declared to her brother Patrice that,
despite the fate that parted him from his sweetheart,
he and she were worthy of envy, "and that pangs

caused by loyalty and affection merit the name of the most delicious happiness." For the rest, the *Doyen de Killerine* is perhaps, of all Prévost's romances, the one in which his manner of writing a book is most fully revealed. He does not write with a certain idea in his mind, or with a fixed goal in view; he allows himself to be guided by events, which intermingle as chance wills, and by the various sentiments which wind about them as a stream follows the windings of a valley.

*Le Pour et Contre*—"a periodical work of a new type, in which the contributors express their views freely upon anything likely to interest public curiosity in the field of the sciences, arts, books, etc., etc., without taking sides and without giving offence to any one"—was constantly true to its title. In form it resembled the English journals of Addison, Steele, and Johnson, with less finish and painstaking, but with much good sense, solid information, and frankness. Several numbers by the plagiarist Desfontaines and by Lefebvre de Saint-Marc, who continued some of Prévost's works, should not be charged to Prévost. English literature is criticised at great length in the persons of the most illustrious writers; we find there very full notices of Roscommon, Rochester, Wycherley, and Savage; copious and thoughtful analyses of Shakespeare; a translation of Dryden's *Mark Antony,* and of a comedy by Steele. Prévost had studied on the spot, and he held in unreserved admiration

England, her manners, her politics, her women, and her stage. The works, then recently published, of Le Sage, Madame de Tencin, Crébillon Fils, and Marivaux, are reviewed by their rival, as they successively appear, with an unerring accuracy of taste which always rests upon a basis of good-will. We feel that in secret he prefers the older writers, d'Urfé, and even Mademoiselle de Scudéry; but there is no trace anywhere of literary sensitiveness or of professional jealousy. He even does not hesitate on occasion (a display of generosity which it will be found difficult to credit) to quote approvingly, by their names, his brother journals, *Le Mercure de France* and *Le Verdun*. By way of compensation, when Prévost has occasion to speak of himself and of his own books, he does it with excellent grace, and does not haggle over words of praise. I find in number 36, volume iii, a review of *Manon Lescaut,* which ends thus:

"What art was requisite to interest the reader and arouse his compassion with respect to the fatal misfortunes which befall that corrupt creature! . . . The character of Tiberge, the chevalier's friend, is admirable. . . . I say nothing of the style of this work; there is neither cant, nor affectation, nor sophistical reflections; it is Nature herself who writes. How insipid a stiff and bedizened author appears in comparison! This writer does not run after wit, or, rather, after what is called by that name. It is not a laconic, constipated style, but flowing, copious, and expressive. It is all descriptions and sentiments, but lifelike descriptions and natural sentiments."

Once or twice Prévost was called upon to take the field in his own defence, and he always acquitted himself with dignity and moderation. Attacked by a

Jesuit in the *Journal de Trévoux*, on the subject of
an article on Ramsay, he replied so temperately that
the Jesuits realised their mistake and disavowed that
first onslaught. He took up with more acrimony the
slanders of Abbé Lenglet-Dufresnoy; but his moral
justification demanded it, and we owe to that fortunate exigency some of the elucidations of the incidents
of his life that we have made use of. A fact which
we have not mentioned as yet, and which was a
result of the same episode, is that, after his stay in
Holland, Prévost had not recovered from that inclination for the tender passion whence so much suffering
befell him. His face, they say, and his accomplishments had touched the heart of a young Protestant of
high lineage, who wished to marry him. " To escape from this indiscreet passion," adds his biographer
of 1764, Prévost crossed to England; but, as he took
the lovelorn damsel with him, we are justified in the
conjecture that he defended himself no more than
half-heartedly against so insane a passion. Lenglet
brutally accused him of allowing himself to be ab-
ducted by a charmer. Prévost replied that such ab-
ductions suited only the Médors and the Renauds,
and he drew, by way of refutation, the following
portrait—a portrait of himself:

" This Médor, so dear to the fair sex, is a man of thirty-seven to
thirty-eight years of age, who bears upon his face and in his temper the
marks of his earlier sorrows; who sometimes passes whole weeks in
his library, and employs seven or eight hours of each day in study;
who rarely seeks opportunities to make merry and even declines those

that are offered him; and who prefers an hour's conversation with a judicious friend to all that is called worldly pleasure and agreeable pastimes.  He is a civil fellow, as the result of an excellent education, but not at all gallant; of a gentle, but melancholy disposition; sober and orderly in his conduct.  I have described myself faithfully without looking to see whether the portrait flatters or wounds my self-esteem."

*Le Pour et Contre* offers us also a multitude of anecdotes of the day and strange happenings—veritable rough drafts of novels, and material therefor ; the story of Dona Maria, and the life of the Duc de Riperda are the most noteworthy.  An English scholar, Mr. Hooker, had conceived the idea of drawing, in an English journal, an ingenious parallel between the place of retirement of Cassiodorus of old, Sir Philip Sidney's Arcadia, and the land of Forez in the time of Celadon.[1]  Cassiodorus, already advanced in years, as we know, and out of humour with the Court by reason of the disgrace of Boethius, went into retirement at the monastery of Viviers, which he had built on one of his estates, and there devoted himself, with his monks, to the study of ancient manuscripts, to the cultivation of the land, and to the exercises of religion.  Prévost descants with pleasure upon the joys of that diversified life in common; he evidently recognises his ideal in Cassiodorus's monastery; it is his Saint-Germain-des-Prés, his La Flèche, but with infinitely more sunshine, comfort, and entertainment. And as for the resemblance to Arcadia and Celadon's country, which the English writer points out with a

[1] [The lover of the beautiful Astrée, in d'Urfé's famous romance of that name.—Tr.]

touch of malice, he does not balk at it for an instant,
for, he says, he is convinced that "in Arcadia and in
the land of Forez, with such principles of equity and
charity as the people of those countries are represented
to hold, and with morals so pure as those attributed
to them, they would need nothing but more accurate
ideas on the subject of religion to make them very
acceptable to Heaven."

After about six years of exile, Prévost received permission to return to France in the garb of a secular
ecclesiastic.　The Cardinal de Bissy, who had known
him at Saint-Germain, and the Prince de Conti, proved
to be most useful patrons; the latter appointed him his
almoner.　Thus re-established in a life of tranquillity,
and raised above want, Prévost, who was still young,
divided his time between the composition of numerous
works and the cultivation of the brilliant society in
which he sought relaxation.　The labour of writing had
become so familiar to him that it was no longer labour;
he could let his pen run and carry on a conversation
at the same time.　We are bound to say that the voluminous writings with which the last half of his life
overflows show the effects of this extreme facility,
become a matter of habit.　Whatever he undertakes,
whether it be a compilation, a romance, a translation
of Richardson, Hume, or Cicero, a *Histoire de Guil-
laume le Conquérant,* or a *Histoire des Voyages,* the
style is always the same, agreeable, but monotonous
in its fluency, always running on, and too swiftly to

be coloured by the variety of subjects touched upon. All differences are wiped out, all inequalities levelled, all raised surfaces smoothed down, in that swift stream of unvarying elegance. We will mention only one among the last productions of his prolix pen, the *Histoire d'une Grecque Moderne,* a pretty little romance, of which the plot is as subtle as it is vague. A young Greek woman, destined at first for the seraglio, then ransomed by a French nobleman, who wished to make her his mistress; her resistance to her emancipator's love, being perhaps less insensible to others than to him; this *perhaps* above all, which is never solved, which the proof flutters about, grazes again and again, but never succeeds in grasping;—in all this there is material for a charming and delicate work in the style of Crébillon Fils; Prévost's, although a graceful production, is executed a little too much at hazard.

Prévost was living thus, happy in study, in a select circle of friends, and in tranquillity of the senses, when a slight service in the way of correction of proofs, rendered to a satirical newsmonger, compromised him when he least expected it, and sent him off to Brussels (1741). From Brussels he went to Frankfort. All the powers in those places became interested in him. The offers of Frederick, King of Prussia, who was then recruiting academicians and soldiers, sought him out, but did not tempt him overmuch. It was the moment when the Diet of the Empire was assembled at Frankfort to elect an emperor. The

Maréchal de Belle-Isle, who was in the city, on the point of setting out for Bohemia, took the trouble to write in Prévost's behalf to Cardinal de Fleury. Negotiations were entered into, especially with M. de Maurepas, the Minister for Paris, in whose department the affair belonged, and who ought, it would seem, to have been less severe than most men in the matter of thoughtless evil-speaking and satire.

Abbé Prévost was a persuasive apologist, and as in this case the offence was trivial, M. de Maurepas allowed himself to be touched. On his return he resumed his position with the Prince de Conti, who set him at work arranging the material for a history of his family, while Chancellor d'Aguesseau employed him in editing the *Histoire Générale des Voyages*.[1] Amid these sources of favour, and of wealth as well, his disinterestedness never wavered; he refused to take part in schemes which would have been most profitable to him; he turned over his profits to his publisher, with whom, it has been observed (and I can well believe it), he was always on the most cordial terms. Indeed, I am afraid that, like some other too easy-going and reckless men of letters, he put himself at the mercy of the speculator. For him, he said, a garden, a cow, and two hens were enough.[2] A small house that he

---

[1] Chamfort relates that Chancellor d'Aguesseau had formerly given Abbé Prévost permission to print the first volumes of *Cléveland*, only on the express condition that Cléveland should turn Catholic in the last volume.

[2] Jean-Jacques, who had the same aspiration, but who did not

had bought at Saint-Firmin, near Chantilly, was his perspective of the future here on earth, the narrow but smiling horizon within which he proposed to confine his old age. He was on his way thither through the forest one day, alone (it was November 25, 1763), when a sudden attack of apoplexy brought him to the ground, unconscious. Some peasants came along; he was carried to the nearest village, and an ignorant surgeon, thinking that he was dead, proceeded at once to open his body. Prévost, aroused by the scalpel, recovered consciousness only to die in frightful agony.[1]

confine himself to it, had occasion, at the beginning of his career, to meet Abbé Prévost quite often at the house of their common friend Musard, at Passy; he mentions him in the *Confessions* (part ii, book viii), with an expression of regret for happy moments passed in a select company. Enumerating the distinguished men whom the excellent Musard had made his friends, he says: " At their head I place Abbé Prévost, a very amiable man of simple manners, whose heart gave life to his writings, which deserve immortality, and who had in company none of the vivid colouring which he imparted to his works." We may be permitted to believe that Abbé Prévost formerly had had that *colouring* in conversation, but that he had lost it to some extent as he grew older.

[1] [Although the official death certificate gives apoplexy as the cause of the death, and states that the body was not inspected by the officials until the following day, November 26th, there is very strong evidence, outside of the common tradition, in favour of the version in the text. In a later essay, apropos of the unveiling of a statue of Prévost, at Hesdin, in October, 1853, Sainte-Beuve, after quoting one of the orators of that occasion in contradiction of the story, adds: " However, I have before me a note written by Abbé Prévost's grand-niece, Mademoiselle Rosine Prévost, and dictated to her by her father, who was eighteen years old at the time of the abbé's death; and he must surely have been accurately informed of all the circumstances by his

The prior and monks of Saint-Nicolas-d'Acy, near Genlis, learning that Abbé Prévost was no more, and remembering that he had been a Benedictine, charitably, and also, no doubt, to assert their right, claimed his mortal remains; so he was taken to their house and buried, as if he had not ceased to be one of them. Dom Prévost's returning at last to the fold, and his interment in the convent close, or beneath the flags of the cloister, puts the final and concluding touch to the vicissitudes of his life.

Thus ended, by a catastrophe worthy of Cléveland, that romantic and restless existence. In literature Prévost belongs to the fading but still noble generation which immediately followed and completed the age of Louis XIV. He is a writer of the seventeenth century writing in the eighteenth; he is a contemporary of Le Sage, the younger Racine, Madame de Lambert, and Chancellor d'Aguesseau; and, in criticism, of Desfontaines and Lenglet-Dufresnoy. Of painters and sculptors that generation can count very few, and it does not worry over the lack; its only musician is the tuneful Rameau. Against the background of this

brother, who was with their uncle at the time. Now it is said in this note, that 'one day, when Abbé Prévost was returning from Chantilly to Saint-Firmin, where he lived, an attack of apoplexy laid him at the foot of a tree in the forest; that some peasants who came along took him to the curé's house in the nearest village; that the officers of justice were summoned in a great hurry, and ordered that the body be opened at once; and that a cry from the unfortunate man, who was not dead, stopped the knife and froze the spectators with horror.'"— Tr.]

peaceful decline of genius, Prévost stands out more
distinctly than any other.   Antedating by his style the
reign of analysis and philosophy, he does not copy,
and in copying enervate, a style made illustrious by
some formidable predecessor; his style is an invention
of his own, no less natural than original, and in that
interval between the imposing groups of the two
centuries, the glory that he radiates recalls him alone.
After Louis XIV, after that finical elaboration of taste
and of sentiments, he revivifies the type that d'Urfé and
Mademoiselle de Scudéry had prematurely introduced;
and although in his work there is still too much con-
ventionality, prosiness, and chimerical stuff, he often
attains, and affords his readers glimpses of, the secret
paths of genuine human nature.   In the series of
painters of the heart and good-humoured moralists, he
holds a place from which he could not disappear
without leaving a very perceptible void.[1]

[1] The following parallel between Manon Lescaut and Carmen, taken
from M. Sainte-Beuve's essay on Mérimée, has seemed to be of sufficient interest to be added here:

"This Carmen is simply a more highly spiced Manon Lescaut, who
debauches her Chevalier des Grieux, a man as weak and as easily
seduced as Don José, although of an entirely different type.   It is
interesting to read the two little novels side by side, when one has
once thoroughly grasped the identity of the subject in conjunction
with the difference in manners and costumes.   Abbé Prévost's story
has already ceased to be of our time or our civilisation; we can still
overlook Manon's lack of heart, but it is hard to forgive the chevalier's
degradation, and nothing less than the author's perfect naturalness
will avail to lead us on to the true emotion through the debasing
scenes through which he conducts us.   M. Mérimée has chosen his

course more frankly, or at all events with more deliberation. At the very outset he presents his two characters as rascals; thereafter it is simply a question of degree; it is especially interesting to see how love is born, how it demeans itself, and how it goes to pieces, or persists in spite of everything, in such strong, stern natures, in such untamed hearts. Poor Don José, bewitched by that demon of a Carmen, passes through vicissitudes analogous to those of the Chevalier des Grieux; but the latter's misdeeds are mere peccadilloes compared to the atrocities into which the other is led when he becomes a gypsy bandit. The conclusion differs in this respect: in Abbé Prévost Manon ends by being touched by her chevalier's devotion and by raising herself to his height; whereas Carmen, after a certain moment, feels her fierce passion vanish and no longer loves. However, there is a resemblance even to the end, and Don José, after killing his mistress, buries her in the ravine as piously as Des Grieux buries his in the sand of the desert. A natural consequence of the super-abundance of colouring and energy that M. Mérimée has employed in his tortuous study of the brigand and the gypsy, is that the author, like a clever man who knows his constituency, has deemed it advisable to enclose his romance in a setting of pleasantry and sarcasm. He was travelling as an antiquary, his only object being to solve an archæological and geographical problem concerning the battle of Munda, fought by Cæsar against Pompey's sons, when he fell in with the brigand who afterward told him his story; and the romance ends with a short chapter in which the antiquary appears once more, and the philologist disports himself a little on the subject of the language of the gypsies. In Abbé Prévost, on the other hand, everything is ingenuous, and so fluent, so far from seeming displaced, that we wonder to this day, when we observe the narrator's air of kindliness, and his absence of merriment, whether the episode is not authentic, and a simple copy of the truth. M. Mérimée is a consummate artist; Abbé Prévost is not an artist at all, even when he is so unexcelled a painter of nature."

# Madame de Lambert,

## 1647?—1733,

### and

# Madame Necker,

## 1739—1794.

## Madame de Lambert

### and

## Madame Necker.

I HAVE long had it in mind to couple together these two clever women, who held salons of so distinctly literary a type, one at the beginning, the other at the close, of the eighteenth century, and to place their profiles in the same medallion. They have in common a pronounced taste for things of the mind, and for common sense heightened by a certain turn of phrase, distinctive, concise, and novel, which one need only be ill-disposed to confound with affectation and preciosity. In both, morality is the dominating element ; decorum and duty regulate manners and tone. Madame de Lambert, amid the debauchery of the Regency, opens under her roof a place of refuge for conversation, for clever badinage, for serious discussions. Fontenelle presides over that refined and polite circle, to which it is an honour to be admitted. Madame Necker, born far from Paris and coming thither from French Switzerland, of which she was the glory, desired nothing so much as to

39

find in Paris a salon exactly like Madame de Lambert's,
—that is to say, one where intellect would be made
welcome, and where no sentiment worthy of respect
would be outraged. That was the type of salon
and the surroundings which would have been best
suited to her character. Being obliged, by the much
more promiscuous social customs of the period, to do
without it, and to open her house to almost everybody who was celebrated in society, for all sorts
of reasons, she at all events introduced therein the
greatest possible degree of decency and regularity;
she made her own selection of the objects of her
special admiration and esteem; in her salon Buffon
occupied almost the same position that Fontenelle
had occupied in Madame de Lambert's. But these
similarities, which I do no more than mention, will
appear more clearly by a careful study of the two
characters.

Nothing, or almost nothing, is known of the first
sixty years of Madame de Lambert's life. She died
in 1733, at the age, so it was said, of eighty-six,
which would fix the date of her birth about 1647.
Her name was Anne - Thérèse de Marguenat de
Courcelles. Her father, who was a *maître des comptes*,
was of Troyes, and Courcelles is the name of a small
fief that he owned near that town. She lost her
father when she was very young. Madame de
Lambert's mother, the daughter of a rich bourgeois

A. THERESE DE MARGUENAT
DE COURCELLES MARQUISE DE LAMBERT
née à Paris en 1647. et y mourut en 1733.

Des plus rares esprits sans cesse environnée,
Et de mille vertus ornée :
Le Ciel qui la chérit en elle nous fait voir
Une autre Athenais par son profond sçavoir.

## MADAME DE LAMBERT

*From a copper engraving*

of Paris, was an arrant coquette, in whose honour it
may be said that her *historiette* is among the most
scandalous in Tallemant des Reaux. She was much
more engrossed by the Brancases, the Miossens, the
Chevalier de Grammont, and all the amiable young
noblemen to be found at Court, than by her worthy
husband, whose brain was weak, and who even
ended by being confined in a single room as a fool.
This *historiette* of Tallemant arouses grave suspicions
(to say no more) concerning Goodman Courcelles's
claims to paternity, and it would not be safe to come
too quickly to a conclusion as to the child's father,
even if there were more physical resemblance between
them.

About that time Bachaumont fell in love with
Madame de Courcelles. When her husband was
dead, he lived with her several years, then married
her. This Bachaumont was the same who was
Chapelle's companion in his famous *Voyage ;* a
man of pleasure and of much wit. He is said to
have been very fond of his step-daughter. What
the influence of her step-father's circle upon the
young woman may have been, we can easily imagine; but we are reduced to guessing. Fontenelle
tells us that, at that time, "she often stole away
from the amusements suited to her years, to go off
and read by herself, and accustomed herself, of her
own motion, to make little extracts of what impressed
her most. Even then these were either shrewd

reflections on the human heart, or ingenious turns of phrase,—but generally reflections."

To my mind the life of undisguised dissipation led by Madame de Lambert's mother indicates an influence of another sort, which is often seen in such cases, and which may be called influence by contraries.   How many times has the sight of a frivolous and disreputable mother driven a judicious and sensible daughter into a class of reflections bordering upon the rigorous and severe !   Everything seems to indicate that this was the effect which her mother's evil example produced upon Madame de Lambert.   A weak mind would have allowed itself to be led, and would have followed that example; a sensitive and strong mind transformed it into a moral lesson;   it revenged itself nobly by well-doing.   Madame de Lambert throughout her life made it her duty to respect propriety all the more because she had seen it outraged all about her in her childhood.   Worldly esteem and an honourable name — these she made the principal aim and object of her whole conduct.

It seems that she was heir to a considerable estate through her father.   Married in 1666 to the Marquis de Lambert, an officer of merit who afterward became a lieutenant-general, as his father had been before him, she entered a social circle more in conformity with her elevated instincts, and she retained nothing of her earlier surroundings except a very ardent inclination for intellectual pursuits.

In her *Avis d'une Mère à son Fils,* which has come down to us, we may see what a lofty conception she had of military renown, and how thoroughly she espoused that religion of loyalty, devotion, and self-sacrifice. "I regret every day," she says to her son, "that I never saw your grandfather. Judging from the praise which I have heard bestowed on him, no one ever had in a greater degree than he the eminent qualities of a soldier and the genius for war. He acquired such esteem and such authority in the army, that he did more with ten thousand men than others did with twenty."

One day, at the siege of Gravelines, Maréchal de Gassion and Maréchal de La Meilleraie, who were in command, had a quarrel, and their enmity went so far as to disrupt the army; their respective troops were on the point of coming to blows when the Marquis de Lambert, then only a major-general, threw himself between the two factions, and in the king's name ordered the troops to halt. "He forbade them to recognise those officers as their commanders. The troops obeyed; the two marshals, La Meilleraie and Gassion, were obliged to withdraw. The king heard of this performance," says Madame de Lambert, "and spoke of it more than once with enthusiasm." It was by such examples that, on entering her new family, she uplifted her own heart, then strove to mould those of her children. After that, all that remained of Bachaumont and of the habits of her early education tended only to culture and to refinement of mind. Among the words and ideas which come most frequently from her pen when she begins to write, I note especially *morals, innocence,* and *glory.*

Insisting upon this principle of emulation and of noble ardour, she went so far as to say to her son: "You cannot be too eager to rise, or sustain your aspirations with too flattering hopes. Nothing is less becoming in a young man than a certain modesty which causes him to think that he is incapable of great things. This modesty is listlessness of the heart which prevents it from making a start and travelling swiftly toward glory." You imagine that, in the words of that mother, sprung from a wealthy and licentious bourgeoisie, you are listening, in anticipation, to Vauvenargues advising some young friend. Thus it is that energetic souls acquire new vigour under precisely the same circumstances in which others become enervated and corrupted. The excellent M. Droz, in his criticism of Madame de Lambert's writings, is impressed by the dangerous and even absurd tendency of such a scheme of morality, which openly preaches ambition. I beg his pardon, but Madame de Lambert knew that, at the time when she was writing, the peril, for that warlike youth, lay rather in an excess of dissipation and effeminacy. Fénelon, criticising these same *Avis* of Madame de Lambert to her son, said: "Honour, the purest probity, and knowledge of the human heart, are predominant in this discourse.  .  .  .  I might not be altogether in agreement with her as to the full measure of the ambition which she demands of him; but we should very soon be in accord concerning all the virtues whereby she would have that ambition supported and tempered."

Madame de Lambert lost her husband in 1686; two years earlier she had gone with him to Luxembourg, when he was appointed governor of that province, and she had aided him to win the hearts of the people in that newly conquered country. "He had a light hand," she says, "and governed by love alone, never by exerting his authority." She had devoted all of her individual estate, which was considerable, to the advancement of her husband's fortunes, and to maintaining an honourable establishment. When he died she transferred her attention to the interests of her children, grievously jeopardised by tedious and distressing law-suits which she had to carry on against her own family. "There are so few untainted great fortunes," she writes to her son, "that I forgive your ancestors for not leaving you one. I have done what I could to adjust our affairs, in which nothing is left to women but the glory of saving." This regret because of the secondary rôle to which women are reduced will manifest itself more than once in Madame de Lambert. She was adroit enough to win her lawsuits, to obtain her property and her children's by conquest, so to speak; and not until then did she give rein to her inclinations by setting up in Paris an establishment which brought together literary people and people of fashion, and which gradually became one of the best and most prominent houses in the capital, and so continued from about 1710 to 1733, or more than twenty years.

I have told elsewhere how the salons of the seventeenth century, Madame de La Sablière's and Ninon's, came to an end. If one desired to write a formal history of the salons of the eighteenth century, one must begin with Madame de Lambert's. About the same time, but a little later, came Madame de Tencin's; then Madame Geoffrin's and Madame du Deffand's; and so in due course we should arrive at Madame Necker's. But Madame de Lambert unquestionably inaugurates and gives the tone to the new epoch. Some private testimony will enable us to form a pertinent judgment of her salon, almost as if we ourselves had been admitted to it.

" I have just met with a very grievous loss in Madame la Marquise de Lambert, who has died at the age of eighty-six," wrote the Marquis d'Argenson (1733). " Fifteen years ago she did me the honour to invite me to her house, and I became one of her intimate friends. Her house reflected honour upon those who were admitted to it. I went there to dinner regularly on Wednesdays, which was one of her days. In the evening there was always company; we talked, and there was no more thought of cards than at the famous Hôtel de Rambouillet, so extolled by Voiture and Balzac. She was wealthy, made an excellent and benevolent use of her wealth, conferred benefits on her friends, and especially on the unfortunate. A pupil of Bachaumont, she had never had other associates than people of fashion and the brightest minds, and she knew no other passion than a constant, almost Platonic affection."

MADAME NECKER
*From a portrait by Duplessis*

D' Argenson adds that she tried to persuade him to enter the lists for the Académie Française.    She assured him of the votes of her friends, who were very numerous in that association.    "Some people," he says, "have even tried to cast ridicule upon a most unquestionable fact, namely, that it was difficult for a man to be admitted to the Académie unless he were presented at her house and by her.    It is certain that she made fully one-half of our present academicians."

This influence of the salons on the Académie Française, and the importance which that body was beginning to recover, are among the peculiar signs which mark the progress of the eighteenth century.    For it is a fact that the Académie Française has not had the same weight at all periods of its existence.    It enjoyed great consideration at its creation and in its early days: society and literature, despite an occasional protest here and there, recognised in it the director of the language and of good usage, and even a court of last resort in matters of taste.    But thirty years after its foundation, when a youthful and daring literature made its appearance under Louis XIV, when the Boileaus and the Racines, the Molières and the La Fontaines, had really regenerated French letters and poetry, the Académie found itself somewhat behind the times, and it remained so, more or less, during the last thirty-five years of the century.    It is customary, in the Académie, to live to a ripe old age; that custom has not been laid aside, and, taken in conjunction with so many other privileges, it certainly has its value. But the result of this academic longevity was that, in the second half of the seventeenth century, the institution did not take in new blood so rapidly as the public could have wished.

Boileau and La Fontaine waited a long time before they were of the Académie, and even when they were admitted, many of the old school were still members, while there were already slipping in some advocates of a new style, which was not the most pure. Fontenelle was a member betimes; his growing influence, combined with that of La Motte and other friends of Madame de Lambert, helped to impart to the Académie Française something of that philosophic character which was destined to become very perceptible during the eighteenth century, and to make up for the inadequacy thenceforth of its earlier grammatical or purely literary rôle.

But we are talking of Madame de Lambert's salon. When they saw the men of letters so assiduous in their visits to her, and Messieurs de l'Académie dining with her twice a week, her envious detractors did not fail to accuse her of keeping a *bureau d'esprit.* "It was," says Fontenelle, "the only house, with a very few exceptions, which had kept clear of the epidemic of gambling, the only house where people met to converse with one another sensibly, and even wittily, according to circumstances. And so those people who had their reasons for taking it ill that there should be conversation anywhere discharged ill-humoured remarks against Madame de Lambert's house when they had an opportunity." She was not insensible to such shafts, for she cared for public opinion before everything. I find some of these same animadversions, not from an enemy, but from the pen of a friend, M. de La Rivière, who was Bussy-Rabutin's son-in-law, and who had retired in his old age to the Institution de l'Oratoire. He was a rather clever man, with a facile and somewhat ornate style, but, toward the end, he became most scrupulously religious. In many passages of his *Letters,* he presents Madame de Lambert in a somewhat novel light.

"She was," he says, "my oldest friend and my contemporary. She was born with much intelligence; she cultivated it by persistent reading; but the fairest jewel in her crown was a noble and luminous simplicity, which, at the age of sixty, she thought it best to lay aside."

Elsewhere he says :

" She had a gripe of *bel-esprit.* It was a disease which took her suddenly, and of which she was not cured when she died. She gave herself to the public, she associated herself with Messieurs de l'Académie, and set up at her house a *bureau d'esprit.* I omitted nothing to save her from the ridicule attached to the trade of *bel-esprit,* especially among women; I could not convince her. As I was born with simple tastes, by inclination and perhaps by necessity, I did not choose to appear to be a party to such a false step, and I took leave of her. I was twenty-five years without entering her house, except for a single time when I went to see her to prepare her for her journey to eternity [that is to say, to induce her to confess]. Nevertheless she retained her esteem and affection for me to the end. She came to see me and wrote to me from time to time; my replies were always aimed at her conscience."

It will be observed that religious austerity has much to do with this judgment of M. de La Rivière. One is tempted to wonder whether it really was Madame de Lambert who was suddenly attacked with the disease of *bel-esprit* at sixty years, or whether it was not rather he who was seized with an increase of severity and scruple. However that may be, he is a good man to listen to with respect to her, and he unsuspectingly awards Madame de Lambert high praise when he observes that, notwithstanding all the rather harsh criticisms which he addressed to her, she always retained her friendship and indulgence for him.

This same M. de La Rivière, humble as he has lived to become, is very careful to recall the fact that, when Madame de Lambert was writing her *Avis* to her son, and to her daughter, she was assisted by one of her friends, who was no other than himself. He suggested to her several sentiments and ideas, which she was pleased to transform, he says, into precious stones and *cut diamonds*. But it is precisely this clean, sharp-cut, and original style, which to-day gives distinction and value to these maternal counsels of Madame de Lambert. They are often well conceived, but they are expressed even better.

Her few writings appeared during her lifetime, and originally without her participation, although the extreme care with which she had edited them seems to imply that she had had the public in mind. She had lent her manuscripts to friends, who, according to custom, were indiscreet. Her *Avis à son Fils* first appeared in 1726, in Père Des Molet's *Mémoires de Littérature,* under the title of *Lettre d'une Dame à son Fils sur la vraie Gloire.* The *Avis à sa Fille* also was about to appear without her sanction, when she decided to publish an edition of both opuscula, in 1728. But it was much worse when the manuscript of her *Réflexions sur les Femmes,* a much more audacious work, and of a nature to arouse the scoffers, fell into the hands of a publisher, and began to circulate among the public at large ; she hastily bought up the whole edition, or what was left of it, but was unable to prevent its being reprinted abroad. Thenceforth she had no choice but to make the best of praise and criticism alike, and to become an authoress at her own risk, with all the honours of war.

The *Avis d'une Mère à son Fils,* which is addressed to a young man already fairly started in the career of arms, a colonel of twenty-four years, and which was written, I suppose, about 1701, is marked by great elevation of thought and a piquant turn of phrase. I have said that glory is the goal openly advocated by the moralist, who, herein, is rather ancient than modern, and more in accord with Plutarch than with the gospel. Religion is there defined, for the first time, after the manner of the eighteenth century, and we detect thus early an accent that seems a precursor of Jean-Jacques. " Above all these duties" [of humanity and citizenship] says the mother to her son, "is the worship which you owe to the *Supreme Being*. Religion is intercourse established between God and man, by God's favour to man, and by man's worship of God. Lofty souls entertain for God sentiments and adoration of a special kind, which does not resemble that of the common herd : everything issues from the heart and goes straight to God." She declaims against the "libertinage" that is fashionable among young men. This word "libertinage," in the language of the seventeenth century, always means the license of the mind in matters of faith, and Madame de Lambert uses it in that sense.

"Most young men of to-day think that they gain distinction by assuming an air of libertinage, which injures them with sensible persons. It is an air which does not imply superiority of the mind, but derangement of the heart.

"One does not attack religion when one has no interest in attacking it. Nothing makes one happier than to have one's mind convinced and one's heart touched : that is a blessing at all times. Even those persons who are not fortunate enough to believe as they ought, bow to established religion ; they know that what are called *prejudices* fill a great place in the world, and that they must be respected."

Speaking of her last illness, M. de La Rivière says somewhere, ingenuously enough: "She fell ill ; she was eighty-six years old ; I was alarmed and I went to see her, to hear her confession. She carried the disease of the mind [*maladie de l'esprit*], to the last extreme, for she chose for her confessor Abbé Couet, who was a man of much wit [*beaucoup d'esprit*], and was known as such." Madame de Lambert, who did not readily part with her common sense and her reasoning power, even in these religious matters, hit upon some noble words at the end of her treatise *De la Vieillesse,* where she said : " Lastly, things are in repose when they are in their place: *the place of man's heart is the heart of God.* When we are in his hand, and our wills are submissive to his, our anxieties cease. There is no safer refuge for man than the love and fear of God." One could speak no more eloquently, nor think more worthily. In these words the idea of religion is ennobled ; it is no longer a mere respectable sentiment, but the loftiest of human proprieties, the end and the limit of our duties. Despite the fine concluding sentence,[1] it is none the less quite clear to us that Madame de Lambert's religion is rather an exalted form of the intellect than an interior spring welling constantly from the heart, or a positive revelation. She speaks of the Supreme Being; she is capable of raising herself to him, or even of resting upon him; but, however that may be, hers is no longer the religion of the seventeenth century, and Fénelon, after reading Madame de Lambert, had need to be more indulgent on this point than Bossuet would have been.

We continue to point out the precursory signs in

[1] A friend calls my attention to the fact that this reflection, which surprised me a little as coming from Madame de Lambert, is in fact simply a quotation, an extract more or less altered in arrangement, from something that she had read. It is found at the end of Marsollier's *Vie de l' Abbé de Rancé.*

her work which indicate the transition to a new epoch. She constantly urges her son to aim high in everything, and at the same time to cling to reality and not to appearances. "Let your intimacies be with persons who are above you; in this way you will accustom yourself to be respectful and courteous. With our equals we grow careless; the mind drowses." This is a keen and true remark. But this superiority, she continues, should not be gauged by rank alone, for there are real and individual grandeurs, and grandeurs by creation. To the latter we owe only *outward respect;* "We owe esteem and *the respect born of sentiment* to merit. When fortune and virtue combined have placed a man in high station, his is a twofold empire, which demands a twofold submission." But how rare this conjunction is! At a distance those who are favoured by fortune inspire awe. "Common report exaggerates their merits, and flattery deifies them. Draw near them and you find mere men. How many common people [*peuple*] we find at Court!" What she says to her son, she will repeat to her daughter. She would have her happy too, she would have her learn to think healthy thoughts, to think differently from common people on what is called morality and happiness in this life. "I call *peuple,*" she adds, "all those whose thoughts are low and vulgar; *the Court is full of them!*"

Those philosophical reflections, which, at a later period, will glide without difficulty into declamation

and intemperance, may be discerned in Madame de
Lambert in a state of well-defined analysis. The word
" mankind " occurs often in her writings. "Mankind,"
she says to her son, " suffers because of the extreme
distance which fortune has placed between one man
and another. Merit is what should separate you from
the common people, not dignity nor haughtiness."
She repeats it in more than one place. Those who
are above him she bids him judge by what they
really are, and not by their outward display. " But
let us not lose sight of an infinite number of unfortun-
ates who are below us. You owe to chance alone
the difference that exists between you and them."
She repeats the same counsel to her daughter. " Accustom yourself to be kind and humane to your servants. One of the ancients has said that we should
regard them *as unfortunate friends.* Remember that
humanity and Christianity make all men equal." Evidently the time draws near when humanity and equality will be preached on all sides: she was one of the
first to turn her thoughts to those things, to have a
presentiment of them, and to name them, before Louis
XIV had vanished.

We find in Madame de Lambert some thoughts
which one would think that she had borrowed in anticipation from the moralists who followed her. One
would say that she has Vauvenargues in mind, although he did not come until somewhat later, when
she says: "I will exhort you much more earnestly,

my son, to work upon your heart than to perfect your mind: the true grandeur of man lies in the heart." On the other hand, if she anticipates her successors on some points, she echoes her predecessors on others, and it would not be difficult to find in her writings some of the thoughts of Pascal, La Bruyère, and La Rochefoucauld, unadulterated. Herein she resembles the old moralist Charron, who is content to combine ideas and express them in fitting words, no matter whence they may come to him, provided that he finds them judicious and to his liking.

In this first of her writings, addressed to her son, we readily distinguish in her and credit her with some vigorous, lofty, and refined qualities—a way of looking at things which implies much discernment and power of analysis, and a way of saying things which is never commonplace. The only fault in these counsels, to one who reads them, is that they allow no repose; the tissue is too compact and always in a state of tension. She herself tells us the secret in speaking to her daughter: "Tell few stories; tell them in a refined and concise style; let what you say be new, or let your turn of phrase be novel." It was this novelty which some well-meaning contemporaries of Madame de Lambert took for neologism, and which caused her to be accused of pretentiousness. As for us, who are less sensitive, and whom these novelties of a century ago barely affect and certainly do not scandalise, we will acknowledge that her style overflows with most

happily chosen words, of a clear and vivid signification.

Her most noticeable failing, in the long run, is the
constant affectation of analysis, the fondness for sentences with several members or compartments, which
compel the mind to grasp complicated relations.  She
forces those who read her to work.  For example, in
one place she defines all the virtues according to the
degree in which they are at variance with self-esteem
[*amour-propre*].  "All the vices favour self-esteem,
and all the virtues agree in combating it: valour *exposes* it, modesty *debases* it, generosity *despoils* it,
moderation *disappoints* it, and zeal for the public welfare *immolates* it."  This is wonderfully well put; but
in Madame de Lambert's time, it did not require a
large number of such phrases to fatigue any one who
was not endowed at birth with a mind of psychologi-
cal leanings, and more or less unpractical.

They called that preciosity, and a return to the
Hôtel de Rambouillet; one might as truly say that
it was in the direction and in the style of Madame
Necker's salon.  In my eyes Madame de Lambert
stands for the mean term between those two salons;
she is midway between them and is already turning
her eyes in the direction of the more modern one.

The ideas that she expresses concerning the rôle of
women and their condition are of a nature now and
then to cause surprise, even while they arouse profound esteem for the author.  Madame de Lambert,

like Mademoiselle de Scudéry, considers that nothing
is so ill-advised as the education commonly given to
young women.   "Their destiny is to please, and they
are given lessons in the art of pleasing only."   She,
on the contrary, the daughter of such a mother as we
have described, realised betimes the need that there is
for women to be reasonable beings, and to be armed
against their passions.   She insists that a woman
*must know how to think*.   She distrusts the sensitive
part of her organisation.   "Nothing is more prejudicial to happiness than a sensitive, ardent, and too
quickly kindled imagination."   Showy virtues do not
fall to the lot of women; it seems to distress her a
little to observe that fact, as well as "the nothingness, to which," she says, "the men have striven to
reduce us."   Women must resign themselves, therefore, to practise the modest virtues, and such virtues
are difficult, "because glory does not help us to
practise them."

The advice that Madame de Lambert gives her
daughter is especially noteworthy for its extraordinary comprehension of all the tender and vulnerable points of the sex, and for the extreme dread
which leads her to call to her assistance all possible
precautions and all possible resources.   One would
say that this woman, who waited until she was sixty
years old before making people talk of her, must have
previously put down many inward struggles, many
revolts; that she must have fought long and hard.   It

was for herself above all, it was to train and inure herself, that she wrote those judicious *Avis,* before transmitting them to her children. It was said in the preface to an English translation of her works, that in what she had written about women she had apologised for herself. She replied proudly: "I have never had occasion to make an apology." It was added that she had revealed a tender and sensitive mind. "I do not deny it," she replied; "it is only a question of being able to make the use of it that I have made."

This use is sufficiently indicated by the *Avis* themselves, so subtly unfolded and so forcibly defined; she exalted her courage, she fortified her reason, she avoided opportunities and risks; she indulged her tastes sparingly, and she put constraint upon her sensibility, in order to make it enduring and of as long duration as the longest life. "When we have a sound and healthy heart," she thought, "we make the best of everthing and everything is transformed into pleasure. . . . We spoil our taste by amusements; we become so accustomed to intense pleasures that we cannot descend to simple ones. We should dread these great commotions of the mind, which pave the way for ennui and distaste." She says some excellent things on this subject of the moderation and temperance of healthy minds— such things as could have been conceived only by an ardent mind which had partly triumphed over itself.

One fancies that one can detect in more than one of these bits of counsel the beginning of a confession, something like a personal revelation, checked in time.

"Attached to every vagary of the heart there is a pang and a sense of shame which implore you to stop it."

"It is not always our errors that ruin us, but our way of conducting ourselves after we have committed them."

Passion increases with every look backward ; to forget is the only sure remedy for love."

And there are a multitude of other thoughts by virtue of which Madame de Lambert deserved to be called the La Bruyère of women. She shares that honour with Madame de Staal de Launay.

I know nothing of Madame de Lambert's face, and they who wrote of her in her old age forgot to mention it. But as she had "a very pretty mother," and a daughter to whom she was able to say, "You were born not without attractions," it is to be believed that she herself was not altogether devoid of charm. Her virtue is the more praiseworthy if that be so.

In the "Reflections" properly so called, which she wrote concerning women, and which are distinct from the *Avis à sa Fille,* she gives herself a somewhat freer rein. She boldly attacks Molière for the ridicule that he cast upon learned women. She shows that, since women have been laughed at for laying claim to intellect, they have substituted de-

bauchery for learning. "When they found themselves assailed for innocent diversions, they argued
that, shame for shame, they had better choose that
which would pay them better, and they abandoned
themselves to pleasure." This little work of Madame
de Lambert, in which there is more than one idea
worthy to be discussed, must not be separated from
the circumstances that inspired it: it was written to
avenge her sex and to demand from it an honourable
and vigorous employment of the mind in face of the
orgies of the Regency. "These are my *débauches
d'esprit,*" said Madame de Lambert. At the sight of
the Duchesse de Berry, the Regent's daughter, and her
gross immoralities, she went back in her imagination
to Julie, Duchesse de Montausier.

Madame de Lambert preferred to those shameless
women of the Regency even the learned Madame
Dacier herself, whom she considered an authority on
the subject of the honour of the sex. "She knew
how to combine learning and the proprieties of life,"
she says ; "for in these days modesty has been
degraded, shame is no longer felt for vice, and
women blush for nothing save knowledge." In the
dispute that arose between that erudite person and
La Motte on the subject of Homer, Madame de
Lambert, although she leaned toward the side of her
friend La Motte, who was the more courteous and
refined, tried to hold the balance and to bring about
a reconciliation, which was effected a little later by

the intervention of M. de Valincour. Madame de
Lambert would have liked right well to filch from
him the credit of that arbitration, and to be able to
give to the two adversaries, at her house, that famous
dinner of reconciliation of which a witty guest said:
"We drank Homer's health, and everything went
off well."

When the Duchesse du Maine was in Paris, she frequently attended Madame de Lambert's Tuesdays, and
then there was a superabundant expenditure of *bel-
esprit,* and a contest of gallant conceits. In the works
of La Motte there is a whole volume concerning these
society trifles. On ordinary Tuesdays, the conversation at Madame de Lambert's was more serious and
more placid, although still very trenchant. The Marquis de Sainte-Aulaire, after the refinements of the
little Court of Sceaux,[1] surfeited by the lavish outlay
of wit there, sportively exclaimed:

> " Je suis las de l'esprit, il me met en courroux,
>   Il me renverse la cervelle;
> Lambert, je viens chercher un asile chez vous
>   Entre La Motte et Fontenelle." [2]

A queer position that, to assign to the unartificial,
some one may say, and between two strange neigh-

[1] See the essay on the Duchesse du Maine in Vol. I.; especially pp.
44–46.

[2] I am weary of wit, it rouses my bile,
      It turns my brain topsy turvy;
    Lambert, I come to take refuge with you,
      Between La Motte and Fontenelle."

bours. But everything is relative, and when one is suffocating with heat, a change of a few degrees, on going into another room, immediately produces the effect of the coolest of spring breezes. Let us add, that M. de Sainte-Aulaire was quite at home in Madame de Lambert's salon; for if it is true, as has been said, that "she knew no other passion than a constant and almost Platonic affection," he was its object.

Among the many bright men who frequented her salon—of whom I may mention Mairan, the Abbé de Mongault, the Abbé de Choisy, the Abbé de Bragelonne, Père Buffier, and Président Hénault—Madame de Lambert had chosen a second favourite in the person of M. de Sacy, the elegant translator of the younger Pliny, in whom she found a combination of all the virtues and all the accomplishments, *les mœurs et les grâces*. The society of her other friends was agreeable to her, but that of M. de Sacy was necessary. More than forty years later, d'Alembert, writing in his *Éloges Académiques* that of M. de Sacy, drew a touching picture of the friendship between him and Madame de Lambert, and while drawing it, he recalled to his own mind, by an evident allusion, his liaison with Mademoiselle de Lespinasse, whom he had recently lost.

The literary conclusion concerning Madame de Lambert, that talented person, at once so refined and so right-minded, who made so noble a use of her talents and her fortune, was pronounced long ago by another friend of hers whom I have already mentioned, the judicious Marquis d'Argenson.

" Her works," he wrote, " contain a complete course in morality most admirably adapted for the use of society and of the present. More or less affectation of preciosity is blended with it; but what noble thoughts, what refined sentiments ! How beautifully she speaks of the Duties of Women, of Friendship, of Old Age, of the difference between *Consideration* and *Reputation !* It is a book to be read and reread over and over again."

Thus far I have barely mentioned Madame Necker, inscribed her name by the side of Madame de Lambert's and facing it, to indicate my plan, and to open a perspective. I come now to this second figure, and once more I have to deal with virtue, morality, and veneration of the intellect, in an exemplar more interesting than is commonly supposed.

To form a just estimate of Madame Necker is an undertaking not free from difficulty. Her failings are of those which most readily give offence in France,— they are not French failings; and her good qualities are of those which too frequently are placed second to matters of tact and taste, for they are qualities of the mind and the temperament. It is my desire to deal equitably with both, and to judge that talented person with entire freedom, but always with consideration and with respect. One may judge a public man, dead or alive, with some severity; but it seems to me that a woman, even when dead, provided that she has not ceased to be a woman in all the essential qualities, is always our contemporary to some extent; she is so especially when she has perpetuated herself to our own day by a posterity of renown, of virtue, and of charm.

In order rightly to appreciate Madame Necker, who in Paris was never aught but a transplanted flower, it is proper to view her in her first bloom and on her natal soil.  Madamoiselle Suzanne Curchod was born about 1740, at Crassier in the Pays-de-Vaud, the frontier of France and Switzerland.  Her father was pastor, or minister, of the Holy Gospel; her mother, a native of France, had preferred her religion to her country. She was reared and nourished in that country-parsonage life, in which some poets have laid the scene of their most exquisite idylls, and she imbibed there, together with the virtues of the fireside, an inclination for serious studies.  She was beautiful, with that pure, virginal beauty which is at its best in early youth. Her long and rather straight face was animated by brilliant colouring, and softened by blue eyes instinct with candour.  Her slender figure had as yet only a modest dignity, without stiffness, and without affectation.  Such she first appeared to Gibbon during a sojourn that she made at Lausanne.  The future historian of the Roman Empire was himself very young at that time; his father had sent him to Lausanne to be educated anew and to be cured of " the errors of popery," into which the young Oxford student had allowed himself to be led.  Gibbon passed five years in that agreeable exile, from the age of sixteen to twenty-one.  In June, 1757 (he was then twenty), he first met Mademoiselle Suzanne Curchod, whom the whole town of Lausanne called "La belle Curchod," and who could not appear at a party or at the play without being surrounded by a circle of adorers. Gibbon wrote that evening in his Journal this sentimental and classic note: "I have seen Mlle. Curchod—Omnia vincit Amor, et nos cedamus Amori." In his *Memoirs* he goes into more detail and draws for us a most flattering and most lifelike portrait of Mademoiselle Curchod, as she was at that time.

"Her father," he says, "in the solitude of a lonely village, devoted himself to giving his only daughter a liberal and even a learned education. She surpassed his hopes by her progress in the sciences and languages; and in the brief visits that she paid to some of her friends at Lausanne, Mademoiselle Curchod's wit, beauty, and learning were the subject of universal applause. The tales that I heard of such a prodigy aroused my curiosity: *I saw and I loved.* I found her learned without pedantry, lively in conversation, pure in sentiment, and refined in manners; and that first sudden emotion was only strengthened by the familiarity and observation of a more intimate acquaintance. She allowed me to pay her two or three visits at her father's house. I passed several happy days there, among the mountains of Franche-Comté, and her parents honourably encouraged the intimacy."

Gibbon, who had not yet acquired that grotesque ugliness which afterwards developed, and who already combined "the most brilliant and most diversified intellect with the gentlest and most equable of dispositions," declares that Mademoiselle Curchod allowed herself to be genuinely touched ; he himself went so far as to speak of marriage, and it was not until after his return to England that, having met with an ob-

stacle to that union in his father's will, he abandoned
it. But the whole affair passed off, so far as Gibbon
was concerned, with an equanimity and calmness,
even in disappointment, which makes one smile.
Seven years later, on his return from Italy, he met
Mademoiselle Curchod again in Paris, newly married
to M. Necker, and was greeted by her with a mixture
of cordiality and pique.

"I do not know, Madame," wrote Madame Necker to one of her
Lausanne friends (November, 1765), " whether I have told you that I
have seen Gibbon; I was moved beyond all expression by that pleasure,—not that I still retain any inclination for a man, who, in my
opinion, hardly deserves it, but my feminine vanity never had a more
complete or more honourable triumph. He stayed in Paris two
weeks; I had him at my house every day; he had become gentle,
yielding, humble, modest even to timidity. A constant witness of my
husband's affection, his wit, and his playful humour, and a jealous admirer of opulence, he directed my attention for the first time to that
by which I am surrounded; at all events it had never before made any
other than an unpleasant impression on me."

Mademoiselle Curchod, then, was, in the year 1758,
at the age of eighteen, one of the brightest flowers,
one of the marvels of that Pays-de-Vaud which Rousseau was ere long to bring into fashion in the first
Parisian society by *La Nouvelle Héloïse*. Rousseau,
however, found a way to be unfair to that pleasant
province, even while he depicted it as the setting of
an earthly Paradise.

"I can honestly say," he wrote in a celebrated
passage of the *Confessions,* " 'Go to Vevay, visit the
country thereabout, sail on the lake, and tell me if

nature did not make that fair land for a Julie, for a Claire, and for a Saint-Preux; but do not seek them there.' "   And I will say, and all who have known and dwelt in that province will say with me: " Yes, seek there, if not Julies and Saint-Preux, at all events women of the type of Claire; I mean by that, women with a certain turn of wit, a blending of gravity and gaiety, at once natural and artificial, quite capable of argument, of study, even of dialectics ; yet vivacious, rather given to surprises, and by no means devoid of lighter accomplishments and charm."

Mademoiselle Susanne Curchod was, in her blending of qualities, one of those complex yet ingenuous natures, which are far from being unattractive when one meets them amid such surroundings, on the slopes or in the valleys of those terraced green hills which border the Lake of Geneva on the Swiss side.

Voltaire, just returned from Prussia, and before he settled permanently in the suburbs of Geneva, made a trial of this novel sort of life at Lausanne, where he passed the winters of 1756, 1757, and 1758.   He was amazed to find there a taste for things of the intellect which he helped to develop, but which he had not to create.

"Among the gossips of Paris," he wrote, "it is commonly supposed that all of Switzerland is a barbarous country; people would be much surprised to see *Zaïre* played at Lausanne much better than it is played in Paris; they would be even more surprised to see two hundred spectators who are as good judges as there are in Europe. I have caused tears to flow from every Swiss eye."

Abate what you please of this praise, make every allowance for courtesy and hospitality, and something will still remain.  It was amid these surroundings that Madame Necker, still unmarried, completed her educa-cation in the flower of her youth, and became a distinguished figure.

Having lost her venerated father about this time, and being left alone with her mother, who was without means, she aroused the profound interest of all who met her; and as the greatest respect for learning and education prevails in that French-Swiss province, it was suggested that she should give lessons in languages and in those branches of learning which she had studied in the paternal parsonage.  She did so with success, with great distinction; she gave lectures, as has always been the custom in Switzerland; she had pupils of both sexes; and a few years ago there could still be seen, in a little valley near Lausanne, the platform or mound of verdure, erected by way of rostrum or throne by the students of the neighbourhood, from which the fair orphan of Crassier awarded praise or prizes, or it may be, on fine days in summer, delivered her lectures in the open air.

During these years Mademoiselle Curchod lost her mother, who had witnessed all her triumphs and had taken joy in them.  Thereupon her friends became more than ever troubled concerning the future of that lovely, virtuous, and learned young woman, who was nearly twenty-four years old.  It was decided that she should go to Paris, under the wing of a society woman, Madame de Vermenou, who, happening to pass through Geneva, had seen her and become enamoured of her talents. Madame de Vermenou, who was a widow, was sought in marriage by M. Necker, a banker, already rich, a member of the Compagnie des Indes, and at this time thirty-two years of age; she had not been able to make up her mind to give him a favourable answer. But he had no sooner seen at Madame de Vermenou's house the young lady whom she had brought with her from Switzerland than he realised that his fancy had changed its object, and it was Mademoiselle Curchod who, after a sojourn of a few months at Paris, became Madame Necker, in 1764.

In a series of letters written by Madame Necker to one of her friends in Lausanne, we have a narrative of her thoughts and impressions in the new world in which she was embarked. She has at the outset the feeling of being transplanted and denationalised. Her taste for intellectual things finds satisfaction there, but the cravings of her heart begin to cause her suffering. "How barren of affection this country is!" she cries. When she is better informed she will withdraw that charge, and, a few years later, will say: "Despite my prepossessions, I have found in the heart of Paris people of the purest virtue and capable of the tenderest affection." But this discovery requires more than a day. Her health is impaired at the very beginning;

no one can divine the cause of her indisposition, but it is attributable to homesickness and to the nervous fatigue which will not fail to grow worse with the years, in this novel situation where fortune requires to be purchased by such a multitude of duties and exacting social conventions.

Madame Necker had formed an idea of the authors and clever men and women of Paris solely from books, and she found that the society in which she had to steer her craft was far more diversified, varied, and full of subtle distinctions. "When I arrived in this country," she says, "I thought that letters were the key to everything, that a man cultivated his mind by books alone, and was great only in proportion to his knowledge." But the sort of conversation that coincided with that idea was little in vogue except *en tête-à-tête,* and she very soon discovered her mistake.

"I had not a word to say in company," she adds; "I did not even know the language. Called upon by my sex to fascinate men's minds, I was entirely ignorant of all the different shades of self-esteem, and I offended it when I thought to flatter it. What we used to call frankness in Switzerland became egotism in Paris; negligence in trifles was non-observance of the proprieties here; in a word, for ever out of tune with my surroundings and abashed by my blunders and my ignorance, never able to find the right word, and foreseeing that my present ideas would never harmonise with those that I was obliged to acquire, I have buried my little store so that I may never see it again, and have set to work to earn my living and to save a little if I can."

It is this painful effort which manifests itself in all that Madame Necker has written, and which helped to undermine her health prematurely. No brain ever worked harder or suffered more than hers.

Placed, within a few months of her arrival in France, at the head of an establishment where she received all those who were most in vogue of Parisian men of letters, eager to prove herself competent and successful in her efforts, a disciple and rival of Madame Geoffrin, she was forced constantly to draw upon herself, upon her health, upon her cherished habits, upon her other tastes.

"I must take this opportunity to make a confession," she wrote in 1771 to a friend in Switzerland; "it is this—that, from the day of my arrival in Paris I have not lived for a single instant on the stock of ideas that I had previously acquired; I except the matter of morals, but I was obliged to make my mind over *entirely new* with respect to the human character, with respect to the circumstances of life, and with respect to conversation."

And, in truth, if we reflect a moment, apart from the excellent Thomas, with whom she became acquainted at the very first, and who met the demands of the serious and somewhat solemn tendencies of her mind; Marmontel, who had the good sense to form a just estimate of her; and, somewhat later, Buffon, who knew enough to appreciate her homage, and who repaid it in admiration,—apart from these, who were the men of letters with whom she had to deal, and whom she was most desirous to entertain regularly and to gather about her?

There was little Abbé Galiani, "who could not forgive her for being virtuous, and for maintaining *the frigid demeanour of modesty."*    There was Diderot, who wrote to Mademoiselle Voland, in August, 1765: "There is a Madame Necker here, a pretty woman and a *bel-esprit,* who fairly dotes on me; she persecutes me to get me to come to her house.    Suard is paying court to her," etc.    There was that crowd of *beaux-esprits,* all more or less licentious and irreligious,—Abbé Arnaud, Abbé Raynal, and Abbé Morellet, to whom she applied among the first to start her salon.

" The conversation there was very well," Morellet tells us, "although somewhat constrained by the rigid morality of Madame Necker, in whose presence many subjects could not be mentioned, and who was especially distressed by liberty of opinion in religious matters.    But on literary subjects the conversation was very interesting, and she herself talked very well indeed."

We can imagine the constant labour and striving of Madame Necker's faculties in the presence of this entirely unfamiliar society, especially when the circle of her connections widened more and more as M. Necker began his upward course.    To enumerate all those whom she received in her salon at Paris or in her park at Saint-Ouen, we should have to give a list of the élite of France.[1]

[1] [Among their friends was the Marquise de Créqui, the alleged author of certain *Mémoires,* the real authorship of which is a mystery.    In an essay on Madame de Créqui, Sainte-Beuve says: " She goes there [to the Neckers'] to dine once or twice, but on that head she has a veritable grievance against them which prevents her from going again: they dine at the undue hour of *half-past four ;* the Marchioness was accustomed to dine at two."—Tr.]

It has been said that M. Necker made himself noticeable at first in his wife's salon only by his attitude of observation and by a disdainful, or, perhaps, prudent silence upon subjects as to all of which he was not equally well informed. He emerged from this silence only on rare occasions, with some sharp sally, some malicious or joking sentence with which he marked as it passed a blunder or an absurd remark. That serious-minded man had a shrewd and quizzical turn of mind which was peculiar to him, and he proved it afterwards by certain writings which bear witness to a minute and searching observation. Madame du Deffand, that severe and formidable judge, who afterward became intimate with the Neckers, found the husband much to her liking and gave the wife credit for intellect and talent; she said of him, however, that with all his good qualities he lacked a single one, and that the one which makes a man most attractive, "a certain facility which, so to speak, supplies wit to those with whom he is talking; he does not assist one to develop one's thoughts, and one is more stupid with him than when alone or with other people." It would be impossible to define better the effect produced by that type of mind, aloof, exalted, isolated, and unsympathetic,—the *doctrinaire* mind, to call it by its name,—of which M. Necker was the fountain-head among us. Madame Necker, beneath her cold and constrained exterior, loved her husband with lofty passion, with adoration, and he returned her love in kind. Not by any means the least striking singularity of the period was that altar to honourable and decent wedlock, erected in the heart of Paris and in the centre of the philosophical sect.

"I am very fond of some of our modern philosophers," said Madame Necker, "but I am not fond of their philosophy." In a letter in which she apologises for her inability to introduce to the philosophers two young men from Zürich, she represents them as unable to control themselves in their speech, and as accustomed to work in the morning in their studies and to talk all the rest of the day.

"The morning is devoted to study, and they exercise such entire liberty of thought that they cannot endure to meet a strange face in the houses they frequent; for he who says liberty of thought implies a violent desire to talk. I see some of them, and luckily their morals, which are very respectable, correct the impression produced by their principles; otherwise it would be preferable to renounce the society of such people."

But to renounce it would have cost her too dear; her great merit is that she was able to reconcile her passionate love for intellectual things with perfect integrity of principle amid her perilous surroundings.

Strangely enough, despite their enforced silence on religious subjects, free thinkers like Diderot found themselves even more at ease in Madame Necker's salon than in Madame Geoffrin's. In the latter it was social circumspection, strict observance of the proprieties, which took precedence of everything else; at Madame Necker's it was virtue and an unfailing

amiability, which made itself felt even amid disagree-
ments and reproach.

It was in Madame Necker's salon, and under her
inspiration, that the idea of erecting a statue to Voltaire was first suggested, in 1770. He wrote her
several entertaining letters and even one or two amorous madrigals on that subject.   Pigalle was chosen to
execute the patriarch's statue; but when she learned
that the sculptor proposed to make him absolutely
nude, Madame Necker made a great outcry.   Not so
had her modesty understood the commission.

In matters of taste, Madame Necker, being not at
all sure of herself, and forming her opinion only after
reflection, as is usually the case with persons who
have passed their youth elsewhere than in Paris, believed, when she came thither, that she had simply
to take lessons, as in everything else.   "The only
advantage of this country," she wrote after living here
a year, "is that it trains the taste, but it is at the expense of genius; a sentence is twisted and turned in
a thousand ways, and the idea examined from every
standpoint."   And she thought to acquire taste herself
by subjecting her ideas to that species of test, we
might almost say of torture.   In reality she would
have liked, not, as she says, to make herself over entirely new, but to combine two types of intellect, to
blend in some way the intellect of her canton with
ours.   Unluckily the graft with her always continued to
be refractory, and her success was very far from perfect.

If one opens the posthumous *Mélanges* of Madame
Necker, after laying aside some work of the seventeenth century, one seems to enter an entirely new
world, and to have to do with a different language.
"She did not try," some one has said, in describing
Madame de Caylus's style of writing and her agreeable
carelessness. Surely no one will ever say that on
reading Madame Necker's collected works. At every
turn we meet with comparisons which, far from explaining her thought, often obscure and enigmatical in
itself, do but make it still more obscure; the faint
gleam that we may have caught a glimpse of vanishes.
Some of these comparisons are exceedingly odd. For
instance, wishing to describe people who are not
equable in disposition or in sensibility, and who scat-
ter themselves about here and there as if they had
several distinct minds, she says that " they resemble
crabs, one of whose claws may be cut off and the loss
be not apparent after two or three days, because they
have several centres of feeling." She is fond of mythological similes, and some of them are very far-fetched.
Speaking in praise of her husband, and arguing that
his life has become indispensable to the public weal,
she says: "It is the *brand of Meleager* upon which
his ministerial life hangs." [1] This brand of Meleager

[1] [The Parcæ entered the chamber of Althæa, Meleager's mother, and
told her that her son would live until the brand then on the fire should
be consumed; Meleager having slain Althæa's brothers as a result of a
dispute over the carcass of the Calydonian boar, she flew into a rage
and thrust the fatal brand into the fire, and Meleager died.—Tr.]

recurs in more than one passage. In a word, we are much too conscious that comparisons, in the works of this clever woman, do not present themselves unbidden, that they are not born under her feet and from the womb of the subject that she is discussing, that they are not suggested by their pertinency at the moment, but that she produces them from some more ancient storehouse, from some notes of conversation where she had them in reserve. So that they cause surprise before all else, and afford no enlightenment.

It would be unjust not to recognise, beside this artificiality, all that is natural in her writings, all that distinguishes her from other women in that age of corruption and sham sensibility. Her sensibility is genuine; it is drawn from the purest moral sources; and when we come to a question of mental elevation, it is both pleasant and profitable to listen to her. Would not one fancy that she was thinking of Madame de Lambert and remembering something of hers that she had read, when she said: "Happy the man who has never found pleasure except in sudden and reasonable impulses! he will be sure of being entertained as long as he lives." She turned her thoughts betimes to the decline of life and to the moment when external charms fade away. Every day adds to her distaste for fashionable society, where everything seems to be artificial, and where her heart finds so little nourishment. She goes back to the past, she loves to live again therein. While she felt at first

all that she lacked in Paris, she nevertheless appreciated that the life there soon becomes indispensable to
those who have once tasted it. "It is certain," she
writes, "that one may and should be happier elsewhere; but for that to be so one must know nothing
of the fascination which, while it does not give happiness, poisons for ever all other kinds of life." When
she wrote these words she was still half under the
spell (1773).

Her husband's first ministry, which must of course
have elated her, was also the moment when she began
to lose her illusions.

"My heart and my regrets," she wrote to a friend in July, 1779,
"seek constantly a universe where beneficence is the first of virtues.
How am I undeceived, concerning ourselves especially! I expected to
see the age of gold under so pure an administration; I see only the age
of iron; all our aspirations are reduced to doing as little harm as
possible."

And so from that moment regret for the past laid hold
upon her.

"Regret for the past," she cries, "always turns my glances toward
that Being for whom there is no past. I seem to see Him surrounded
by all the hours that we have lived, and I seek by his side both the
moments and the persons who seem no longer to exist for us ; thereupon my heart becomes tranquil, my wandering and despairing
thought finds a refuge."

She did not, as so many women do, regret her
fleeting youth and fading beauty. One day, however
(she was thirty-four years old), she allowed something
like a faint lament to escape her:

"I have much difficulty," she wrote to a friend, "in accustoming
myself to all sorts of change; age, which seems to come so slowly,

took me by surprise by that selfsame noiseless tread ; I fancy that I am in a new world, and I do not know whether the brief instant of my youth was a dream, or whether the dream is just now beginning."

But she soon made the best of it, and the resources of middle age were all in readiness.

" As my tastes in my younger days were vastly different from those which engross me now, I felt but slightly the incommodities of the transition; it came about by slow degrees, and I have never failed to find substitutes for what I have lost. And so, when I look in the glass at my faded complexion and my sunken eyes, and when, on looking into myself, I find a mind more active and more steadfast, then, if it were not that Time has robbed me of the objects of an affection which will end only with my life, I should not know whether I ought to complain of him."

The first ministry of her husband, or, as she said less familiarly, of her *friend,* afforded her an opportunity to develop her virtues and to put them in practice on a grand scale. In 1778 the patients in the hospitals were by no means well treated; it will suffice to say that it was the custom to put more than one in the same bed, and the hospital founded by Madame Necker was originally designed "to demonstrate the possibility of caring for patients *alone in bed,* with all the attention of the most tender-hearted humanity, and without exceeding a fixed price." The experiment was tried in a small hospital of only a hundred and twenty patients. Madame Necker, the foundress, continued to be for ten years the manager and vigilant steward. She deserved to have her share of public praise in a passage of M. Necker's report to the king

in January, 1781. Although worldly malice might find
food for ridicule in this formal laudation by a husband of
his helpmeet, I must confess that in this case the smile
dies on the lips, in view of the loftiness of the object
and the magnitude of the benefaction.

I do not propose to follow her in the details of her
life and of her various journeys, undertaken for the
most part to restore her health, which was impaired by
nervous paroxysms indicating the travail of the mind.
The duties of her position, the conventions of society,
unceasing watchfulness of herself and of her surroundings, a sensitiveness which was coerced and often
held in subjection, silently and with intense suffering
—all these did their part toward wearing out Madame
Necker before her time. Two enthusiastic friendships
were predominant in her life next to her worship of
her husband. The more exalted of these friendships,
which was itself similar to worship, was that which
bound her to M. de Buffon. The other was for
Thomas, that estimable and moral writer, whom it is
the fashion to laugh at to-day, but who was possessed
of distinguished literary talents and touching qualities
of the heart.

Madame Necker's daughter, who was to be the
illustrious Madame de Staël, was already growing up
and escaping from her. As lively and impulsive as
her mother was self-restrained and cautious, fluttering in all the breezes of the age, and endowed with
a genius which was destined to venture upon many

paths, she surprised and disturbed that wise mother, and suggested to her this involuntary thought: "Children ordinarily feel little gratitude for our anxieties in their behalf; they are young twigs that lose patience with the stalk that joins them, unmindful of the fact that they would break if they were detached from it." M. Necker, in the intervals of his serious business, delighted in his daughter's outbreaks and took pleasure in encouraging them. It has been said that Madame Necker was made unhappy by this preference, and that the wife was more vulnerable than the mother was proud.

The events of M. Necker's second ministry left her far behind, and on every occasion when there was any room for hesitation she was with the party that advocated retirement. So that it was some consolation for her, amid so many subjects of distress, to find herself in 1790 at Lausanne or Coppet, in sight of her beautiful lake, and not far from the graves of her parents. During these last years, and while '93 was sowing its crop of horrors in France, she composed a touching work which has found favour even with those who have shown themselves most severe upon Madame Necker's type of intellect,—I mean her *Réflexions sur la Divorce,* which appeared soon after her death. In this work, which she wrote with a hand already failing, Madame Necker proposed to do battle with the French law of divorce and to point out wherein it is opposed to the principal aims of nature in the organisation of society, and of morality.  Strong in her own example, in her own life of virtue and piety, she pleads for the indissolubility of the marriage tie; she cannot conceive how a fundamental institu- tution can be thus left to the mercy of human whims and physical charms.   "For the first charm of youth," she says, "is only a first bond which supports two plants newly set side by side, until, having taken root there, they live wholly upon the same substance." Depicting the happiness of a loyal husband and wife, especially that of the father who, seeing that he lives anew in the features of his children, reads therein the chastity of his wife, in the genuineness of her emotion she attains the perfection of expression and colouring:

" Sometimes indeed a dearly loved husband sees all of himself in the features of his children.   Nature, who thus becomes the guarantor and interpreter of conjugal love, delights to sanctify with her inimit- able brush the chaste passion of a loyal wife; and every glance that a fond father casts upon sons who resemble him, falls with renewed tenderness upon their mother."

These are captivating thoughts, set forth in most natural terms.   Side by side with them, to be sure, Madame Necker repeats some of her earlier faults. She carries to excess mythological comparisons, his- torical illustrations, Meleagers, Arrias, and Pætuses. She most inopportunely cites Henri IV in connection with the picture by Rubens representing the lying-in of Marie de' Medici.   Henri IV and Marie de' Medici are unfortunate examples to recall, apropos of marital fidelity.   We observe still the same lack of delicacy

of touch in respect to the association of ideas and the
relevancy of the nice distinctions in her comparisons.
But these failings are more readily redeemed here than
elsewhere; the subject inspires her; it is elevated and
ingenious; and when she comes to the consideration
of marriage late in life, to that final goal of consolation, and sometimes of happiness too, in that disin-
herited age, her words are noble and strong: "The
happiness or unhappiness of old age is often only
the essence of our past life." And describing, after the
experience of her own heart and after her ideal, the
final happiness of a husband and wife,

"Who love ev'n to the last despite th' unwilling years,"

she traces for us the image, and confides to us the
secret, of her own destiny; that truly delightful passage
should be read from beginning to end.

"A husband and wife who are attached to each other mark the
stages of their long life by pledges of virtue and reciprocal fondness;
they fortify themselves with the past and make of it a rampart against
the attacks of the present. Ah! who could endure to be cast alone
upon the unknown shore of old age? Our tastes are changed, our
minds are enfeebled, the testimony and the affection of another person are
the only proofs that we still exist; sentiment alone teaches us to recognise ourselves; it bids Time relax his sway for a moment. And so,
far from regretting the world which shuns us, we shun it in our turn;
we escape from selfish projects which no longer appeal to us; our
thoughts increase in magnitude like shadows at the approach of night,
and a last ray of love, which is now wholly divine, seems to form the
transitional stage between the purest sentiments that we are capable
of feeling here on earth and those which will inspire us in heaven.
Watch, Almighty God, over the friend, the only friend who shall receive our last breath, who shall close our eyes, nor fear to bestow a
farewell kiss on lips cold in death!"

I have thought it well to quote at length this curious specimen of a fervid and solemn sort of eloquence,— a most curious specimen, in very truth, if we reflect that it is a product of the last half of the eighteenth century, of that social hierarchy which was already on the verge of dissolution, and that it was written by a person who had lived in the midst of that society thirty years and had not allowed herself to be tainted or infected for a single instant. It was like going back to Philemon and Baucis, but in the only way in which it could be done at that time, namely by means of a certain amount of declamation. It is at all events perfectly sincere; it may readily be mistaken for eloquence, and at the close it is even more than that,—it is a prayer.

Madame Necker had sung her swan's song; she died in May, 1784, in a country house near Lausanne; she was only fifty-four years old. In a *Notice* written by her grandson may be read some affecting details of her last hours. But, even outside her domestic circle, Madame Necker deserves to be remembered in our literature and to hold a more distinguished place therein than has generally been accorded her down to the present time. France owes to her Madame de Staël, and that magnificent gift has made us too prone to forget everything else. Madame Necker, with certain faults which offend at first sight and at which it is easy to arouse a smile, had her own sources of inspiration, and a strongly marked personality. Entering Parisian society with the distinct purpose to be a *femme d' esprit,* and to join hands with the *beaux esprits* of the time, she was able to preserve her moral conscience, to protest against the false doctrines that were poured upon her from all directions, to preach by her own example, to be loyal to her duties in the centre of fashionable society, and by way of atonement for some too subtle ideas and some affected turns of phrase, to leave behind her more than one monument of her beneficence, a spotless memory, and a few eloquent pages.

As for her daughter, although Madame Necker admired her, she certainly would have liked her to be altogether different, and it is difficult to follow in her career the influence of her mother. But it is much less difficult to trace this influence in some others of her descendants, and Madame Necker's cast of mind, softened and mellowed after the first generation, has surely counted for much in the elevated form of thought, and in the moral principles, always conspicuous, of an illustrious family.

# Denis Diderot.

## 1713–1784.

## Denis Diderot.

I HAVE always loved the correspondence, the conversation, all the details of the character, the morals, the biography, in a word, of great writers; especially when such a comparative biography does not already exist, prepared by another, and one has to construct and compose it for oneself.

You seclude yourself for a fortnight with the writings of some illustrious dead man—poet or philosopher; you study him, you turn him this way and that, you question him at your leisure; you make him pose for you, so to speak; it is almost as if one passed a fortnight in the country making a portrait or a bust of Byron, Scott, or Goethe; only one is more at ease with one's model, and the *tête-à-tête,* at the same time that it demands a little more attention, imparts much more familiarity. Each feature in turn comes forward and of its own motion takes its place in the countenance you are striving to reproduce; just as one star after another becomes visible and begins to shine in its appointed place in the panorama of a lovely night. With the vague, abstract general type, which alone was apparent at the first glance, becomes blended and incorporated by degrees a real, well-defined individuality, more and more accentuated, shining with ever-increasing brilliancy; you feel the birth of the likeness and watch its growth; and on the day, the moment, when you have seized the familiar trick, the revelatory smile, the imperceptible blemish, the secret and distressing wrinkle which hides itself in vain under the hair already growing thin,—at that moment analysis vanishes in creation, the portrait speaks and lives, you have found the man.

There is always pleasure in this sort of secret study, and there will always be a place for the works which a keen and sincere enthusiasm may produce as a result of such study. Always, in our opinion, good taste and art will give opportuneness and some lasting quality to the briefest and most specialised works, if, while setting forth but a narrowly restricted portion of nature and of life, they are stamped with that unique seal of the diamond, the imprint of which is recognisable at a glance, which is handed down unchangeable and perfect through the ages, and which one would try in vain to describe or to counterfeit.

Thus much we, as a literary critic, felt that we must say before setting about a careful study of art and a close scrutiny of the great men of the past; it has seemed to us that, despite all that has taken place in the world and all that is still taking place, a portrait of Regnier, of Boileau, of La Fontaine, of André Chenier, of any

DENIS DIDEROT
*Bronze by Pigalle*

one of those men whose peers are in all ages very rare, would be no more a puerile matter to-day than a year ago; and by turning our attention at this time to Diderot, philosopher and artist, by following him closely in his attractive private life, by watching him speak and listening to his thoughts in his most unreserved moments, we shall at least have gained, in addition to the acquaintance of one more great man, the pleasure of forgetting for a few days the distressing spectacle of the society in which we live, so much poverty and turbulence among the masses, so much ill-defined alarm and such consuming selfishness among the higher classes; governments devoid of ideas and of grandeur; heroic nations sacrificed; the sentiment of patriotism dying out and nothing broader to take its place; religion fallen back into the depths from which it must conquer the world anew, and the future becoming more and more veiled in mist, concealing a shore which does not yet appear.[1]

It was not altogether so in Diderot's time. Then the work of destruction was just beginning to cut to the quick in philosophic and political theory; the task, notwithstanding the difficulties of the moment, seemed quite simple; the obstacles were clearly defined, and the assailants rushed to the assault with admirable concert and with hopes at once boundless and near fulfilment.

[1] [The essay from which this passage is taken was written in 1831. —Tr.]

Diderot, who has been so diversely judged, is, of all the men of the eighteenth century, the one whose personality sums up most completely the philosophic revolt with its broadest and most sharply contrasted characteristics. He paid little attention to politics, which he left to Montesquieu, Jean-Jacques, and Raynal; but in philosophy he was in a sense the soul and the mouthpiece of the century, the guiding theorist *par excellence.* Jean-Jacques was a spiritualist, and at times a sort of Socinian Calvinist; he denied arts, sciences, trade, perfectibility, and in all these directions clashed with his age rather than reflected it. In several respects he stood by himself in that licentious, materialistic society, dazzled by its own brilliancy. D'Alembert was prudent, circumspect, moderate, and frugal in doctrine, weak and timid in temperament, a sceptic in everything except geometry; he had two faces, one for the public, another in private life,—a philosopher of the school of Fontenelle. Buffon did not lack faith in himself and his ideas, but he was not lavish of them, he elaborated them in private and put them forth only at intervals, beneath a pompous style, the grandiloquence of which was, in his eyes, its surpassing merit.

Now, the eighteenth century is justly considered to have been lavish of ideas, familiar in speech, and quick to act, all things to all men, with no aversion for dishabille; and when it got overheated in fervid talk, holding forth in some salon for or against God,—faith!

then it did not hesitate, the dear old century, to remove its wig, like Abbé Galiani, and hang it on the
back of a chair. As for Voltaire, that indefatiga-
ble bear-leader, whose adroitness in action was so
marvellous, and who was in that respect a practical
philosopher, he bothered his head very little about
constructing, or even adopting the whole of the
metaphysical theory of that day; he confined himself
to what was most clear, he hastened where the need
was most urgent, he aimed at the tallest, wasting none
of his shots, and worrying men and gods from afar,
like a Parthian with his whistling arrows. In the
pitiless vigour of his common sense, he even went so
far as to rail lightly at the labours of his epoch, by
whose aid chemistry and physiology were seeking to
elucidate the mysteries of the human organism.

Thus the philosophical faculty of the age needed, in
order to become individualised in a single genius, a
brain to conceive more patient and more serious than
Voltaire's; it required more abundance, more rapidity
of outflow and more solid elevation of thought than
could be found in Buffon, more amplitude and glowing resolution than in d'Alembert; a sympathy for the
arts, sciences, and trade, which Rousseau had not.
Diderot was the man,—Diderot, a rich and fertile
nature, open to seeds of all sorts, fertilising them in
his breast, and transforming them almost at random
by an instinctive and undefined force; a vast, bubbling
mould, wherein everything was in a state of fusion,

wherein everything was crushed, wherein everything was in a ferment; a capacity more all-embracing than any other of his time, but active, consuming and vivifying at once, arousing and inflaming everything that came in its way, and sending it forth again in torrents of flame, and of smoke as well; Diderot, passing from a stocking-machine, which he takes apart and describes, to d'Holbach's and Rouelle's crucibles, and Bordeu's *Considérations;* dissecting, if he will, man and his senses as skilfully as Condillac, splitting the slenderest hair without breaking it, then abruptly returning to the bosom of creation, of space, and of nature, and boldly carving from the vast metaphysical geometry some ample fragments, sublime and luminous pages, which Malebranche or Leibnitz might have signed with pride if they had not been Christtians [1]; a mind of intelligence, of audacity, and of conjecture, alternating between fact and fancy, wavering between majesty and cynicism, kindly even in its disordered state, and, like his epoch, lacking naught of harmony save a divine ray, a *fiat lux,* a guiding idea, a God. [2]

Such had to be, in the eighteenth century, the man adapted to preside over the philosophic workshop,

[1] *Christians?* The word is more applicable to Malebranche than to Leibnitz.

[2] Grimm compared Diderot's brain to nature as Diderot conceived it: rich, fertile, gentle and wild, simple and majestic, kindly and sublime, but without any predominant principle, without a master, and without God.

the leader of the undesciplined army of thinkers, the
man who had the power to organise them as volun-
teers, to call them together at his pleasure, to urge
them on by his effervescent energy in the conspiracy
against the still subsisting order of things. Between
Voltaire, Buffon, Rousseau, and d'Holbach, between
the chemists and the *beaux-esprits,* between the geo-
metricians, the mechanicians, and the men of letters, between these last and the artists, sculptors, and
painters, between the partisans of the ancient taste
and innovators like Sedaine, Diderot was the connecting link. He it was who best understood them as a
body and as individuals, who judged them with the
best grace and carried them most considerately in his
heart; who, with the least obtrusion of self and of
self-sufficiency (*quant-à-soi*), passed most freely from
one to another. He was therefore well adapted to be
the shifting centre, the pivot of the whirlwind; to lead
the line to the assault with inspiration and in unison,
and with a something tempestuous and imposing in
his bearing. The head erect and slightly bald, vast
forehead, the temples bare, the eye aflame or moist
with a great tear, the neck bare, and, as he says,
"uncovered, the back broad and full," the arms out-
stretched to the future;[1] a mixture of grandeur and

---

[1] [" 'His high, open, and gracefully rounded brow,' says Meister,
'bore the imposing imprint of a vast, luminous, and fruitful mind.'
He adds that Lavater thought that he detected indications of a timid,
unenterprising spirit; and there is ground for the statement that, with
all his daring intellect, Diderot's springs of conduct and action were

pettiness, of exaggeration and reality, of fiery enthusiasm and human sympathy; such as he was, and
not as he was misrepresented by Falconet and Vanloo,
I imagine him in the theoretic movement of the century, worthily leading those men who seem to be
of his family, those leaders whose ascendancy is un-
marred by arrogance, whose heroism is disfigured by
impurity, but glorious despite their vices, veritable
giants in the *mêlée,* and in reality better than their
lives: Mirabeau, Danton, Kléber.

Denis Diderot was born at Langres, in October,
1713; his father was a cutler. For two hundred years
that trade had been hereditary in the family, together
with the humble virtues, the piety, good sense, and
honour of the olden times. Sprung from that sturdy
bourgeois stock, but having received from nature a
disposition of the most expansive sort, Diderot was
the black sheep of the family, and he became its glory.

Being the oldest of the children, Denis was at first
intended for the clerical profession, to succeed an

rather weak. By exerting a little adroitness one could do with him
whatever one chose; and with all his sudden and quickly kindled impetuosity, he lacked faith in himself. 'The whole profile,' continues
the same Meister, 'was distinguished by a manly, sublime beauty; the
contour of the upper eyelid was most delicate; the usual expression
of his eyes was sweet and sympathetic; but when he began to get
heated, they seemed to emit sparks. His mouth expressed an attractive blending of shrewdness, grace, and good-nature.' Such was the
man who was wholly himself only when he became animated and
excited, which happened so easily."—Sainte-Beuve, in an essay of
later date than that from which the passage in the text is taken.—Tr.]

uncle who was a canon. He was sent betimes to the Jesuit school of the town and made rapid progress there. These first years, the home life and his childhood, which he loved to recall, and which he celebrated in several passages in his writings, left a deep imprint upon his impressible nature. In 1760, at Baron d'Holbach's in Grandval, dividing his time between the most fascinating company and the essays on ancient philosophy which he was preparing for the *Encyclopédie,* those incidents of long ago came back to his mind, with tears; in reverie he followed back the course of his *melancholy and tortuous fellow-citizen,* the Marne, which he imagined there, before his eyes, at the foot of the slopes of Chenevières and Champigny; his heart swam in memories, and he wrote to his friend Mademoiselle Voland :

"One of the sweetest moments of my life, and I remember it as if it were yesterday, was when my father saw me coming home from college, my arms full of the prizes I had won, and my shoulders covered with the wreaths which had been awarded me, and which, being too big for my head, had slipped down over it. As soon as he caught sight of me, he left his work, came to the door, and began to weep. It is a touching thing to see a good man and a stern shed tears!"

Madame de Vandeul, Diderot's only daughter, whom he loved so dearly, has left us several anecdotes of her father's childhood, which we will not repeat, but all of which bear witness to the quick susceptibility, the vivacity, and the easy-going kindness of heart of that precocious character. Diderot differs from the other great men of the eighteenth century in that he had a *family,* an altogether bourgeois family, that he loved them dearly, and that he always clung to them with effusion, heartiness, and joy. When he had become a fashionable philosopher and a famous personage, he still had his dear father, the *forgeron* [blacksmith], as he called him, his brother the abbé, his sister the housekeeper, and his darling little daughter, Angélique; he talked about them all in a charming way; he was not content until he had sent his friend Grimm to Langres to embrace his aged father. I can find little trace of anything of the sort in Jean-Jacques, in d'Alembert (for a good reason),[1] in the Comte de Buffon, or this same M. de Grimm, or in M. Arouet de Voltaire.

The Jesuits tried to attach Diderot to their order; he had a vein of ardent piety; he was tonsured when he was about twelve, and they even tried to take him away from Langres, so that they might dispose of him more at their ease. This little incident induced his father to take him to Paris, where he placed him at the Collège d'Harcourt. Young Diderot showed himself to be a good scholar and above all an excellent comrade. It is said that he and Abbé de Bernis dined more than once at a cabaret, for six sous a head.

---

[1] [D'Alembert is supposed to have been the son of the famous Madame de Tencin, and to have been left by her at the *Enfans Trouvés*, where he was brought up.—Tr.]

On leaving the college he led, in the Paris of that day (1733–1743), the ordinary life of a young man hard pressed for funds, trying many a trade but unable to decide upon any, accepting work from every hand, reading, studying, devouring everything with avidity, giving lessons in mathematics, which he learned as he went along; walking in the Luxembourg in summer, "in a grey plush redingote, with torn wristbands, and black cotton stockings darned behind with white thread"; going into the shop of Mademoiselle Babuti, the pretty bookseller on Quai des Augustins, (who later became Madam Greuze), with the *quick, ardent, wild manner* which was characteristic of him at that time, and saying to her : "Mademoiselle, La Fontaine's *Contes,* if you please, and a Petronius," and so on. In a word, both before his marriage and after, Diderot continued beyond reason to lead that life of chance, of opportunity, of expedients, of toil, and of constant improvisation. His genius—for he had genius; it is impossible to give any other name to diverse faculties of such breadth and such power— adapted itself to it so perfectly, that one hardly knows to-day whether he would have been suited for any other régime, and one is tempted to believe that by thus distributing himself about and pouring himself forth in all directions and to all comers, he fulfilled his destiny better than he could have done otherwise.

He first entered the office of an attorney, M. Clement de Ris, a compatriot, to study jurisprudence

and the laws, which very soon became a bore.   This
dislike for the law led to a quarrel with his father, who
realised the necessity of curbing, of taming by study,
a nature so enthusiastic, and who urged him either to
choose some profession or to return to the paternal
fireside.   But young Diderot was already conscious of
his powers, and an irresistible vocation led him away
from the beaten paths.   He ventured to disobey the
indulgent father whom he venerated, and alone, without assistance, at odds with his family (although his
mother aided him secretly and at long intervals), living
in a garret, still dining for six sous, we find him attempting to construct for himself a life of independence and of study; geometry and Greek aroused his
ardour, and he dreamed of the glories of the stage.

Meanwhile every sort of work that presented itself
was welcome; the trade of journalist, as we understand it, did not exist at that time, else he would certainly have taken it up.   One day a missionary ordered
of him six sermons for the Portuguese colonies, and
he supplied them.   He tried to adjust himself to the
post of private tutor to the sons of a rich financier,
but that life of dependence became intolerable to him
after three months.

It is pleasant to come across the grey plush redingote again in the *Neveu de Rameau*.   How bitterly
must he, who at a later date so eloquently regretted
his "old robe de chambre," have regretted that grey
plush redingote, which would have retraced for him

that whole period of youth, of poverty, and trials!
How proudly he would have hung it in his study, dec-
orated as that study was with modern luxuriousness!
How earnestly and how much more justly he would
have exclaimed at sight of that relic, of the sort that
he loved so dearly:

> " It reminds me of my first trade, and pride halts at the door of my
> heart. No, my friend, no, I am not corrupted. My door is still open
> to the need that appeals to me for aid; it finds in me the same amia-
> bility; I listen to it, I advise it, I sympathise with it. My heart is not
> hardened, my head is not exalted; my back is broad and full as of yore.
> There is the same tone of frankness, the same sensibility; my magnifi-
> cence is of recent date, and the poison has not yet begun to work."

And what would he not have added, if the everlasting
plush redingote had been at hand, precisely the same
as when he wore it on that Shrove Tuesday, when,
having fallen to the lowest depths of poverty, exhausted by walking, fainting from lack of food, and
succoured by the compassion of an inn-keeper's wife,
he swore that, so long as he had a sou in his pocket,
he would never turn a poor man away, and that he
would give his all rather than expose a fellow-creature
to a day of such agony!

His morals, amid that life of uncertainty, were not
what one might imagine; we learn, from an avowal
that he made to Mademoiselle Voland, the aversion
which he early conceived for facile and perilous pleasures. This young man, abandoned to his own resources, in dire need, of an ardent temperament,
whose pen afterward acquired the reputation of

impurity; who, according to his own testimony, knew his Petronius more than well, and could recite without a blush three-fourths of Catullus's little madrigals, —this young man escaped the corruption of vice, and at the most passionate age succeeded in saving the treasures of his senses and the illusions of his heart. This good fortune he owed to love.

The girl whom he loved was one who had known better days, a poor working-girl, who lived honestly with her mother, by the work of her hands. Diderot became acquainted with her as a neighbour, fell madly in love with her, won her heart, and married her (he was then thirty years old) despite the economic remonstrances of her mother; but the marriage was celebrated secretly, to avoid the opposition of his own family, who were deceived by false reports. Jean-Jacques, in his *Confessions,* expresses himself most contemptuously concerning Diderot's Annette, to whom he much prefers his own Thérèse. Without deciding between these two companions of great men, it seems to be the fact that, although she was a good sort of woman at bottom, Madame Diderot was a busybody, of mediocre intellect and slight education, incapable of understanding her husband or of answering the requirements of his affection. All these unpleasant drawbacks, which time developed, disappeared at the beginning in the glamour of her beauty. Diderot had by her as many as four children, of whom only one, a daughter, lived to grow up. After one of her first lyings-in, he despatched the mother, and the little one too, no doubt, to his family at Langres, in order to compel a reconciliation. This pathetic expedient was successful, and all the prejudices which had endured for years vanished in twenty-four hours.

But Diderot, crushed by new burdens, forced to toilsome drudgery, translating for booksellers an occasional English book, a History of Greece, or a Dictionary of Medicine, very soon became disenchanted with the woman for whom he had so heavily handicapped his future. Madame de Puisieux (another blunder) during ten years, Mademoiselle Voland, the only one worthy of his choice, during the whole of the second half of his life, and a few such women as Madame de Prunevaux for short periods, engaged him in close liasons which became, as it were, the very tissue of his private life.

Madame de Puisieux was the first: a coquette, and an impecunious one, she added to Diderot's burdens, and it was for her that he translated the Essay on Merit and Virtue, and wrote the *Pensées Philosophiques,* the *Interprétation de la Nature,* the *Lettre sur les Aveugles* and *Bijoux Indiscrets,* a better assorted and less serious offering. Madame Diderot, neglected by her husband, became more confirmed in her by no means refined tastes; she had her coterie, her little circle of intimates, and Diderot thenceforth acknowledged no other domestic tie than the education of his daughter.

After such an experience one can readily understand

how it was that that one of the philosophers of the age who best appreciated family morality, who performed most religiously the duties of father, son, and brother, had at the same time such a slender conception of the sanctity of marriage, which is, however, the keystone of all the rest. One can readily see by what personal feeling he was inspired when he made the Otaheitan say in the *Supplément au Voyage de Bougainville:*

"Can you imagine anything more absurd than a command which forbids the change that is born in us, which enjoins a constancy that cannot exist, and which destroys the liberty of the male and the female by binding them together for ever; than a fidelity which confines the most fickle of pleasures to a single individual; than an oath of immutability between two creatures of flesh and blood, beneath a sky which is not the same for two successive instants, in caverns which threaten destruction, at the base of a cliff that is crumbling away, at the foot of a tree that is falling apart, on a rock that moves and totters?"

It was Diderot's strange destiny, albeit easily explained by his ingenuous and contagious exaltation of mind, to have felt or inspired during his life sentiments so disproportionate to the real merit of the persons concerned. His first, his most violent, passion bound him for ever to a woman who had no real sympathy with him. His most violent friendship, which was as passionate as love, had for its object Grimm, a refined, keen, agreeable intellect, but a hard and selfish heart.[1] And lastly, the most violent ad-

[1] This is too severe a judgment of Grimm; I have since formed a more favourable opinion of him, on studying him at close range. [The relations between Diderot and Grimm are discussed more fully in the essay on the latter.—Tr.]

miration that he inspired came from Naigeon—Naigeon, the idolatrous worshipper of his philosopher, as Brossette was of his poet; a sort of addle-pated disciple, a fanatical beadle of atheism. Wife, friend, disciple—thus Diderot went astray in his choice of all three; La Fontaine could have been no more unlucky than he. However, except as to his wife, it seems that he himself never realised his mistakes.

Every man endowed with great talents, if he has come into the world at a time when they can make themselves known, owes to his epoch and to mankind a work suited to the general needs of that epoch, a work which will assist the march of progress. Whatever his private inclinations, his caprices, his slothful humour, or his fancy for incidental writings, he owes to society a public monument, on pain of disregarding his mission and squandering his destiny. Montesquieu by the *Esprit des Lois,* Rousseau by *Émile* and the *Contrat Social,* Buffon by the *Histoire Naturelle,* Voltaire by the grand total of his labours, bore witness to this sanctified law of genius, by virtue whereof it devotes itself to the advancement of mankind; nor did Diderot, whatever may once have been said too thoughtlessly, fail to do his part.[1]

His great work, his own special work, so to speak, was the *Encyclopédie.* As soon as the booksellers who first conceived the idea of it had laid their hands

[1] This is a partial retractation, a correction of what I had previously written in an article in the *Globe*.

on him, they were confident that they had their man; the idea instantly expanded, took on body and life. Diderot seized upon it so eagerly and presented it in such an attractive light that he succeeded in winning the approbation of the pious Chancellor d'Aguesseau, and in inducing him to give his assent, his patronage, to the undertaking; d'Aguesseau was its earliest patron.[1]

It was originally intended to be nothing more than a translation, revised and augmented, of Chalmers's English Dictionary—a bookseller's speculation. Diderot fertilised the original idea and boldly conceived the scheme of a universal compendium of human knowledge in his day. He took twenty-five years (1748–1772) to carry it out. He was the living corner-stone within of this collective structure, and also the target of all the persecution, of all the threats from without. D'Alembert, who had joined him mainly from self-interest, and whose ingenious Preface assumed far too much, for the benefit of those who read only prefaces, of the surpassing glory of the whole undertaking, deserted when it was half executed, leaving Diderot to contend against the frenzy of the pietists, the cowardice of the booksellers, and to struggle beneath an enormous increase of editorial labour.

[1] [Elsewhere Saint-Beuve quotes M. de Malesherbes to this effect: " Chancellor d'Aguesseau was advised of the project [of the *Encyclopédie*] ; he not only approved it, but he revised and improved it, and *chose M. Diderot for the principal editor.*" Malesherbes was censor at the time.—Tr.]

The history of philosophy, which he treats at second hand, it is true; the description of the mechanic arts, in which perhaps he displays more originality ; three or four thousand plates which he caused to be drawn under his own eye ; in a word, the responsibility and superintendence of the whole affair were never able to engross him or to quench the sparkle of his energy. Thanks to his prodigious activity, to the universality of his knowledge, to the manifold adaptability which he acquired at an early age, in poverty,—thanks above all to his moral power to rally his associates about him, to inspire and arouse them, he completed that daring edifice, threatening in its massiveness, yet built according to rule. If we seek the name of the architect, his is the name that we must read upon it.

Diderot knew better than any one else the defects in his work; he even exaggerated them to himself, considering the time spent upon it; and believing that he was born for the arts, for geometry, for the stage, he deplored over and over again that he had wasted his life over a matter the profit of which was so paltry and the glory so promiscuous. That he was admirably constituted for geometry and the arts, I do not deny; but surely, things being as they then were, a great revolution, as he himself observed,[1] being under way in the sciences, which were descending from the higher geometry and from metaphysical contempla-

[1] *Interprétation de la Nature.*

tion, to include in their scope morality, belles-lettres, natural history, experimental physics, and trade; furthermore, art in the eighteenth century being falsely turned aside from its more elevated aim, and debased to serve as a philosophical speaking-trumpet, or as a weapon in the conflict;—amid such general conditions, it was difficult for Diderot to employ his powerful talents more profitably, more worthily, and more memorably than by devoting them to the *Encyclopédie*. He aided and hastened, by that civilising work, the revolution that he had noted in the sciences.

Diderot, in his first *Pensées Philosophiques,* seems especially indignant at the tyrannical and waywardly savage aspect which the doctrine of Nicole, Arnauld, and Pascal gave to the Christian God; and it is in the name of misjudged humanity and of a saintly commiseration for his fellow-men that he begins the daring criticism in which his impetuous fervour will not allow him to stop. So it is with the majority of unbelieving innovators: at the starting-point the same protestation of a noble purpose makes them one.

The *Encyclopédie,* then, was not a peace-bringing monument, a silent cloistral tower, with scholars and thinkers of every variety distributed among the different floors. It was not a pyramid of granite with an immovable base; it had no feature of those pure and harmonious structures of art which ascend slowly during centuries of fervent devotion toward an adored and blessed God. It has been compared to the impious Babel; I see in it rather one of those towers of war, one of those siege-machines, enormous, gigantic, wonderful to behold, such as Polybius describes, such as Tasso imagines. There are ruinous portions, and unsymmetrical, much plaster, and firmly cemented and indestructible fragments. The foundations do not extend into the ground; the structure wavers, it is tottering, it will fall; but what does it matter? To apply here an eloquent observation of Diderot himself: "The statue of the architect will remain standing amid the ruins, and the stone that is detached from the mountain will not shatter it, because its feet are not of clay."

Diderot's atheism, although he flaunts it at intervals with a deplorable flourish of trumpets, and although his adversaries have too pitilessly taken him at his word, can generally be reduced to the denial of an unkind and vindictive God. In truth, it often seems that all that he lacks is a ray of light to illuminate everything; and one might well say of Diderot's atheism, as he himself said of those two landscapes of Vernet, in which everything is darkened and obscured by the coming of night: "Let us wait till to-morrow when the sun will have risen."

If the *Encyclopédie* was Diderot's great social work and his principal work, his principal glory in our eyes to-day is the having been the creator of earnest, impassioned, eloquent criticism; it is by his work in this direction that he survives and that he must be ever dear to us all, journalists and extemporaneous writers on all subjects. Let us salute in him our father and the earliest model of the race of critics.

Before Diderot, criticism in France had been exact, inquisitive, and shrewd with Bayle, refined and exquisite with Fénelon, straightforward and useful with Rollin; I omit in modesty the Frérons and Des Fontaines. But nowhere had it been lively, fruitful, searching,—if I may so express it, it had not found its soul. Diderot was the first who gave it a soul. Naturally inclined to overlook defects and to take fire at good qualities,

"I am more affected," he said, "by the attractions of virtue than by the deformities of vice; I turn gently away from the wicked and *I fly to meet the good*. If there is in a literary work, in a character, in a picture, in a statue, a beautiful spot, that is where my eyes rest ; I see only that, I remember only that, all the rest is well-nigh forgotten. What becomes of me when the whole work is beautiful! "

This propensity to extend a cordial welcome, to universal condescension and to enthusiasm, doubtless had its risks. It has been said of him that he was singularly fortunate in two respects, "in that he had never fallen in with a bad man or a poor book." For if the book were poor, he made it over and unconsciously attributed to the author some of his, Diderot's, own inventions. Like the alchemist, he found gold in the crucible because he had put it there. However, it is to him that is due the honour of having first introduced among us the fruitful criticism of *beauties,* which he

substituted for the criticism of *faults;* and in this respect Chateaubriand himself, in that part of the *Génie
du Christianisme* where he eloquently discusses
literary criticism, simply follows the path blazed out
by Diderot.

Abbé Arnaud said to him: "You have the reverse
of dramatic talent: it should transform itself into all
the characters, and you transform them all into yourself." But if it be true that Diderot was nothing less
than a dramatic poet, that he was in no wise competent for that species of sovereign creation and of
transformation altogether impersonal, he had by way
of compensation, and in the very highest degree, that
power of *semi*-metamorphosis which is the game and
the triumph of criticism, and which consists in putting
oneself in the author's place and at the point of view
of the subject that one is examining, in reading every
written work *according to the mind that dictated it.*
He excelled in taking to himself for a time, and at his
pleasure, the mind of another person; in gathering
inspiration from it, often to better effect than that
other himself had done; in arousing the enthusiasm
not only of his own brain, but of his heart; and at
such times he was the great modern journalist, the
Homer of the profession, intelligent, ardent, effusive,
eloquent, never at home, always abroad; or if it happened that he received others at his home and amid
his own ideas, then he was the most open-hearted,
the most hospitable of mortals, the most friendly to all

men and to everything, and gave to all his circle, readers no less than authors or artists, not a lesson but a fête.

Such an one does he appear in his admirable *Salons de Peinture*.   One day Grimm, who supplied several sovereigns of the North with the latest news of literature and the fine arts, asked Diderot to write for him a report on the Salon of 1761.   Diderot had theretofore turned his attention to many subjects, but never to the fine arts in particular.   At his friend's request he undertook to observe and scrutinise for the first time what he had never up to that time done more than casually glance at; and the result of his observations and reflections gave birth to those pages of admirable *causerie* which really created criticism of the fine arts in France.

I am aware of one objection which is commonly made to such noble discourses upon art, and to which Diderot's *Salons* are peculiarly obnoxious.   It is that they are *beside* the subject, that they discuss it from the literary, the dramatic standpoint, which is the standpoint dear to the French.   Madame Necker wrote to Diderot: "I continue to be infinitely entertained by reading your *Salon; I do not care for painting except in poetry;* and that is how you have had the skill to interpret all the works, even the most commonplace, of our modern painters."   That is praise indeed, and, according to some people of intelligence, it is the severest kind of criticism.

"It is a fact," they say, "that it is a peculiarity of the French to judge everything with the mind, even forms and colours. It is true, that, as there is no language to express the delicate refinements of form or the various effects of colour, whenever one undertakes to discuss them, one is forced, for lack of power to express what one feels, to describe other sensations which can be understood by everybody."

Diderot is more open than others to this reproach, and the pictures which he sees are generally simply a pretext and a motive for those which he makes of them, and which he imagines. His articles almost invariably consist of two parts: in the first, he describes the picture that he has before his eyes; in the second, he suggests his own. Such talkative writers, however, when they are, as he was, saturated with their subject, imbued with a lively appreciation of art and of the things which they are discussing, are at the same time useful and interesting: they guide you, they make you pay attention; and while you follow them, while you listen to them, while you go along with them or take another road, the sense of form and colour, if you have such a sense, awakens, takes shape, and becomes sharpened; unconsciously you become in your turn a good judge, a connoisseur, for mysterious reasons which you cannot describe and which there are no words to express.

To how great a degree Diderot is a *littérateur* in his way of criticising pictures, we may discover at the very outset. A painter has represented "Telemachus on Calypso's Island": the scene shows them at table, where the young hero is narrating his adventures, and Calypso offers him a peach. Diderot considers that this offering a peach by Calypso is an *absurdity,* and that Telemachus has much more sense than the nymph or the painter, for he continues the tale of his adventures without accepting the proffered fruit. But if the peach were gracefully offered, if the light fell upon it in a certain way, if the nymph's expression were consistent with her act, if, in a word, the picture were a Titian or a Veronese, that peach might have been a chef-d'œuvre, despite the *absurdity* which the mind thinks that it detects therein; for in a picture, the narrative of adventures, which we do not hear, and which the offer of the peach runs the risk of interrupting, is only secondary; we have no use for our ears, we are all eyes.

In a great number of instances, however, Diderot has some just observations, strikingly true, which he offers less as a critic than as a painter. For example, addressing M. Vien, who has painted a Psyche holding her lamp in her hand and surprising Cupid in his sleep, he says:

" Oh! how little sense our painters have! how little they know nature! Psyche's head should be bent over Cupid, the rest of her body thrown back, as it is when we creep toward a place we are afraid to enter and from which we are all ready to fly; one foot resting on the ground, the other barely touching it. And that lamp— ought she to let the light fall on Cupid's eyes? Should she not rather hold it away and interpose her hand so as to shield the light? Besides, that would be an excuse for arranging the light in the picture in a very fetching way. These fellows do not know that the eyelids are transparent in some sort; they have never seen a mother come at night to look at her child in the cradle, with a lamp in her hand, and afraid of waking him."

In all this Diderot is a great critic, and in that kind of general criticism which no art can possibly escape on the pretext of technique.

"It seems to me," he says, " that when one takes up the brush, one should have some powerful, ingenious, delicate, or interesting idea, and should have in mind some definite effect, some impression to be produced. . . . There are very few artists who have ideas, and there is hardly a single one who can dispense with them. . . . There is no middle way—either interesting ideas, an original subject, or wonderful workmanship."

This wonderful workmanship, which is, after all, the condition without which the idea itself cannot live; this exceptional and superior execution which is the hall-mark of every great artist—when Diderot detects it in one of them, he is the first to feel it and to interpret it for us by words no less wonderful,—unusual words from a wholly new vocabulary of which he is, as it were, the inventor. And, in general, all the powers of improvisation, of picturesque and quick imagination, with which he was endowed; all his stores of bold, profound, and ingenious conceptions; the love of nature, of the country, and of family; even his sensuality, his decided tendency to touch and describe forms; the sentiment of colour, *the sentiment of the flesh,* of blood and of life, " which is the despair of colourists" and which came to him as his pen flew—all these priceless qualities of Diderot found employment in those *feuilles volantes* which are still his surest title to the admiration of posterity.

He surpasses himself whenever he speaks of Vernet and of Greuze. As an artist, Greuze is Diderot's ideal; he is a sincere, sympathetic painter, a painter of the family and the drama, affecting and straightforward, slightly sensual, yet moral at the same time. And so, when Diderot falls in with him, he makes fast to him, translates him, interprets him, explains him, adds to his meaning, and never again releases his hold of him. "I am a trifle long, perhaps," he says, "but if you knew how I am enjoying myself while boring you! I am like all the other bores in the world." The analyses, or rather the *paintings,* which Diderot has given us of the " Village Bride," the "Girl Weeping for her Dead Bird," the "Beloved Mother," and the rest, are masterpieces, little poems appropriate to the pictures and printed on the opposite page as it were. Diderot frequently says of a painter, "He paints freely (*large*), he draws freely." The same may be said of himself as a critic; he spreads his colours freely; his criticism is effusive. Even when describing to us with keen delight some family idyl of Greuze, he finds a way to mingle some tones of his own. In his analysis of the "Girl Weeping," he does more, he introduces a complete elegy of his own invention. That child, who seems to be weeping for her bird, has her secret, she is weeping for something very different.

"Oh! what a lovely hand," cries the intoxicated critic as he gazes at her; "what a lovely hand! what lovely arms! Observe the accuracy of the detail of those fingers, and those dimples, and that soft flesh, and the reddish tint of the finger tips caused by the pressure of the head, and the fascination of it all. One would draw near to that hand to kiss it, were it not that one respects the child and her grief."

And, even while enjoining upon himself respect for the child's grief, he does draw near; he begins to speak to her, to raise, as gently as he can, the veil of mystery:

"Why, my dear, your grief is very great, very profound. What means this dreamy, melancholy expression? What! all for a bird? You are not weeping, you are in deep affliction; and your affliction is accompanied by thought. Come, my dear, open your heart to me; tell me the truth: is it really this bird's death that has withdrawn you so entirely and so sadly into yourself?"

And so he goes on and transfixes the idyl with his elegy. Thus the picture is, with him, simply a pretext for reverie, for poetic thoughts.

Diderot is the king and the god of those half-poets who become and appear whole poets in criticism; all that they need is an external fulcrum and a stimulus. Observe that, in analysing this picture, and others of Greuze's works as well, Diderot delights in noting therein, or in introducing, a faint vein of sensuality amid the moral meaning—a vein which is really there, perhaps, but which at all events he loves to trace out, to point his finger at, and which he is tempted to magnify and exaggerate rather than pass over. The curves of the breast, the fulness of contour, even in the family pictures, even in wives and mothers, he recurs to again and again, he delights to let his glance and his pen rest upon them, not as a critic or an artist, not as a fastidious libertine either (Diderot is not depraved), but as a natural, materialistic man, and sometimes a little indelicate. That is a weak side in him, a vulgar and even rather ignoble side. This excellent man, sincere, exalted, warm-hearted, this critic so animated, so ingenious, so keen, who has above all else a mania for preaching *morality,* is utterly unable, in presence of an object of art, to content himself with elevating and determining our idea of the beautiful, or even with satisfying our sensitiveness to impressions; he does more, he disturbs our senses a little. And so when you see at times on his brow a reflection of the Platonic ray, do not trust to it; look closely, there is always a satyr's foot.

We have divers fugitive writings of Diderot, brief narratives, tales, skits, which it is the fashion to call chefs-d'œuvre. A chef-d'œuvre! there is always more or less courtesy in the use of this word with respect to Diderot. The chef-d'œuvre properly so-called, the finished, definitive, complete work, in which good taste sets the measure of the movement and sentiment, is not his forte: the superior quality, always scattered about in his work, is nowhere concentrated, nowhere set in a frame and glowing with a steady radiance. He is, as we have seen, much more truly *the man of the sketch.*

In the short pieces written for a purpose, such as

the *Éloge de Richardson* or the *Régrets sur ma Vieille Robe de Chambre,* he has much grace of expression, happy thoughts, original conceits; but the emphatic manner recurs and manifests itself in spots, the apostrophe spoils the naturalness for me. There are gusts of emphasis here and there. In this direction he lays himself open to caricature to some extent, and that fact has been made use of without compunction in the portraits, generally overcharged, which have been drawn of him. Diderot is altogether successful, and without art too, when he makes no preparation, and has no particular object in view, when his thoughts escape him, when the printer is at his elbow, waiting for him and hurrying him; or when it is time for the postman to come, and he writes in haste, on a tavern table, a letter to his friend. It is in his *Correspondance* with that friend, Mademoiselle Voland, and in his *Salons,* written for Grimm, that we find his most delightful pages, the outspoken, rapid sketches in which he lives again just as he was.

Diderot set forth his views on the substance, the cause, and the origin of things in the *Interprétation de la Nature,* under the shelter of Baumann, who was no other than Maupertuis; and even more explicitly in the *Entretien avec d'Alembert* and the strange *Rêve* (Dream) which he attributes to that philosopher. It is sufficient for our purpose to say that his materialism is no dry geometrical mechanism, but a confused vitalism, fruitful and potent, a spontaneous, unceasing, evolutionary fermentation, wherein, even in the least atom, delicacy of feeling, latent or patent, is always present. His opinions were those of Bordeu and the physiologists, the same that Cabanis afterward expressed so eloquently. From the way in which Diderot appreciated external nature, *natural* nature so to speak, which the experiments of scientists had not as yet distorted and falsified—the woods, the streams, the charm of the fields, the harmonious beauty of the sky, and the impression that they make on the heart— he must have been profoundly religious by nature, for no man was ever more sympathetic and more accessible to universal life. But this life of nature and of created beings he purposely left undefined, vague, and in some sort diffused about him, hidden in the heart of the seeds, circulating in the air-currents, fluttering over the tree-tops, breathing in the puffs of wind; he did not gather it about a central point, he did not idealise it in the radiant example of a watchful, guiding Providence. However, in a work which he wrote in his old age, a few years before his death, the *Essai sur la Vie de Sénèque,* he gratified himself by translating the following passage from a letter to Lucilius, which filled him with admiration:

" If there is before your eyes a vast forest, peopled by ancient trees, whose tops ascend to the clouds and whose interlacing branches conceal the heavens from you, that immeasurable height, that profound silence, those masses of shadow which the distance makes more dense and unbroken,—do not all these signs *hint* to you the presence of a God ? "

It was Diderot who underlined the word *hint* (*intimer*).

I am delighted to find in the same work a criticism of La Mettrie which indicates in Diderot some slight forgetfulness perhaps of his own cynical and philosophical extravagances, but also a bitter distaste for and a formal disavowal of immoral and corrupting materialism. I like to have him reprove La Mettrie for not having *the first idea of the true fundamentals of morality,* "of that enormous tree whose head touches the heavens and whose roots reach down to hell, in which everything is bound together, in which modesty, reserve, courtesy, the most trivial virtues, if such there be, are attached as the leaf is to the twig, which one dishonours by stripping it."

This reminds me of a dispute concerning virtue that he had one day with Helvetius and Saurin; he writes to Mademoiselle Voland a charming description of it, which is a picture in a few words of the inconsequence of the age. Those gentlemen denied the innate moral sense, the essential and unselfish motive of virtue, for which Diderot argued.

"The amusing part of it," he adds, "is that the discussion was hardly at an end before those excellent folk began unconsciously to use the strongest arguments in favour of the sentiment they had been combating, and to furnish the refutation of their own opinions. But Socrates, in my place, would have extorted it from them."

He says in one place, referring to Grimm: "The severity of our friend's principles is thrown away; he distinguishes two sorts of morality, one for the use of sovereigns." All these excellent ideas concerning virtue, morality, and nature recurred to his mind with greater force than ever, doubtless, in the meditative seclusion, the solitude which he tried to arrange for himself during the painful years of his old age. Several of his friends were dead; he often felt the loss of Mademoiselle Voland and Grimm. To conversation, which had become fatiguing, he preferred his dressing-gown and his library on the fifth floor, under the eaves, at the corner of Rue Taranne and Rue de Saint-Benoît; he read constantly, meditated much, and took the keenest pleasure in superintending his daughter's education.

In his old age Diderot wondered whether he had made a good use of his life,—whether he had not squandered it. Reading Seneca's treatise *De Brevitate Vitæ,* especially the third chapter, where the reader is appealed to so earnestly: "Come, review your days and your years, call them to account! Tell us how much time you have allowed to be stolen from you by a creditor, by a mistress, by a patron, by a client. How many people have pillaged your life, when you did not even dream what you were losing!" Diderot, thus reminded to search his conscience, wrote as his only comment: "I have never read this chapter without blushing; *it is my history.*" Many years earlier he had said to himself: "I am not conscious of having as yet made use of half of my powers;

up to this time I have only fiddle-faddled." He might
have said the same thing when he died. But, as an
antidote, an alleviation of these ill·concealed regrets
of the writer and the artist, the philosopher and the
moralist in him rejoined: " My life is not stolen from
me, I give it voluntarily; and what better could I do
than bestow a portion of it upon him who esteems me
enough to solicit that gift ? " It was in precisely the
same frame of mind that he wrote somewhere or
other these kindly and admirable words:

" A pleasure which is for myself alone touches me but little and lasts
but a short time. It is for myself and my friends that I read, that I reflect, that I write, that I meditate, that I listen, that I observe, that I
feel. In their absence my devotion refers everything to them    I think
unceasingly of their happiness. If a beautiful line impresses me, they
know it at once. If I have fallen in with a fine drawing, I promise
myself to tell them about it. If I have before my eyes some entranc-
ing spectacle, I unconsciously think how I shall describe it to them. I
have consecrated to them the use of all my senses and all my faculties,
and that perhaps is the reason that everything is exaggerated, everything is glorified a little in my imagination and in my language;
sometimes they reprove me for it, the ingrates! "

We, who are of his friends, of those of whom he
thought vaguely at a distance, and for whom he wrote,
we will not be ungrateful. While regretting that we
find too often in his writings that touch of exaggeration which he himself admits, a lack of discretion and
sobriety, some laxity of morals and of language, and
some sins against good taste, we do homage to his
kindness of heart, his sympathetic nature, his generous intellect, his shrewdness and breadth of view and

of treatment, his freedom and delicacy of touch, and the admirable vigour, the secret of which he never lost throughout his incessant toil. To all of us Diderot is a man whom it is encouraging to observe and to study. He is the first great writer in point of time who definitely belongs to modern democratic society. He points out to us the road and the example to follow: to be or not to be of the *Académie,*[1] but to write for the public, to address the whole people, to be always in haste, to go straight to the reality, to the fact, even when one has a mania for reverie, to give, give, give, with no purpose ever to take back; *to wear oneself out rather than rest,* is his motto. And that is what he did to the very end, with energy, with devotion, with a sometimes painful consciousness of this constant loss of substance. And yet, through it all, and without a too manifest effort to that end, he succeeded in saving, of all these scattered fragments, some enduring ones, and he teaches us how one may make his way to the future and to posterity, and arrive there, though it be only as débris from the shipwreck of each day.

Diderot's beneficent life, replete with good counsels and good works, must have been a source of the

[1] [Diderot was never a member of the Académie Française. In an essay on Duclos, Sainte-Beuve quotes a letter (1760) of Voltaire to Duclos, in which the latter (then Secrétaire Perpetuel of the Académie) is urged to use his influence with Madame de Pompadour to obtain Diderot's election, on the pretext that his assistance would be of great value in compiling the *Dictionnaire de l'Académie.*—TR.]

greatest inward consolation to him; and yet, perhaps, at certain times, there came to his lips this saying of his old father: "My son, my son, an excellent pillow is that of reason; but I find that my head rests even more softly on that of religion and the laws."

He died in 1784.

# Jean-Jacques Rousseau.

## 1712–1778.

## Jean=Jacques Rousseau.

IN 1803 there was published for the first time the correspondence of Jean-Jacques Rousseau with a contemporary of his, a woman of intellect, and one of his enthusiastic admirers, Madame de La Tour-Franqueville. This correspondence, into which Rousseau entered against his will, and in which, from the first day to the last, every letter was extorted from him, as it were, is nevertheless noteworthy and interesting in that it is connected, that it forms a complete whole, that it was not intended for the public eye, and that it shows us Jean-Jacques *au naturel*, from the morrow of *La Nouvelle Héloïse* down to the time when his mind became hopelessly impaired. In it we can study, in an abridged form, the increasing progress of his oddities and his moods, interspersed with delightful lapses, and with rare but charming gleams of his former self. In it we can study at the same time the public of that day, and, if I may use the phrase, *Rousseau's women,* in the person of one of the most distinguished and certainly the most devoted of them all.

Every great poet, every great novelist has his procession of admirers, especially women, who surround him, who exalt him to the skies, who adore him, who would gladly sacrifice themselves for him, and who (I humbly beg their forgiveness), if they were allowed to have their way, would, unwittingly, soon have him torn in pieces like Orpheus. But it is in that circle of admirers, where everything is reëchoed again and again, and exaggerated, that it is sometimes convenient and interesting to observe an author and to study him. Tell me who admires you and I will tell you what manner of man you are—at least with respect to the form of your talent and your tastes.

We have had in our day many instances of these diverse processions, which we have watched as they passed by. But it was Rousseau who inaugurated this great revolution in France, and who definitively brought women into the game. He stirred up in his own interest that moiety of the human race, theretofore self-restrained and not indiscreet; the enthusiasm of the sex for him was unprecedented. How shall we describe that universal revolt which broke out after *La Nouvelle Héloïse*, after *Émile* (1759-1762), which anticipated the Revolution of '89, and which, at a long distance, paved the way for it? Madame de Staël, Madame Roland—will not they soon appear in the front rank of those whom I call Jean-Jacques's women? More modest, or less in the public eye, but no less generous and devoted, Madame de La Tour-Franqueville was one of the first: she opens the procession, and she deserves to be assigned a place by herself in the renown of him to whom she consecrated

JEAN JACQUES ROUSSEAU
*Bust by Houdon*

herself, for he, ingrate that he is, does not say a word
of her in his *Confessions.*

It was two years after *La Nouvelle Héloïse*
appeared, and while it still had public sentiment
ablaze and was playing havoc with excitable imaginations.   Rousseau, forty-nine years of age, living in retirement at Montmorency, was enjoying
that last interval of repose (a sorely perturbed repose) before the publication of *Émile,* which was to
revolutionise his life.   Late in September, 1761, he
received a letter, unsigned, in which the writer said
to him: "You must know that Julie is not dead, and
that she lives to love you; this Julie is not myself;
you will see that from my style; I am at most her
cousin, or rather her friend, even as Claire was."   It
was a friend of Madame de La Tour who thus assumed
the rôle of Claire, and who betrayed to Jean-Jacques
his latest admirer, herself worthy to be admired.
After a somewhat tedious eulogy of this unknown
Julie and of her right to enter into relations with the
great man, she told Rousseau how he might reply.
He did reply, and on this first occasion by return mail,
without waiting to be urged.

No matter how great a misanthrope and bear one
may be, one is always susceptible to such alluring
advances of a new and at the same time mysterious admiration.   But, in this first letter, he takes his precautions and depicts himself thus early, with his strange
variations of moods: "I trust, madame, despite

the beginning of your letter, that you are not an author, that you have never had an idea of being one, and that it is not a battle of wits to which you propose to challenge me—that being a kind of fencing for which I have no less aversion than incapacity." Thereupon he enters seriously into this prolonged game of Claire, Julie, and Saint-Preux; he makes no pretence, as good taste would require a well-bred writer to do, of treating lightly the personages of his invention; he continues to show them respect, and to speak of them to his correspondent as if they were real exemplars. "To the editor of one Julie you make known the existence of another, who really exists, and whose Claire you are. I am overjoyed for your sex, and indeed for my own; for, whatever your friend may say, as soon as there are Julies and Claires, there will be no lack of Saint-Preux; tell her so, I entreat you, so that she may be on her guard." Then he suddenly takes fire at the idea of finding somewhere a replica of the inseparable friends of whom he has dreamed; the apostrophe, that figure of speech which is his favourite literary trick, breaks forth. "Charming friends!" he cries, "if you are such as my heart imagines you, may you, for the honour of your sex and the happiness of your lives, never find a Saint-Preux! But if you are like other women, may you find none but Saint-Preux!"[1]

[1] [Bernardin de Saint-Pierre once asked Jean-Jacques if Saint-Preux were not himself. " No," was the reply, " he is not altogether what I was, but what I would have liked to be."—Tr.]

All this, read in cold blood to-day, by men of a generation which has never felt the same enthusiasm, seems a little peculiar and provokes a smile.   On his recovery from this romantic outburst, Rousseau goes into the realties of life more than was necessary, exhibiting to those two young women, whom he did not know, all the details of his physical ills, his infirmities. "You speak of making my acquaintance; you are, doubtless, unaware that the man to whom you write, afflicted by a cruel and incurable disease, struggles every day of his life between pain and death, and that the very letter that he is writing to you is often interrupted by diversions of a very different sort." When we know what sort of disease Rousseau's was, we are slightly surprised at this direct allusion to it. Montaigne, to be sure, speaks of a similar malady that he had, but he speaks of it to his readers, that is to say, to everybody; whereas in this case Rousseau mentions it in a private letter to two young women to whom he is writing for the first time; that is going a little beyond Montaigne!

Madame de La Tour was a person of merit and of virtue.   Married to a man far from worthy of her, from whom she finally separated by the advice and with the consent of her family, she did not misuse her ill-fortune to the point of thinking that she had the right to console herself.   She has one fault, however, in common with all the women of this school of Rousseau: she speaks not alone of her sensibility and her charms, but of her character, of her *principles,* her *morals,* and her *virtue.* I do not know whether the women of the seventeenth century had more or less of all those things; but as a general rule they did not talk about them themselves; and that is more agreeable, more becoming, in fact, whether because it is better not to call attention to what one lacks, or because there is good taste and good grace in allowing others to discover what one has.

Madame de La Tour's enthusiasm for Jean-Jacques is not artificial, it is sincere, and yet there is something false in it, as there is in its object and hero himself. She works herself up and raves about the purity of her passion, about the beauty of the motive which actuates her. She would fain make of the aging and infirm misanthrope a genuine Saint-Preux, an ideal Saint-Preux, all soul and all mind, all flame. The instinct of her sex, that is to say, her common sense, whispers to her now and then, it is true, that she has little to expect from him, that she can with difficulty extort a reply from him, that it is hardly becoming, after all, for a woman to throw herself thus at the head of a surly fellow (great writer though he be), who troubles himself not at all about her and who spurns her. Then suddenly, ignoring the disadvantages, she cries: *"He is a man!* What difference does it make? Ought the paltry distinction between the sexes to be considered in a commerce of which the soul pays all the expenses?" There is the false note, there the

impossible begins. Why, it is sex and nothing else
(do you not realise it ?) which, constantly brought to
the surface, or understood, vaguely hinted at, and felt,
makes the charm of such correspondences, even the
purest, from which you anticipate nothing else than
that selfsame charm.

Madame de La Tour's friend, the *soi-disant* Claire,
who had begun the correspondence in her friend's
name, was the first and only one to abandon it. She
became disgusted with Rousseau's gusts of temper,
which were in truth severe on certain days, especially
when the two friends demanded letters, answers,
which they did too often. One day, when he had
been harassed and reproached by the two friends for
the infrequency and brevity of his replies, Rousseau,
annoyed beyond endurance, wrote the following letter
to Madame de La Tour:

"MONTMORENCY, 11 January, 1762.

"Saint-Preux was thirty years old, in good health, and intent only
upon his pleasures; nobody resembles Saint-Preux less than J.-J.
Rousseau. On receipt of a letter like the last, Julie would have been
less offended by my silence than alarmed at my condition; at such a
time she would not have amused herself by counting letters and
underlining words; nobody resembles Julie less than Madame de ——
[La Tour]. You have much wit, Madame, you are very glad to
display it, and all that you want of me is letters: you are more repre-
sentative of your quarter than I thought.

"J.-J. ROUSSEAU."

Observe that Madame de La Tour lived on Rue
Richelieu, in the Palais-Royal quarter, and that Rousseau's closing allusion was nothing less than a vulgar

insult.  Madame de La Tour's friend, "Claire," had
had enough.  "I have given myself three smart blows
on the breast," she wrote to her friend, "because I
was fool enough to bring you two together.  Socrates
said that he looked at himself when he wanted to see
a madman.   Let us give that receipt to our animal."
In the last letter that she had written to Rousseau,
this Claire, who had perhaps more wit, or at all
events a less reserved and sharper wit than Madame
de La Tour, had discharged at the eloquent bear the
most cruel phrase that he could hear.   "Bah !" she
had said, "you are made just like other men."   Molière's Dorine could have thought of nothing better.

In truth, Rousseau's great pretension, the germ of
his malady and of that of his successors, was precisely
this, that he was not cast in the mould of other men.
"I am not made like any man that I have ever seen;
I venture to believe that I am not made like any man
alive."  These words of Rousseau, at the beginning
of his *Confessions,* all those who are afflicted with
Rousseau's disorder say or think.

Madame de La Tour did not follow her friend
Claire's example; she did not lose courage.  It was
not her brain alone that had become enthusiastic for
Rousseau: she loved him sincerely, ardently, irration-
ally, with the devoted passion of a woman who had
never before had an object upon which to place her
romantic affections.  A few sentences from him, in
his early letters to her, sentences wholly literary, the

significance of which she exaggerated and which she read again and again, had led her to think that she had succeeded in occupying for an instant some corner in his heart, which was open to nobody since Madame d'Houdetot had passed that way.   She resumed the correspondence alone, unknown to Claire; she became—what a woman becomes so easily when she loves—importunate, persistent, often maladroit; she was a torment.   Constantly humiliated, she returned again and again to the charge, never disheartened. Proud and sensitive, she received many a wound, which, however, never prevented her from forgiving.
[7] The name "Julie," which Rousseau had bestowed upon her at first, was taken from her; he called her nothing but "Marianne."[1]   She submitted to this painful diminution of evidences of regard, already so rare and so dearly bought, and continued to show gratitude for what she did obtain.   Sometimes he forgot even the name Marianne, and did not know what to call her when he wrote to her; she had to refresh his memory.   No matter, she still found means to grasp at the slightest marks of affection, and to be moved by things that certainly were not worth the trouble.

The interval of two or three years, during which

---

[1] [Marianne was the heroine of the inordinately long (11 volumes) novel of that name published by Marivaux in 1738–1741, to which, rather than to that author's plays, is said to be due the coining of the word *marivaudage,* which means great subtlety and refinement of expression.—Tr.]

Rousseau, having taken refuge in Switzerland, lived at Motiers (1762–1765), was the time when the correspondence was most regular and afforded most consolation to poor Marianne. One day, after receiving from her a letter in which she drew a pleasing portrait of herself, Rousseau wrote to her: "How delightful it will be to me to hear all the pleasant things you write, said to me by such a lovely mouth, and to read in those deep blue eyes, fortified by black lashes, the friendship which you express for me!"

That was the supreme moment. "Do you know that your letter is charming," Madame de La Tour replies, "and that, in order not to deem you too charming yourself, I have been obliged to remember the many clouds with which you have darkened the beautiful days that you have sometimes given to me? If it were more equal, my intercourse with you would be too absorbing; such as it is, it absorbs me enough to give me both pleasure and pain; more would be too much."

Let us be just: there are moments when we understand Rousseau's annoyance, when we almost share it; for Madame de La Tour is very exacting, although she seems not to suspect it. One day she sends him another portrait of herself, this time a miniature. She attaches to this gift an importance perfectly natural in a woman, in a woman who loves, who would fain be loved by a man who has never seen her; but that feeling betrays itself by over-much solicitude. She in-

sists that Rousseau *at the very moment* that he receives
the portrait, or the letter accompanying it (and even
though he does not send his answer for a week), shall
sit down to write—what?—his first impression of
her. She wishes to seize this first impression all
a-quiver, when it has made but one leap from the
heart and mind to the paper. Rousseau obeys, but in
few words, and too coldly to suit the sensitive Marianne: "So here it is at last, the portrait that I have
so justly longed for! It comes just when I am surrounded by strangers and tiresome visitors. I thought
that I ought to notify you of its receipt, and to set
your mind at rest about it." Poor Marianne is in
despair and frantic to receive so little. "Your lacon-
icism distresses me, my friend." She would like to
know what he thinks of her in the portrait; she is at
great pains to inform him that it does not flatter her;
that everybody thinks that she is better-looking than
it makes her. In a word, she is a woman. Alas! all
this rests upon an illusion, upon the theory that because she loves she must be loved equally. Madame
de La Tour did not know that, since Madame d'Houdetot's day, Rousseau's heart had no more flame to give
forth. And so, despite all her efforts, she can find no
lodging in that contracted and embittered heart.

She strives to insinuate a soothing quality, a secret
consolation into that glorious passion of hers; that
would have been difficult, doubtless, at any time, but
it certainly was too late at the time when she made

the attempt. Rousseau tells her so in every tone;
he enumerates his physical ills, the persecutions of
which he is, or believes himself to be, the object, the
bores, the spies, and Heaven knows what else!

"And with all the rest," he adds, sensibly enough, "a man who
hasn't a farthing of income cannot live on air, and he must be at some
pains to provide himself with bread. But I am amused at my simplicity, in trying to make a Parisian woman listen to reason concerning
a situation so different from her own—a woman who is an idler by
profession, and who, having no other occupation than to write and
receive letters, thinks that her friends should pay no heed to anything
else."—" I know," he says again, with no less truth than bitterness,
"I know that it is not in the human heart to put itself in the place of
other people in respect to its demands upon them."

At this time Rousseau's reason was already seriously
impaired; he was beginning, not only to appear mad
in the vague general sense of the word, but actually
to be mad, in the exact, medical sense. His correspondence with Madame de La Tour during his sojourn in Switzerland bears traces of the irritation, the
over-excitation of *vanity,* in other words, of that trait
which, in madness of this sort, is at once the cause
and the symptom. "You say that I am not indifferent to anybody," he wrote one day to Madame
de La Tour; "so much the better! I cannot endure
lukewarm people, and I much prefer to be hated to
the death by a thousand and to be loved in the same
way by a single one. *Whoever is not passionately
fond of me is unworthy of me.''* Then the diseased
chord begins to vibrate. He can contain himself no

longer; the spring is released. "A person may not care for my books," he adds, "I have no fault to find with that; but *whoever does not love me because of my books is a knave;* no one can ever drive that out of my mind!" His mind, therefore, was already attacked. One has a sense of humiliation for what is called human talent or genius, when one reflects that it was after this time that Rousseau wrote some of his divinest pages, the first books of the *Confessions,* the fifth "Promenade" of the *Reveries.* That wounded organism seemed in only the better trim to produce some of its most delicious fruits.

Induced by the persecution to which he was subjected in Switzerland to go to England and entrust himself to the hospitality of David Hume, Rousseau returned for a moment to Paris (December, 1765). A *Life of Hume* has recently been published in Edinburgh, which places this episode of Rousseau's life in its proper light. In this connection Hume's letters are invaluable, impartial testimony. The cold temperament of the English sage was at that time outspoken in favour of him who proposed to be his guest. To no purpose did the *philosophes* inform him that Rousseau would be at odds with him before he reached Calais. Hume would not believe a word of it, he had found him so mild, so courteous, so modest, so naturally vivacious, and of so pleasant a humour in conversation.

[1] [Written in 1850—Tr.]

" He has," he said, " more of the manners of a man of the world
than any of the literary men here, except M. de Buffon, whose air,
carriage, and attitude correspond more nearly to those of a Marshal of
France than to one's idea of a *philosophe*.   M. Rousseau is of small
stature and would be rather ugly were it not that he has the finest features in the world, or at all events the most expressive."

Hume called him "the pretty little man"; he did
not even see over-much affectation in the Armenian
costume which Rousseau wore at that time on the
pretext that his infirmity made it necessary.   But this
same David Hume judged him most justly when, a
month or two later, and before their falling-out, finding that Rousseau was determined to shut himself up,
alone, in the country, he prophesied that he would be
as unhappy there as he was anywhere else.

" He will be absolutely without occupation," he wrote to Blair,
" without society, and almost without diversion of any sort.   He has
read very little during his life, and he has now renounced reading altogether.   He has seen very little, and he has not the slightest curiosity to see and observe.   He has studied and reflected, strictly speaking,
very little, and has, in truth, only a very slight stock of knowledge.
He has simply *felt* throughout his life; and in that regard his sensitiveness has reached a point that surpasses anything I ever saw before;
but it affords him a keener sensation of pain than of pleasure    He is
like a naked man, not only stripped of his clothes, but stripped of his
skin, who, thus flayed to the quick, should be forced to contend with
the inclemency of the elements which incessantly keep this world in
turmoil."

Certainly it is impossible to describe more exactly
Rousseau's condition, mental and physiological; and
with a guest of such unhealthy susceptibilities, thus
abandoned to solitude, " without occupation, without
books, without society [except that of the wretched

Thérèse [1]], and *without sleep,*'' Hume must have been the less surprised at the result.

Meanwhile I have forgotten Madame de La Tour, and Rousseau himself came within an ace of forgetting her when he passed through Paris. She waited anxiously for him to advise her of his arrival by a word,—perhaps she even expected a visit from him. "I heard that you were in Paris, my dear Jean-Jacques; I cannot believe it, as I did not learn it from yourself." But "Dear Jean-Jacques" was not in an amiable mood that day. "I have received your two letters, Madame; more reproaches! As I never, in whatever situation I may be, receive anything else from you, I take them for granted and know what to expect. My arrival and my stay here are not a secret, I have not been to see you, because I go to see no one." And he made her, who deemed herself already an old friend, feel that she was only a new friend, one among a multitude, and that she had not as yet succeeded in gaining a real foothold in a corner of his heart.

She made bold, in spite of everything, to present herself at his door, in the Temple, where the Prince de Conti was giving him shelter. She arrived at an hour when she hoped to find him alone, but he was not; she went in, however, and it would seem, from the gratitude which she displayed, that she was not too

[1] [Thérèse La Vasseur, the woman with whom Rousseau lived for many years; he had five children by her, whom he carried, one after another, to the Foundling Hospital.—Tr.]

coolly received: he embraced her when she went away. This was the only occasion when she met the object of her worship, with any satisfaction to herself. Six years later (April, 1772), when Jean-Jacques had returned to Paris, she appeared one morning at his lodgings on Rue Plâtrière, on the pretext that she had music for him to copy.[1]  She did not give her name, and he did not recognise her. She went again two months later and made herself known. She had little success; he gave her her dismissal by letter, and hinted that that third visit was quite enough. A prey to his mania, Rousseau no longer belonged to himself.

And yet Madame de La Tour deserved well of him on a memorable occasion, and he himself had seemed to appreciate her devotion. When, six months after Rousseau went to England, his quarrel with Hume burst out and all Paris took sides for or against him, Madame de La Tour did not hesitate: she was for Jean-Jacques, *whether or no;* it is a woman's right, and her honour, to act blindly in such a case. She published, anonymously, a letter most favourable to her friend's disposition, although she knew so well how unjust and insulting he could be without reason. This letter, which has lost all its interest to-day, bears witness to a fearless pen, capable of virile polemical writing,—the lance of an amazon. "As I read it," wrote Rousseau, "my heart beats fast, and I recognise

[1] [It was by copying music that Jean-Jacques gained a livelihood during his last years —TR.]

my dear Marianne." But this gratitude soon sub-
sided; his heart was already too closely beset by distrust to admit for long any gentle sentiment.

Let us be more just than he was. It was her aspiration to make a place for herself in his heart and to
leave an impression there, and she failed; but at least
let her name be attached to the renown of the man
who so often spurned her, and to whom she devoted
herself without a murmur; may it be given to her (it is
the sole consolation that she would have wished) to
live forever, as a satellite in the radiance of his glory!

Turning now to the consideration of Rousseau from
a literary standpoint, I should like to say a few words
concerning the French language of the eighteenth
century—the language which was in part bequeathed
to that century by the dying seventeenth—as we find
it in that writer through whose influence it made the
greatest progress, and who compelled it to submit to
the greatest revolution it had known since the days of
Pascal—a revolution from which we of the nineteenth
century date our beginnings.

Before Rousseau and after Fénelon there were many
attempts at acquiring styles of writing which were
no longer pure seventeenth-century: Fontenelle had
his style, if style there ever was; Montesquieu had
his,—more robust, more solid, more striking, but a
style none the less. Voltaire alone had none, and
his quick, clear, impetuous language flowed as if its

source were but two steps away. "You think," he writes somewhere, "that I express myself clearly enough; I am like the little brooks,—they are transparent because they are not deep." He said this laughingly; in such wise we tell ourselves many half-truths. But the age demanded something more; it wished to be moved, excited, rejuvenated by the expression of ideas and feelings of which it had no clear conception, and which it was always seeking. Buffon's prose, in the early volumes of the *Histoire Naturelle,* gave it a sort of image of what it wanted, an image more majestic than living, a little out of reach, and too closely attached to scientific subjects. Rousseau appeared: on the day when he really became known to himself, he revealed at the same instant to his epoch the writer best adapted to set forth with novelty, with force, with a logic streaked with flame, the confused ideas which were struggling, striving to be born. In taking possession of this language, which he had had to vanquish and make himself master of, he put a little constraint upon it, he marked it with a ply which it was destined to retain thenceforth; but he gave it more than he took from it, and, in many respects, he strengthened and regenerated it. Since Jean-Jacques it has been the form of the language created and firmly established by him into which our greatest writers have cast their innovations, and which they have striven to improve. The pure seventeenth-century form, as we love to recall it, has been little more than a charming relic of antiquity, and a source of regret to persons of taste.

Although the *Confessions* did not appear until after Rousseau's death, and when his influence was already in the plenitude of its power, it is in that work that it is most convenient for us to-day to study him, with all the merits, the prodigies, and the defects of his talent. We will try to do it, confining ourselves so far as we can to a consideration of the writer, but reserving the right to comment upon the ideas and the character of the man.

The present moment [1850] is not very favourable to Rousseau, who is charged with being the author, the promoter, of many of the ills that we are undergoing. "There is no writer," some one has judiciously said, "better fitted to make the poor man arrogant." In spite of all this, we will try not to be unduly influenced ourselves by this personal feeling, so to speak, which leads men of good judgment to blame him for the painful trials through which we are passing. Men who have such a range and such foresight should not be judged according to the emotions and reactions of a single day.

The idea of writing "Confessions" seems so natural in Rousseau, and so in harmony with his disposition and his talent alike, that one would hardly believe that it was necessary to suggest it to him. It came to him, however, in the first place, from his publisher, Rey of Amsterdam, and also from Duclos. After *La*

*Nouvelle Héloïse,* after *Émile,* Rousseau began in 1764 to set down his *Confessions,* at the age of fifty-two, after his departure from Montmorency and during his sojourn at Motiers in Switzerland. There has just been published, in the last number of the *Revue Suisse* (October, 1850), an opening chapter of the *Confessions,* taken from a manuscript deposited in the library of Neuchâtel ; it is Rousseau's first draft, which he afterward suppressed. This original exordium, which is much less emphatic and less ornate than that which we find in the *Confessions* as published, does not greet us with a blast from "the trumpet of the last judgment," nor does it end with the famous apostrophe to the "Eternal Being." Rousseau sets forth therein, at much greater length, but in philosophical language, his plan of painting himself, and making his confessions *à toute rigueur;* he makes it very clear in what the originality and singularity of his plan consists.

"No one can describe a man's life but the man himself. His inward being, his real life, is known to him alone; but when writing of it, he disguises it; under the name of his life, he writes his apology; he exhibits himself as he wishes himself to be seen, but not at all as he is. The most sincere of men are, at the best, truthful only in what they say; they lie by their reticences, and those things as to which they are silent put such a different face on what they pretend to confess, that by telling only a part of the truth they tell nothing. I put Montaigne at the head of those *sincere hypocrites,* who try to deceive by telling the truth. He exhibits himself with failings; but he ascribes to himself only those which are amiable; *there is no man living who has not some hateful ones.* Montaigne's portrait of himself is a good likeness, but taken in profile. Who can say that a scar on the cheek, or an eye gouged out on the side that he hides from us, would not have changed his aspect completely ? "

He proposes therefore to do what no one before him has ever planned or dared to do. As for style, it seems to him necessary to invent one as novel as his project, and proportioned to the diversity and dissimilarity of the things he has it in mind to describe.

" If I attempt to produce a work written with great care, as others have done, I shall not paint myself but besmear myself with paint.[1] The matter now in hand is my portrait, not a book. I am going to work, so to speak, in the *camera obscura ;* no other art is needed than to follow exactly those lines which I see marked out. And so I choose my own path in the matter of style as in that of subject. I shall not take pains to make it uniform; I shall always use whatever style may come to me; I shall change it according to my whim, without scruple; I shall set down everything as I feel it, as I see it, without choice of words, without embarrassment, without worrying over the mixture. By abandoning myself at once to my recollection of the impression received at the time and to my present feeling, I shall depict the state of my mind twice over, to-wit, at the moment when the event happened to me and at the moment when I describe it; my style, uneven and unadorned, now hurried and now diffuse, now serious and now foolish, now grave and now gay, will itself form a part of my story. In a word, no matter how this work may be written, it will always be, because of its aim, an invaluable book for philosophers; it is, I say again, a document for the comparative study of the human heart, *and it is the only one in existence.*"

Rousseau's error was not the believing that, by confessing himself thus aloud before all men, in a frame of mind so different from Christian humility, he was doing a unique thing, or even a thing of the greatest interest for the study of the human heart; his error

[1] *Je ne me peindrai pas, je me farderai.*

consisted in his belief that he was doing a *useful* thing.
He did not see that he was acting like the physician
who should undertake to describe in an intelligible,
attractive way, for the behoof of worldly and ignorant
people, some strongly characterised mental weakness
or disease; such a physician would be in a measure
blameworthy and responsible for all the maniacs and
fools by imitation and contagion whom his book
would make.

The first pages of the *Confessions* are over-empha-
sised and decidedly painful. I find at the outset "a
hiatus occasioned by a failure of memory." Rousseau
speaks of *the authors of his days;* he bore at his birth
the germ of an *incommodity* which time has aggra-
vated *(renforcée)*, he says, and which now gives him
occasional respites *(rélâches)* only to, etc., etc. All
this is unpleasant; but beware! beside this harshness
of accentuation and these native crudities, what words
are these? what unwonted simplicity, intimate, and
penetrating!

"I felt before I thought; that is the common lot of mankind. I
experienced it more fully than others. I do not know what I did up
to the time I was five or six years old. I do not know how I learned
to read; I simply remember my first books and their effect on me.
. . . My mother had left some novels; we began to read them
after supper, my father and I. At first it was simply a question of
giving me practice in reading by means of entertaining books; but
soon the interest became so intense that we read by turns without in-
termission, and passed whole nights in that occupation. We could
never put a book down until the end. Sometimes my father, hearing the swallows in the morning, would say shamefacedly: *'Let 's go
to bed, I am more of a child than you.'* "

Mark well this swallow; it is the first, and it announces a new springtime of the language; we begin to detect its appearance only in Rousseau. It is from him that the appreciation of nature dates, in the eighteenth century, in France.[1] From him, too, dates, in our literature, the sentiment of domestic life, of that lowly, poor, reserved, intimate life, wherein so many treasures of virtue and amiability are amassed. Despite some details in execrable taste, where he talks about pilfering and victuals (*mangeaille*), how readily we forgive him in consideration of that old ballad of his childhood, of which he remembers only the tune and a few scattered words, but which he is for ever trying to recall, and never succeeds in recalling, old as he is, without a touching delight!

" It is a whim which I do not understand at all, but it is absolutely impossible for me to sing it through without being stopped by my tears. A hundred times I have thought of writing to Paris to have the rest of the words hunted up, that is, if there is still any one who knows them; but I am almost sure that the pleasure I take in remembering the song would disappear in great part, if I had proof that others besides my poor Aunt Suzon used to sing it."

That is the new thing in the author of the *Confessions,* that is what fascinates us by opening before us an unexpected fountain of private, domestic sensibility. And so, when we note with some regret that Rousseau

[1] [In his Essay on George Sand, Sainte-Beuve says: " It was Jean-Jacques who had the glory of first discovering nature and describing it; the natural scenery of Switzerland, of her mountains, lakes, and forests — he aroused enthusiasm for these hitherto unknown beauties.—Tr.]

did force and upturn and, as it were, run the plough through the language, we add instantly that at the same time he fertilised it and sowed it.

A man of the haughty aristocratic stock,.but a pupil of Rousseau, and one who had not much more appreciation and fear of ridicule than he, M. de Chateaubriand, adopted in *René* and in his *Mémoires* this fashion of avowals and confessions, more or less direct, and he produced some astounding and magical effects with it. Let us mark the differences, however. Rousseau has not the initial elevation of mind; he is not altogether —far from it!—what we call a well-born child; he has a leaning toward vice, and towards low vices; he has shameful, concealed appetites, which do not bespeak the gentleman; he has those long periods of a timidity which changes abruptly to the effrontery of a *polisson* and a *vaurien,* as he calls himself; in a word, he has not that safeguard, the sense of honour, which M. de Chateaubriand had, from childhood, standing like an alert sentinel beside his shortcomings. But Rousseau, with all these disadvantages, which, following his example, we do not hesitate to call by their names, is superior to Chateaubriand in the sense that he is more human, more of a man, more easily moved. He has not that incredible austerity (a genuinely feudal austerity, in very truth), and those aberrations of the heart which Chateaubriand displays in speaking of his father and mother, for example. When Rousseau is on the subject of the misconduct of his father,—a worthy man, but fond of pleasure, frivolous, and remarried, who abandons him and leaves him to his fate, —with what delicacy he touches upon that painful subject! how the whole matter is coloured by the heart! I am not speaking of the delicacy of the knight-errant, but of genuine, innate delicacy, the delicacy that springs from morality and humanity.

It is most extraordinary that this inner moral sentiment by which he was inspired, and which held him in such close relation with other men, did not warn Rousseau how far he lowered himself in many a passage of his life, and in many a phrase which he affects. His style, like his life itself, seems to have acquired something of the vices of his early education, and of the evil society which he frequented at the beginning. After a childhood passed respectably in the domestic circle, he is apprenticed, and subjected to harsh treatment, which lowers his moral tone and impairs his sense of delicacy.    The terms *polisson, vaurien, gueux, fripon*, have no power to arrest his course; indeed they seem to flow from his pen with a certain complacency.    His language always retained a trace of the wretched style of his early years.

I distinguish in him two varieties of change in language: one, which is due solely to the fact that he is a provincial and speaks the French of one born out of France.   Rousseau will write, without a qualm, *Comme que je fasse, comme que ce fût,* etc., instead of: *De quelque manière que je fasse, de quelque manière*

*que ce fût,* etc.; his articulation is loud and harsh; at
times he has a touch of *goître* in his voice.　But this
is a defect which we overlook, so completely did he
succeed in triumphing over it in some delightful passages; so thoroughly, by dint of hard work and emotion, did he succeed in imparting flexibility to his
diction, and to that learned and laboured style perfect
suppleness and the semblance of a first gushing outflow !—The other variety of change and corruption
which one may remark in him is a more serious matter in that it has to do with the moral sense; he seems
to have no suspicion that there are certain things
which it is forbidden to express; that there are certain
degrading, disgusting, cynical expressions which the
decent man dispenses with,—which he does not
know.

At some time Rousseau was a servant; one detects
the fact by his style in more than one place.　He has
no dislike either of the word or of the thing.　"If
Fénelon were living, you would be a Catholic," said
Bernardin de Saint-Pierre to him one day, observing
his emotion during some ceremonial of the faith.
"Oh ! if Fénelon were living," cried Rousseau, in
tears, "I would try to be his footman so that I might
earn the right to be his *valet de chambre.*"　The
lack of taste may be detected even in the emotion.
Rousseau is not simply a journeyman in the language,
who has been an apprentice before becoming a master, and who allows the marks of the soldering to

appear here and there; he is, morally, a man who, in his youth, has lived amid the greatest variety of conditions, and whose stomach does not revolt at certain ugly and offensive things when he mentions them. I will say no more concerning this essential vice, this blemish, which it is so painful to encounter and to be forced to denounce in so great a writer and painter, in such a man.

Slow to think, quick to feel, with intense but self-contained appetites, with daily suffering and constraint, Rousseau reaches the age of sixteen, and describes himself to us in these words :

" Thus I attained my sixteenth year, restless, dissatisfied with myself and with everything else, with no liking for my trade, with none of the pleasures of my age, devoured by desires the object of which I did not know, weeping without cause for tears, sighing without knowing why I sighed; in a word, fondly caressing my chimeras, because I saw nothing about me which was of equal value.    On Sundays, after sermon, my comrades used to come for me to go out to play with them.    I would gladly have escaped them if I could; but, once interested in their games, I was more eager and went farther than another; *hard to start and hard to stop.*"

Always at one or the other extreme !   In this passage we recognise the first phase of the thoughts, and almost of the very phrases, of René,[1] of those words which have already become sweet music, and which still sing in our ears:

" My humour was impetuous, my disposition uneven.   By turns noisy and joyous, taciturn and melancholy, I would call my young

[1] [In Chateaubriand's romance of that name, published in 1802.— Tr.]

comrades about me; then, abruptly turning my back upon them, I would go and sit apart, to gaze at the fleeting cloud or listen to the rain pattering on the leaves."

And again:

" In my youth, I cultivated the Muses; there is nothing more poetic, when its passions are new, than a heart of sixteen years. The morning of life is like the morning of the day, full of purity, of images, and harmonies."

In truth René is simply this same youth of sixteen, transplanted, set down in the midst of a different nature and in the bosom of a different social condition; no longer an engraver's apprentice, son of a bourgeois of Geneva (of a bourgeois *of the lower order*), but a chevalier, of noble birth, a traveller *en grand,* enamoured of the Muses: everything, at first sight, assumes a more seductive, more poetic colouring; the unexpected aspect of the landscape and of the framework gives relief to the personality and emphasises an unfamiliar style; but the first hint of the type is there, in the passage that we have quoted, and it was Rousseau who, by looking into himself, found it.

René is a model more flattering to us, because in him all the unpleasant human qualities are veiled; he has a tinge of the colouring of Greece, of chivalry, and of Christianity, whose diverse reflections mingle on the surface. Words, in that masterpiece of art, acquire a new magic; there are words overflowing with light and melody. The horizon is magnified in **every** direction, and the rays from Olympus disport themselves thereon. Rousseau offers nothing comparable to him at first glance, but he is more genuine at bottom, more real, more living. This child of toil, who goes out to play with his comrades after sermon, or to dream alone, if he can; this small youth, with the well set-up figure, the bright eye, the shrewd face, who reprobates all sorts of things more than one likes, has more reality than the other, and more life; he is a good fellow, he is emotional, he has feeling *(des entrailles)*.

The two natures, René's and Rousseau's, have each a diseased spot, too great ardour mingled with inaction and idleness, a predominance of imagination and impressibility which react upon and devour themselves; but of the two Rousseau is the more truly impressible, for he is the more original and the more sincere in his chimerical outbursts, in his regrets, in his pictures of an ideal of felicity within his reach and yet thrown away. When, as he is leaving his native country, at the end of the first book of the *Confessions,* he recalls the simple and touching picture of the obscure happiness that he might have enjoyed there; when he says to us:

"I should have passed, in the bosom of my religion, my country, my family and my friends, a peaceful and pleasant life, such as my temperament demanded, in the monotonous round of work that was to my taste, and of a society after my heart; I should have been a good Christian, a good citizen, a good father of a family, a good friend, a good workman, à good man in all respects; I should have loved my trade, *I should have done it credit perhaps,* and, after a simple and

obscure, but unruffled and happy life, I should have died peacefully
amid my own people; soon forgotten, no doubt, I should at least
have been regretted as long as any one remembered me " ;—

when he speaks thus, he does in truth convince us of
the sincerity of his wish and of his regrets; so instinct
are all his words with a vivid and profound realisation
of the sweet, placid, and honourable charm of private
life!

The first book of the *Confessions* is not the most
remarkable, but Rousseau is exhibited therein from
head to foot, with his self-esteem, his budding vices,
his strange and grotesque moods, his meannesses, his
obscenity (it will be observed that I take note of
everything); with his pride, too, and that rebound
of independence and firmness which raises him again;
with his healthy and happy childhood, his sickly and
martyrised youth, and, one foresees, with all that it
will inspire in him later of apostrophes to society and
of vengeful reprisals; with his tearful sense of the
domestic, family happiness of which he had so little
enjoyment; and none the less with the first whiffs
of spring and those first breaths which are a signal of
the natural awakening destined to burst forth in the
literature of the nineteenth century. We are in danger to-day of being too insensible to these early picturesque pages of Rousseau; we are so spoiled by
bright colours that we forget how fresh and new these
first pictures of nature appeared at the time, and what
an event they were in that society, most intellectual

and refined, it is true, but colourless, as barren of imagination as of genuine sensibility, with no trace in itself of the flowing sap which, with each recurring season, wakes to new life. Rousseau was the first to renew the infusion of that vegetable sap which is powerful to revive the delicate tree that is dying. French readers, accustomed to the artificial air of a salon atmosphere—the *urban* readers, as he calls them —were amazed and entranced when they felt those cool and refreshing mountain breezes from the Alps, which came to give new life to a literature as devoid of vital force as it was distinguished.

It was time; and it is in this view that Rousseau was not a corrupter of the language, but, all things considered, a regenerator.

Before him La Fontaine alone among Frenchmen had known and felt, to that degree, nature, and the charm of reverie off the beaten track; but his example counted for little; they let the good man go and come with his fables, and they remained in the salons. Rousseau was the first who compelled all that fine company to leave the salons, and to forsake the grand avenue of the park for the natural pathway across the fields.

The beginning of the second book of the *Confessions* is delightful and full of vigour. Madame de Warens appears for the first time. In depicting her, Rousseau's style becomes, without awkwardness, softer and mellower, and at the same time we instantly

discover one feature, an essential vein which exists in
him and in his whole style, — I mean sensuality.
"Rousseau had a voluptuous mind," an excellent
critic has said; women play a great part in his life;
absent or present, they and their charms engross him,
inspire him and move him, and something of them is
mingled in everything that he writes. "How did it
happen," he says of Madame de Warens, "that on
accosting for the first time an agreeable, polished, *daz-
zling* woman, a lady of a rank superior to my own, I
found myself on the instant as free from constraint, as
much at my ease, as if I had been perfectly sure of
pleasing her?" This facility, this freedom from constraint, which ordinarily was so uncharacteristic of him
when he was actually in the presence of women, was
always characteristic of his style in describing them.
The most fascinating pages of the *Confessions* are
those relating to this first meeting with Madame de
Warens, and those in which he describes the greeting
of Madame Basile, the pretty shopkeeper of Turin:
"She was finely arrayed and refulgent, and, despite
her gracious manner, that splendour abashed me.
But her very kindly greeting, her sympathetic tone,
her gentle and caressing manners, soon put me at my
ease; I saw that I should succeed, and that made me
succeed the sooner." Have you never felt, in that "re-
fulgence" and in that brilliancy of colouring, a ray of
the Italian sun as it were? And he describes the scene,
vivacious but silent, that scene carried on by gestures,

and interrupted in time, that scene overflowing with blushes and youthful desires.

Add to these passages the excursion in the outskirts of Annecy with Mesdames Galley and de Graffenreid, every detail of which is fascinating.  Such pages were in French literature like the discovery of a new world, a world of sunlight and cool breezes which one has had close at hand without noticing it; they presented a combination of sensibility and naturalness, wherein the touch of sensuality appeared only so much as was permissible and necessary in order to set us free at last from false metaphysics of the heart and from the conventional cant of immateriality.  Sensuality of the brush, to that extent, could hardly give offence; it is sober as yet, and it wears no mask, which makes it more innocent than that sensuality in which many painters have indulged since Rousseau.

As a painter Rousseau has in everything the sentiment of *reality*.  He has it whenever he speaks of beauty, which, even when it is imaginary, as in his Julie, carries with it a body and shape that are quite visible, and is by no means an Iris, floating in the air and intangible.  This sentiment of reality manifests itself in this, that he is careful that every scene that he remembers or invents shall be set, every character that he introduces shall act his part, in a definitely marked locality, the slightest details of which may be fixed in the mind and retained.  One of his criticisms of the great novelist Richardson was that he did not connect

the memory of his characters with some locality which
it would be a pleasure to identify by his descriptions.
Observe, for example, how perfectly he has naturalised
his Julie and his Saint-Preux in the Pays-de-Vaud, on
the shores of that lake about which his heart had never
ceased to wander.    His straightforward, steadfast
mind at all times lent its graving tool to his imagination, so that nothing essential should be omitted in the
design.    Finally, this sentiment of reality appears even
in the care with which, amid all the circumstances and
adventures of his career, happy or unhappy, even amid
the most romantic of them all, he never forgets to mention his repast and to give the details of a healthful,
frugal régime, adapted to give joy to the heart as well
as to the mind.

This last point, too, is an essential one; it is refera-
ble to those natural traits of the bourgeois, of the man
of the people, which I have remarked upon in Rousseau.    He has been hungry in his day; he notes in
his *Confessions,* with a sense of gratitude to Providence, the last time that it was his fate literally to feel
poverty and hunger.    And so he will never forget,
even in the ideal picture of his happiness which he
draws on a later page, to introduce these incidents of
real life and of the common lot, these things of the
entrails.    It is by all these veracious details, combined
as they are in his eloquence, that he seizes us and holds
us fast.

Nature, sincerely *felt* and loved for itself, forms the

groundwork of Rousseau's inspiration, whenever that inspiration is sound and healthy and not diseased. When he sees Madame de Warens again, on his return from Turin, he lives some time under her roof, and from the bedroom which is given him he sees gardens and has glimpses of the open country.   "It was the first time," he says, "since Bossey [the place where he had been sent to boarding-school in his childhood], that I had had *green things before my windows.*" It had been a matter of great indifference hitherto to French literature whether it had or had not *green things* before its eyes; it was Rousseau's part to call attention to that matter.   From this point of view he may be defined in a word: he was the first who introduced *green things* into our literature.   Living thus, at nineteen years of age, under the same roof with a woman whom he loved but to whom he dared not declare his passion, Rousseau gave way to a melancholy "in which, however, there was no touch of gloom, and which was tempered by a flattering hope." Having gone to walk alone outside of the town, on a great holiday, while the people were at vespers, he says:

"The ringing of the bells, which has always affected me strangely, the songs of the birds, the beauty of the day, the soft loveliness of the landscape, the scattered country houses wherein I fancied us two living together, all this made such a vivid, tender, melancholy, and moving impression upon me that I saw myself, as in a trance, transported to that blissful time and that blissful spot where my heart, in possession of all the felicity it could desire, would enjoy it in indescribable ecstasy, without even thinking of sensual pleasure."

Such were the feelings of this child of Geneva at Annecy in the year 1731, when people in Paris were reading the *Temple de Gnide*.[1]  On that day he discovered *reverie,* that new charm which had hitherto been abandoned to La Fontaine as a mere oddity, but which Rousseau was to introduce definitively into a literature until then either dissolute or materialistic. *Reverie*—that is his novelty, his discovery, his America. His dream of that day he realised some years later, in his sojourn at Les Charmettes, in that excursion on Saint-Louis' Day, which he has described as no similar thing had ever been described before:

> "Everything," he says, "seemed to conspire for the bliss of that day. It had recently rained; no dust, and the streams flowing abundantly; a light, cool wind fluttered the leaves, the air was pure, the horizon cloudless, serenity reigned in the sky as in our hearts. We dined at a peasant's cottage and shared with his family, who blessed us heartily. Those poor Savoyards are such kindly folk!"

And he goes on, in this strain of good-humour, of observation, and of artless sincerity, to develop a picture in which everything is perfect, everything enchants, and only the name *Maman,* applied to Madame de Warens, gives offence morally, and causes pain.

That brief moment at Les Charmettes, where it was given to that still novice heart to expand for the first time, is the most divine moment of the *Confessions,* and it will never be repeated, even when he has retired to the Hermitage.  The description of the years

[1] [By Montesquieu; published in 1725  *See* vol. i., p. 128.—Tr.]

at the Hermitage, and of the passion which sought
him out there, has much that fascinates, it is true, and
perhaps more salience than all that has gone before;
he was justified, however, in exclaiming: *" This is
not Les Charmettes."* The misanthropy and distrust
by which he was already assailed followed him in
that period of solitude. He thought constantly of
the society of Paris, of d'Holbach's little coterie ; he
enjoyed his retirement in spite of them, but such
thoughts poisoned his purest enjoyment. His character became soured, and contracted during those
years an incurable malady. Doubtless he did have
blissful moments, then and afterward, until the end;
he found in the island of Saint-Pierre, in the centre of
the Lake of Bienne, an interval of calm and oblivion
which inspired some of his finest pages,—the fifth
"Promenade" of the *Reveries,* which, with the
third letter to M. de Malesherbes, cannot well be distinguished from the divinest passages of the *Confessions.* But in lightness of touch, freshness, and
gaiety nothing in them equals the description of the
life at Les Charmettes. Rousseau's true happiness, of
which no one, not even himself, could rob him, was
the being able to evoke thus and to draw anew, with
the accuracy and vividness which marked his memory
of them, such pictures of youth, even in the midst of
his most disturbed and anxious years.

The *pedestrian journey,* with its vivid impressions
of each successive instant, was another of Rousseau's

inventions, one of the novelties which he imported into literature; it has been much abused since. After enjoying the experience, it first occurred to him, but not until much later, to tell what he had felt. Only at such times, he assures us, when he was travelling on foot, in fine weather, through a beautiful country, without haste, having for the goal of his journey an agreeable object which he was not in too great a hurry to reach,—only at such times was he absolutely himself, and only then did his ideas, which were cold and dead in the study, come to life and take their flight.

"There is a something about walking which vivifies and sharpens my ideas ; I can hardly think when I am still; my body must needs be in motion to set my mind in motion. The sight of the fields, the succession of pleasant prospects, the fresh air, the hearty appetite, the excellent health which I gain by walking, the freedom of the wineshop, the distance from everything that makes me feel my dependence, from everything that reminds me of my situation—all this sets my soul free, gives to my thoughts more audacity, casts me, so to speak, into the immensity of created things, to combine them, to select them, to appropriate them at my pleasure, without fear or constraint. I have all nature at my disposal, as its master."

Do not ask him to write down at such moments the thoughts, sublime, foolish, adorable, which pass through his mind: he much prefers to taste and relish them rather than put them in words. "Besides, did I carry paper and pens about me ? If I had thought of all those matters, nothing would have come to me. I did not then foresee that I should have ideas; they come when it pleases them, not when it pleases me." And so, if we are to believe him, we have naught but

far-off recollections and indistinct fragments of himself as he was at those moments.  And yet, what
could be more genuine, more exact, and more delightful at once !  Let us recall the night that he
passed in the open air on the bank of the Rhone or
the Saone, in a sunken road near Lyons:

> "I lay in voluptuous ease on the platform of a sort of recess or false
> gateway hollowed out of a terrace wall ; the canopy of my bed was
> formed by the tops of the trees ; a nightingale was directly over my
> head, and I fell asleep to his singing; my sleep was delicious, my
> awakening even more so.   It was broad daylight; my eyes, when they
> opened, saw the water, the verdure, a beautiful landscape.   I rose
> and shook myself ; hunger assailed me ; I walked gaily toward the
> town, resolved to spend on a good breakfast two fifteen-sou pieces
> which I still had left."

There we have the natural Rousseau complete, with
his reverie, his idealism, his reality; and that *fifteen-
sou piece* itself, coming after the nightingale, is not
misplaced to bring us back to earth, and to make us
realise to the full the humble enjoyment which poverty
carries hidden within itself, when it is combined with
poesy and with youth.

The picturesque in Rousseau is composed, robust,
and clearly outlined, even in the most delicate passages; the colours are always laid upon a fully perfected design; therein this Genevan is of the pure
French breed.  If he lacks now and then a warmer
light and the brilliance of Italy or Greece; if, as sometimes happens about the lovely Lake of Geneva, the
north wind cools the air and a cloud suddenly imparts

a greyish tinge to the mountain sides, there are days and hours of a perfect, limpid serenity. Some later writers have improved upon this style, have thought to eclipse and surpass it; they have certainly succeeded with respect to some effects of colouring and of sound. However, Rousseau's style still remains the most unerring and robust that we can put forward as a pattern in the field of modern innovation. With him the centre of the language is not much displaced. His successors have gone farther; they have not only transferred the seat of the Empire to Byzantium, but have often carried it to Antioch and to the heart of Asia. In them the imagination in its splendour absorbs and dominates everything.

I have been able simply to point out, *currente cala-mo,* the leading features in the author of the *Confessions,* by virtue of which he remains a master; to salute the creator of *reverie,* who inoculated us with the appreciation of nature and the sense of reality, the father of intimate literature and of interior painting. What a pity that there should be an infusion of misanthropic conceit, and that cynical outbursts should make a smirch amid so many alluring and solid beauties! But these follies and vices of the man are powerless to prevail over his innate merits, or to conceal from us the great talents by favour of which he still proves himself superior to his successors.

Extraordinary man, powerful and bewitching writer, one must constantly play a double part in passing

judgment upon him.    If he was his own executioner,
and if he tormented himself exceedingly, he tormented
the world still more.    Not only did he cast a spell
upon passion—he succeeded, as Byron says, in giving
to madness the aspect of beauty, and in cloaking mistaken acts or thoughts with the celestial colouring of
words.    He first imparted to our language a continu-
ous force, a steadfastness of tone, a solidity of texture,
which it had not before; and therein, it may be, lies
his surest claim to glory.    As for the substance of his
ideas, everything in him is doubtful, everything may
seem, fairly enough, equivocal and suspicious; sound
ideas are constantly blended with false ones, and suffer from the contact.    By encompassing half truths
with a false glamour of evidence, he contributed more
than any other writer to start the arrogant and the
weak upon the pathway of error.    One day, in an
hour of unreserve, while talking about his works with
Hume, and admitting that he was not ill-content with
them in respect to style and eloquence, he happened
to add: "But I am always afraid of going astray in
substance, and that all my theories are overloaded with
extravagant conceits."    That one of his works of
which he thought most highly was *Le Contrat Social,*
which is in fact the most sophistical of them all, and
was destined to have the most revolutionary influence
upon the future.

For us, whatever common sense may tell us, for all
those who are, in whatever degree, of his posterity,

poetically speaking, it will always be impossible not
to love Jean-Jacques, not to forgive him much in favour
of his pictures of youth, his impassioned appreciation
of nature, for that *reverie,* of which he implanted the
genius among us, and to which he was the first to give
expression in our language.

# Friedrich Melchior Grimm.

1723–1807.

# Friedrich Melchior Grimm.

G RIMM'S *Correspondance Littéraire* is one of
the books which I use most freely in these
cursory studies so far as they relate to the
eighteenth century; and the more I have used them,
the more I have found Grimm to be (speaking from a
literary, not from a philosophical standpoint) a sound,
shrewd, solid, well-balanced mind, an excellent critic,
in a word, on a multitude of points, and always first in
his judgments.   Let us not overlook this last feature;
when an author's reputation is established it is an easy
matter to speak fittingly of him;  one has only to
govern oneself by the general opinion;  but at his
début, at the moment when he makes his first attempt and is in a measure ignorant of his own powers,
and as he develops,—to judge him then with tact and
accuracy, to avoid overstating his range, to predict
the extent of his flight, and to divine his limitations,
to offer sagacious criticisms in the face of fashion,—all
this is the attribute of the born critic.   Grimm was
endowed with this faculty of keen judgment, which
is so useful near at hand, and so unapparent at a distance.   If we except the group of encyclopædists,

with which he was too much involved to speak of
them without bias, but whose weak points he realised
none the less, no man of that time had a keener eye
for everything produced by his contemporaries.

Men are not just to Grimm; his name is never mentioned without some uncomplimentary qualification;
for a long time I myself shared the common prejudice
against him, and when I came to ask myself the cause
of it, I found that it rested solely on the testimony of
Jean-Jacques Rousseau in his *Confessions*. But Rousseau, whenever his self-esteem and his diseased vanity are at stake, has not the slightest hesitation about
lying, and I have arrived at the conclusion that with
respect to Grimm he was a liar. His lying was the
more dangerous in that he brought to it the sincerity
of his mania, and a curious array of details: he collected and manufactured a multitude of wretched
trifles concerning his former friend, to transform them
into enormities. Grimm, who saw all this stuff
printed, and who lived a long while after, had too
much self-respect ever to reply to them. For my own
part, having emerged from that hateful labyrinth, I
propose, once for all, to express my gratitude to
Grimm, as to one of the most distinguished of our
critics, and to attempt to present him in his true aspect,
without enthusiasm (he arouses little), without partiality, but without disparagement.

Grimm was German by birth and education, and
one does not detect it in the least while reading him:

FRIEDRICH MELCHIOR GRIMM

his cast of thought and of expression is most perspicuous and wholly French.   Born in Ratisbon in
December, 1723, of a father who occupied a respectable position in the Lutheran Church, he was educated at the University of Leipsic; he had for professor
there the celebrated critic Ernesti, and made the most
of his learned instruction in Cicero and the classics.
Grimm never made a display of erudition, but whenever it was necessary to pass judgment upon anything
relating to the ancient authors, he was more prepared
than the majority of French men of letters; he had
a foundation of solid classicism, after the German
fashion.   He expresses surprise somewhere that Voltaire speaks so disparagingly of Homer in his *Essai
sur les Mœurs,* in which all the honours of the epic
are awarded to modern authors.   "If this decree,"
says Grimm, "had been pronounced by M. de Fontenelle, no one would have heeded it, it would have
been of no consequence; but that M. de Voltaire
should be the one to put forth such an opinion is
something utterly inconceivable."   And he produces
his triumphant arguments, altogether to the advantage
of the ancient poet.   The fact is that Grimm spoke thus
of Homer because he had read him in the Greek, while
Voltaire had simply skimmed him in French.

Grimm's first literary efforts were in German; he
wrote a tragedy which may be found in the collections
of German plays of that day.   Many years after, at
Potsdam, the great Frederick paid him the compliment

of repeating the beginning of it from memory. Born twenty-five years before Goethe, Grimm belonged to the generation preceding the great awakening of German literature, which essayed to take for its model the style of the ancients, or of the modern classics of France and England. This useful and in some sort preparatory generation, which recognised as its literary leader Gottsched, numbered among its most distinguished authors Gellert and Haller. Grimm was scarcely settled in France when he began by publishing in *Le Mercure* a number of letters on the literature of his native land; toward the close of them he mentioned the name of young Klopstock and complimented him on the first cantos of his *Messias*[1]; he predicted for his country the blooming of a new spring. "It is thus," he said, "that within about thirty years Germany has become an aviary of little birds who await only the fitting season to begin to sing. Perhaps that glorious season for the Muses of my fatherland is not far distant." Thirty years later, having received from the great Frederick an essay upon German Literature, wherein that monarch, who was a little behind the times on that point, announced the near approach of glorious days for the literature of his nation, Grimm, replying (March, 1781), respectfully called his attention to the fact that they had already

---

[1] [The first three of the twenty cantos were published anonymously in 1748, when Klopstock was twenty-five years old. The poem did not appear in its complete form until 1773.—TR.]

arrived, and that there was no longer any occasion
for the prediction. Although he had become a Frenchman and had long since declared himself incompetent
to pass judgment in matters relating to Germany,
Grimm had evidently kept an eye upon the great
literary revolution which had taken place in his native
country after 1770; and he himself, naturalised in
Paris, deserves to be recognised, despite the difference
in style and forms, as one of the older and most noteworthy collateral kindred of the Lessings and Herders.

Without fortune and without prospects, Grimm
came to Paris, and was for some time attached to the
suite of the young hereditary prince of Saxe-Gotha;
he next became tutor to the sons of the Comte de
Schomberg, then secretary to the young Comte de
Friesen, nephew of the Maréchal de Saxe. In this
delicate, dependent position, by his tact, his bearing,
and an external reserve which was natural to him and
which he never laid aside except with his most intimate friends, he was able to win respect. He developed betimes the art of decorous demeanour, and he
had need of it; Rousseau is the only person who ever
accused him of insincerity in that respect. Marmontel says in his *Mémoires :* " Grimm, at that time secretary and intimate friend of the young Comte de
Friesen, nephew of the Maréchal de Saxe, invited us
to dinner every week, and at those bachelor dinners
perfect liberty was the rule; but that was a dish of
which Rousseau partook very sparingly."

While working to transform himself into a French-man and Parisian, Grimm had a strain of German romanticism which he had to conceal and stifle. The best and best-informed of his biographers, Meister of Zurich, who was his secretary for many years, and who paints him after nature, and with gratitude, mentions a profound and mysterious passion, in his youth, for a German princess who was then in Paris; that silent passion was near making of Grimm a Werther. Another passion, the object of which we know, was that which he entertained for Mademoiselle Fel, a singer at the Opera. Grimm had an intense love of music; he took sides warmly for the Italian against the French school; therein he showed himself a man of taste, and he maintained his cause with the enthusi-asm of his race and his years.

He declared that in French music, as it was at that time, one quitted the recitative, or *plain-chant,* only to shriek instead of singing. According to him there was no real singing except that of Jelyotte and Made-moiselle Fel, especially the latter; and he lost his temper with those who did not think that she had a pretty throat [*un joli gosier*]. "Ah! What a grand, beautiful voice!" he cried; "a unique voice, always the same, always fresh and brilliant and soft; by her talent she has taught her countrymen that it is possi-ble to sing in French, and with the same courage has dared to impart an expression of her own to Italian music." He never went away from hearing her "that

his brain was not excited, that he was not in that
frame of mind in which one feels capable of saying or
doing fine and noble things." Hence his passion for
her, which is in no wise more surprising than those
which we have observed in certain dilettanti of our
own time for the Sontags and Malibrans; and that
passion does Grimm credit instead of making him
ridiculous, as some persons have amused themselves
by representing him to us.

While Grimm was inveighing against the tedium
and false method of the French Opera, the Italian
actors came to Paris, in 1752, and gave performances
at the Opera itself. It was at the height of the disputes between Parliament and Court; thirty years
later, differences of the same sort led to the Revolution of '89. A wit has said that the arrival of Manelli,
the Italian singer, in 1752, averted civil war from
France, because but for that arrival the idle spirits
would have turned their attention to the disputes between the Parliament and the clergy, and would have
embittered them still more; instead of which they
descended furiously on the musical quarrel, and
wasted their fire on that. At the Opera there was
"the king's corner," and "the queen's corner." The
music-lovers who assembled under the queen's box
were the most enlightened, the most earnest, and the
most zealous for the Italian innovations. Grimm distinguished himself most of all by a satirical pamphlet
entitled *Le Petit Prophète de Boehmischbroda,* which

had great success.   In the guise of a prophecy he told many truths concerning the taste of his contemporaries.   A Voice is supposed to speak to a poor Bohemian composer of minuets.   There is a word of praise for Jean-Jacques, the recent author of the *Devin du Village,* coupled with a sharp thrust.   "A man," said the Voice, "with whom I do whatever I choose, *although he kicks against me."*   Refractory and freakish even in his genius, that is Jean-Jacques to the life, even at the date of the *Devin du Village.*[1]

There were, too, special compliments and distinctions for Voltaire, Montesquieu, etc.   Grimm had stood the test, with respect to wit and style; he had won his spurs in French.   "What is this Bohemian thinking about," said Voltaire, "to have more wit than we ?"   That was a certificate of naturalisation for Grimm.

He was thirty years old.   Having thus mastered the language, admitted to the best society, armed with a keen intellect, and supplied with a great variety of points of comparison, he speedily found himself in a better position than any other to form an accurate judgment of France.   Generally speaking, a keen-witted foreigner, who makes a sufficiently long sojourn among a neighbouring people, is better adapted to pronounce judgment upon that people than a person who is one of themselves, and who consequently is too close to them.   Horace Walpole, Franklin, Galiani, in the

[1] [1752.—Tr.]

eighteenth century, judged us with marvellous and unerring accuracy at the second glance. But Grimm's judgment is more pertinent than that of any of them: he is more at home among us than Horace Walpole; he has not the clever restlessness, the incessant fluttering of Galiani, which leads him to say again and again: "I am and I mean to be entertaining." In him tranquillity and reflection are blended with shrewdness. I find in Grimm a trace of infatuation in only one particular, and that is his connection with Diderot. In the praise which he lavishes upon him, all allowance being made for the partiality of friendship, there is a remnant of Germanism. Grimm, becoming the most French of Germans, was attracted, by a sort of natural affinity, to Diderot, the most German of Frenchmen. Diderot is, in France, the German side of Grimm. Except for that, he was altogether cured of his national failing, and he did not acquire ours.

His literary correspondence with the Courts of the North and the sovereigns of Germany came to him originally through Abbé Raynal, who discharged a part of his burden upon him. It begins in 1753, with a criticism of a work of this same Abbé Raynal, of whom Grimm speaks with perfect freedom, tempering his praise with some true observations. This correspondence, which continued without interruption until 1790, that is to say, for thirty-seven years, and came to an end, so to speak, only with the old social régime of France, under the blows of the Revolution, is a monument all the more valuable because it is without pretension and without any prearranged plan. "Paris," some one has said very truly, "is the place of all others in the world where one has the least freedom of judgment concerning the works of people who hold a certain rank." This was true when it was written, and it is true to-day. Grimm, living in society, escaped this difficulty by favour of the secrecy of his correspondence; but, although publicity is an almost insurmountable barrier to free criticism of contemporaries, secrecy is a snare which tempts one to many rash exploits, and to much evil-speaking. Grimm was high-minded enough and just enough not to fall into that little snare, and not to allow his judgment to give way to passion or to malicious curiosity. In a word, his correspondence was secret, but never clandestine.

He began by informing the princes, his correspondents, very modestly, of the current literary news and of the new books; only by slow degrees did his influence increase and his authority became more extensive. It was firmly established and consecrated when the Empress Catherine of Russia chose him for her favourite and confidential correspondent. At that time the German Courts had their eyes fixed on France; the sovereigns visited Paris incognito, and on returning to their own countries desired to keep in touch with that society, which had fascinated them. Grimm, before he held any official diplomatic post, was in fact the minister resident and *chargé d'affaires* of the Powers to French opinion and the French intellect, at the same time that he was interpreter and secretary of the French intellect to the Powers. He fulfilled his mission, on both sides, most worthily.

We are still at the outset of his career. Rousseau, who was beginning to become famous, introduced him one day to Madame d'Épinay, a clever and attractive woman, very ill-married, wealthy, and young, who, having no one to guide her, was at this time trying her wings somewhat at hazard.

"M. Grimm," she says, "came to see me with Rousseau; I invited him to dine to-morrow. I was very well pleased with him; he is modest and courteous; I consider him shy, for he seems to me to have too much wit for his very noticeable embarrassment to have any other cause. He is passionately fond of music; we played and sang with him all the afternoon, Rousseau, Francueil, and I. I showed him some pieces of my own composition which seemed to please him. If there was anything about him that I did not like, it was his extravagant praise of my talents, which I am abundantly conscious that I do not deserve."

She says that Grimm was thirty-four at that time, but he could not have been so old. He had much success with Madame d'Épinay, who was then in one of those periods when the heart suffers, and when, while vowing to itself that it means to go on suffering, it seeks vaguely to give admittance to hope. Madame d'Épinay loved to write, and in her exercises with her pen she was not long in drawing a portrait of Grimm, which represents him in a very favourable

light, and with features which one feels to be truly
described.

"His face is attractive by reason of a blending of artlessness and
shrewdness; his countenance is interesting, his manner careless and
indifferent. His gestures, his bearing, and his carriage indicate kindness
of heart, modesty, laziness, and timidity.

"His mind is just, searching, and profound; he thinks and expresses
himself with conviction, but incorrectly. Although he is a poor
talker, no one succeeds better in holding the attention of his auditors;
it seems to me that, in matters of taste, no one has a more delicate,
keener, surer tact than he. He has a vein of pleasantry which is
peculiar and which would become no one else.

"He loves solitude, and it is easy to see that the taste for society is
not natural to him; it is a taste acquired by education and by habit.

"This vague tendency to seclusion and self-concentration, combined
with much laziness, causes his opinion to be sometimes hesitating in
public; he never gives judgment against his conviction, but he leaves
it in doubt. He hates discussion and disputation; he declares that
they were invented solely for the salvation of fools.

"One has to know M. Grimm intimately to realise his true worth.
His friends alone are in a position to appreciate him, because he is
himself only with them. Then his whole manner is different; jesting,
merriment, freedom, indicate his satisfaction, and take the place of
constraint and shyness.

"He is perhaps the only man who has the faculty of inspiring confidence without bestowing it."

However prejudiced Madame d'Épinay may have
been in Grimm's favour, the aspect in which she presents him is in perfect accord with what Meister says
of him,—Meister, a man of feeling and discrimination
who wrote of him long after. Meister speaks of the
attractiveness of his face, of his refined and expressive
features, and at the same time he does not disguise
what peculiarities there were in his personal appearance taken as a whole. "He carried his hips and

shoulders a little out of line, but not ungracefully. His nose, although it was rather large and slightly crooked, had none the less a most noticeable expression of shrewdness and sagacity; a lady said of him: 'Grimm's nose is turned, but always in the right direction.'"

It is clear that, with these same features, it would be a simple matter to make of Grimm a very ugly man and a caricature; but those who know to how great an extent expression exempts men from beauty, will rely upon the impressions of a clever woman and a judicious friend.

It is not my purpose to tell the story of the lover or of the Werther in Grimm; I propose simply to clear the character of the man, the honourable man, whom I believe that Rousseau slandered. Grimm's great offence against Rousseau was that he speedily saw through his vanity, and that he did not spare it. On the day of the first performance of the *Devin du Village,* the Duc des Deux-Ponts, on leaving the Opera, accosted Rousseau with much courtesy, and said to him: "Will you allow me to congratulate you, monsieur?" Whereupon Rousseau replied brutally: "Very well, provided that you make it short!" At all events, that was the way in which Rousseau chose to tell the story, in a boasting tone. Grimm, who was present when he told it, said to him laughingly:

" Illustrious citizen and co-sovereign of Geneva (for a portion of the sovereignty of the republic resides in you), may I venture to suggest to you, that, notwithstanding the rigidity of your principles, you should not refuse a sovereign prince the consideration due to a water-carrier, and that if you had greeted a kindly remark from the latter with a retort so abrupt, so brutal, you would have reason to reproach yourself for a most untimely impertinence."

Rousseau (although he denies it) seems to have been more or less in love with Madame d'Épinay by fits and starts, when he was not in love with her sister-in-law, Madame d'Houdetot. Grimm, when he became most closely bound to Madame d'Épinay, had fully made up his mind concerning Jean-Jacques's character; one may say that he was the first of his friends who saw with certainty the early manifestations of his madness, and who called it by its true name. Finding an impulsive, generous woman overflowing with anxiety for the welfare of the unfortunate man of talent, he admonished her somewhat harshly for her imprudence. One day Rousseau went to see Madame d'Épinay. He had received letters urging him to return to Geneva to live; he was offered a place as librarian, with a salary—an honourable and agreeable occupation.

"What shall I decide to do?" he said. "I neither wish nor am able to remain in Paris; I am too wretched here. I would like right well to travel and to pass a few months in my republic; but in this offer that is made me it is a question of taking up my abode there, and if I accept I shall not be at liberty to come away. I have acquaintances there, but I have no intimate relations with any one. Those people hardly know me, and they write to me as to their brother; I know that that is one advantage of the republican spirit; *but I distrust such warm friends, there is some purpose behind it.* On the other hand my heart is touched by the thought that my fatherland longs for me. But how can I leave Grimm and Diderot and you? Ah! my dear friend, how perplexed I am!"

Thereupon Madame d'Épinay becomes warmly interested; she considers; on reflection she finds for Rousseau what he desires above all things—a cottage amid the woods. She, or her husband, owns a small house called the Hermitage, in the forest of Montmorency. She determines to propose to Rousseau that he live there; she will have it arranged suitably, taking care not to seem to do anything expressly on his account. So she invites him to go there to live. Rousseau takes fright, balks,—and accepts. In the joy of her heart she tells Grimm about it.

"I was greatly surprised," she says, "to find that he disapproved the service I had rendered Rousseau, and disapproved it in a style that at first seemed to me very harsh. I attempted to combat his opinion; I showed him the letters we had exchanged. ' I see nothing here,' he said, ' on Rousseau's part, except concealed arrogance in every word. You do him a very ill service by giving him the Hermitage, but you do yourself a very much worse one. Solitude will complete the work of blackening his imagination; all his friends will be, in his eyes, unjust and ungrateful, and you first of all, if you refuse a single time to place yourself at his orders. I see already the germ of his charges against you in the tone of the letters you have shown me. *Those charges will not be true, but they will not be absolutely devoid of truth,* and that will suffice to bring reproach on you.' "

Never was prediction more literally verified than this of Grimm. He understood perfectly that diseased mind, combined with such extraordinary talent; he was constantly opposing the indulgent, erroneous views into which his kind-hearted and too impulsive

friend was misled. "I am convinced," said Madame
d'Épinay of Rousseau, "that there is only one way of
taking that man to make him happy; that is, to pretend
to pay no attention to him and to devote oneself to him
all the time." Grimm began to laugh and rejoined:
"How little you know your Rousseau! reverse your
propositions if you want to gratify him; pay no attention to him, but act as if you thought about him a great
deal; speak of him constantly to other people, even in
his presence, and do not be deceived by the ill-temper
he will show you on account of it." He added, with
perfect justice, and repeated again and again, that, as
he was already afflicted with latent madness, the absolute solitude of the Hermitage would result in turning
his brain and scattering his ideas altogether; and towards the end of Rousseau's stay there, when his suspicions and extravagances were beginning to burst
forth, Grimm wrote: "I cannot tell you too often, my
dear friend, that the least evil of all the alternatives
would have been to let him go back to his native
country two years ago, instead of secluding him at the
Hermitage. I am sure that his sojourn there will cause
us annoyance sooner or later." In fact, that sojourn
did cause, through the venomous pages of the
*Confessions,* an undying calumny.

It does not enter into my plan to discuss that controversy here: when one reads Madame d'Épinay's
*Mémoires* on the one hand and the *Confessions* on the
other, it is clear that the letters cited in those works,

which might throw light on the question, are not reproduced in the same terms; that they have been
altered in one case or the other, and that some one
lied. I do not believe that it was Madame d'Épinay.
As for Grimm's character, which is all that I am undertaking to study and elucidate here, it seems to me
to stand out favourably through his very indifference.
In Madame d'Épinay's *Mémoires,* he constantly exhibits himself to us as being above all paltry disputes,
avoiding meddling in them, and at need showing
little amiability in his advice, and maintaining some
reserve, even in private; not from any ulterior motive,
or from lack of confidence, but simply " because he
likes neither arguments nor useless schemes." Rousseau, being the man that we know him to be, had
more than one reason to bear him a grudge. In the
first place, we know that Grimm and Diderot, without mentioning the fact, paid Thérèse and her mother
a pension of four hundred livres: Grimm never boasted
of it, and Madame d'Épinay discovered it one day by
accident. Now, Rousseau did not like benefactions,
and he liked even less the persons to whom he owed
them. Indubitably, whoever paid a pension to persons who were closely connected with him must be
a great conspirator. In the second place, Grimm's
accurate mind had more than once let the daylight
into Rousseau's pretensions, and touched him on his
most sensitive spot. For example, Rousseau came to
bring to M. d'Épinay the copies that he had made for

him of twelve pieces of music. He was asked if he would undertake to deliver as many more in a fortnight. But Rousseau, instantly blending the self-esteem of the copyist and the indifference of the amateur, replied:

" ' Perhaps yes, perhaps no; it depends on my inclination, my mood, and my health.'—' In that case,' said M. d'Épinay, ' I will give you only six to do, because I must be certain of having them.' —' Very good ! ' retorted Rousseau ; ' you will have the satisfaction of having six which will discountenance the other six ; for I defy you to have any made that will approach mine in accuracy and perfection.'— ' Do you see,' interposed Grimm with a laugh, ' how the conceit of a copyist has gripped him already ? If you should say that not a comma is missing in your writings, everybody would agree, but I 'll wager that there are some notes transposed in your copies.' Although he laughed and accepted the bet, Rousseau blushed ; and he blushed even more when, upon examination, it turned out that Grimm was right."

This took place at Madame d'Épinay's house, at La Chevrette. Rousseau remained deep in thought all the evening; the next morning he returned to the Hermitage without saying a word, and he never forgave Grimm for finding errors in his copies. Such grievances (without going any farther), brooded over in solitude and magnified by a sickly imagination, were likely to give birth to many monsters.

" Being a recluse," Rousseau confesses, " I am more sensitive than other men. If I have a dispute with a friend who lives in the world, he thinks about it for a moment, and then a thousand distractions cause him to forget it the rest of the day. But there is nothing to divert my mind from his treatment of me; unable to sleep, I think about it the livelong night; alone in my daily walk, I think about it from sunrise to sunset; my heart has not a moment's reprieve, and the harsh words of a friend cause me years of sorrow in a single day."

There we have the disease and the wound laid bare.
Grimm's only mistake was, perhaps, that, after a certain day, he treated that wound too much as if it
were physically incurable, and that, in the perspicacity
and strength of his mind, he thought too little of
that other pathetic remark of his former friend: "There
never was a fire in the depths of any heart that a tear
would not put out." It is more than doubtful whether
Grimm could have succeeded in putting out the fire in
Rousseau, even with tears, but he did not try.

Moreover, Grimm was absent from France during
the greater part of Rousseau's stay at the Hermitage
(1756–1757); he had lost his friend the Comte de
Friesen, taken away in the flower of youth, and the
Duc d'Orléans had undertaken to look after his fortunes. That prince had deemed it advisable to place
him in the service of the Maréchal d'Estrées during
the campaign in Westphalia. Grimm was one of the
*twenty-eight* secretaries of that pompous staff. He
has very graphically described that "laborious" and
"very magnificent" life. "We have left the heavy
waggons behind; but for all that, on every day's march,
it takes three hours for our indispensable equipment
to pass. This is a most scandalous state of affairs and
makes me more than ever convinced that the world
is made up of nothing but abuses, which none but
a madman would try to reform." The pillage and
theft that he sees all about him are revolting to him.
"Severity does not restore discipline," he says; "we

are surrounded by men hanged, and yet the slaughter of women and children goes on just the same, when they object to seeing their houses pillaged. But for this campaign," he adds, "I should never have conceived how far the horrors of poverty and the injustice of man can be carried." At the same time, in the infrequent glorious engagements, he is alive to the gallant and noble conduct of our troops. His whole correspondence, during that period, bears witness to an upright and humane heart, which is put to the test of experience, but without closing or becoming hardened.

Grimm had suffered much in his youth, and he could if he chose, he says somewhere, have made out a long list of misfortunes; he preferred to let his mind rest upon the assistance he had found in the interest and good-will of a few generous men. He owed it to this fair-mindedness and moderation that he made so many serviceable friends, and he attracted them no less by his merit than by the steadiness and dignity of his sentiments. At the time of which we are now speaking, when he was in the last years of his youth, his apparent coldness but half concealed a remnant of inward ardour, and his stoicism in no wise diminished the delicacy of his feelings. In the letters written to Madame d'Épinay during that Westphalian campaign, the advantage in the matter of loving attentions and delicate shades of sentiment is not always with his friend. He has no sooner left her than he writes to her from Metz these affectionate, almost feminine words: " How I long to hear from you!  I do not know a single thing that you will do to-morrow; *that has never happened before since I have known you!''*

Good morals suffered severely from these relations that were so easily and so publicly entered into in the society of the eighteenth century.  Madame d'Épinay, although married to a most unworthy husband, was not free; the image of duty was not altogether effaced; she had children, and she prided herself, like a good mother, upon bringing them up well, upon devoting herself to their education.  On this subject she consulted Rousseau, Grimm, all her friends; but did she set them the example of the virtue and respectability that she preached to them ?  Grimm (let us say it to his honour) was not so insensible as one might suppose to this lack of harmony between her morals and her precepts, and he was distressed by it.  "One of the things," he wrote, " which make you most dear to my eyes, my dear love, is the strict watch you keep upon yourself, especially in the presence of your children. Children are keen-eyed! they seem to be playing, but they hear, they see. *Oh ! how many times that fear has embittered the pleasure of moments passed with you !''* Let us ask nothing more than this avowal, let slip by one of the men who prided themselves most upon being free from prejudices; that one half-stifled lament is a homage to duty.

In his relations with Madame d'Épinay Grimm is

from the first, and before all else, a critical guide
and a judicious adviser; those qualities, so essential
even in friendship, are very noticeable in him. "How
judicious are his ideas!" she writes again and again
after listening to him; "how impartial his advice!"
He marks out for her a line of conduct to repair the
extreme injury she has done herself by her inconsequence and her enthusiasm. He gives her the most
accurate opinions and the wisest directions with respect to all the people about her; he warns her of her
own failings. "Do nothing hastily, I entreat you! it
is one of your old failings always to go too fast. My
dear love, nature acts slowly and imperceptibly; it has
given you lovely eyes; use them, and act, I pray you,
as nature does." All his efforts are aimed at matur-
ing "that dear head which has such lovely eyes."
Madame d'Épinay, who was especially blessed with a
keen and profound sense of probity, appreciated his
unerring tact at its true value. "I no longer have
any doubt when M. Grimm has given his opinion."
This oracular character is natural enough to all masters of criticism; Grimm, beneath a polished exterior
and a worldly air, could not keep from expressing it
in his words and in his conduct; he liked to set the
style; he had that rigorous and exacting common
sense which is rarely unaccompanied by some roughness of manner. His friends jestingly called him "the
Tyrant." Was not Malherbe, in his day, called "the
Tyrant of words and syllables"?

Those of Grimm's letters which relate to the rupture with Rousseau when he left the Hermitage are masterpieces of tact and precision, and of healthy views concerning that diseased heart. He imparts to his friend his own perspicacity and his lucidity of judgment. Rousseau, to excuse himself from all gratitude to Madame d'Épinay, pretends to suspect her of some base and heinous act or other,—of an anonymous letter to Saint-Lambert about him,—and he takes that occasion to write her an insulting letter; it is easy to lose oneself in that labyrinth of bickerings and villainies.

"The harm is done," said Grimm; "you would have it so, my poor dear, although I always told you that you would suffer for it. It is certain that all this will result in some devilish scrape which no one can foresee; to my mind it is a very great pity already that you have laid yourself open to receiving insulting letters. One can forgive one's friends for anything except insults, because they can come only from contempt. You are not sensitive enough to insults, as I have often told you; one should feel them and not take vengeance for them; that is my principle."

Madame d'Épinay, having trouble with her lungs, and wishing to have the opinion of Doctor Tronchin, went to Geneva. Grimm, being detained by some urgent work with Diderot, did not join her at once; in the meantime she saw Voltaire, who was then at Les Délices.

"So you have dined with Voltaire?" Grimm writes to her. "I do not see why you should decline his invitations; you must try to stand well with him, and to make the most of him as the most fascinating, the most agreeable, and the most famous man in Europe; *so long as you do not seek to make an intimate friend of him, all will go well.*"

We see how justly he estimated the two most celebrated men of letters of that day, and he knew the
others equally well.

It was about this time (1759) that Grimm's literary
pursuits began to occupy a greater place in his life,
and to become more extended.  The months that he
had passed at Geneva with the invalid, and in daily
familiar intercourse, seemed to him the acme of happiness, which he could never hope to know again.
Like a man of foresight he determined, while continu-
ing to cultivate his friendships, to provide an abundance of occupation for the stern and serious years to
come; he chose to demonstrate that he was no longer
an idle and useless being.  Overtures were made to
him by one of the Northern Courts, which he does not
name, to enter into a correspondence with it.   "It is
the sort of occupation that I like," he says, " and it
suits me especially in that it puts me in a position to
show what I am able to do."  He had first to obtain
the consent of the Duc d'Orléans, in whose service he
still was.  The correspondence which he had carried
on up to that time, and which we have from 1753,
was not in his own name perhaps, but in Raynal's.
However that may be, he becomes more and more
the domestic critic in ordinary and the literary chronicler of the age.  The voluminous collection of his
sheets, despite errors and patchwork, despite the
pieces by different hands which have found their
way into it, forms a solid work and deserves to be

inscribed in Grimm's name. It was his mind that dictated the principal parts of it, and it is not difficult to follow therein an original train of thought, which resembles neither La Harpe's nor Marmontel's, which is of an entirely different order from theirs, and which, in its best moments, need not fear comparison with Voltaire's. I will try to lay hold of it and to make it apparent to the reader in a few decisive particulars.

France, it seems to me, owes Grimm reparation; too often he has been paid for the consecration of his services and his talents to our literature only by an altogether unjust and in some respects inhospitable judgment.

Grimm's *Correspondance* is generally considered rather solemn, a little cruel in its impartiality, and even slightly satirical; but Grimm had, to start with, genuine enthusiasm and that love of the beautiful which is the inspiration of true criticism. In a letter written in 1752, against the opera of *Omphale,* he says: "I confess that I consider the admiration and respect which I entertain for all real talent, of whatever sort it may be, as my greatest blessing next to love of virtue." It was not long since Grimm had come from Germany when he wrote that sentence. At the beginning of his *Correspondance* he continues to hold the same sentiments; his tone and his meaning are nothing less than frivolous; in the secrecy which is assured him he sees only an additional reason for using absolute frankness. "Love of truth demands this strict justice as an indispensable duty," he says, "and even our friends will have no ground for complaint, because criticism whose only objects are justice and truth, and which is not inspired by the shameful wish to find that bad which is good, may indeed be mistaken and obliged sometimes to retract, but can never offend anybody."

In Grimm's day it was still the custom to call articles written about books "Extracts," and these extracts, sanctioned and sanctified by the example of the *Journal des Savants,* were in most cases confined to an exact and dry analysis of the work in question; "on the pretence of giving its substance, they produced only a skeleton of it." Grimm was not in favour of that heavy, mechanical sort of criticism, which is of the same type as the report of a police magistrate. According to him, good books should not be studied by extracts, but should be read. "Poor books need only to be forgotten; so that it is simply bothering us to no purpose to give us extracts from them; and in good policy, journalists should be forbidden to mention a book, good or bad, when they have nothing to say about it." *To examine and rectify* — that is his object in his letters, "and that should be the aim of all journalists." Herein Grimm is an innovator to a certain extent, and he assuredly places newspaper criticism where it belongs.

It is interesting to observe the excesses and extremes of the type. The first method adopted by the

*Journal des Savants,* the oldest of the literary journals, was one extreme; it consisted in a statement pure and simple, a sort of description of the book, in many cases differing little from a table of contents. The purpose, however, and the utility of this method, at a time when communication was less easy than to-day, was to keep the scholars of the various countries posted concerning new works, and to offer them at least reliable and faithful extracts, pending the time when they could procure the work itself. Another extreme in the opposite direction, into which some have fallen in our own day (and I am speaking now of serious criticism, of that of some English and French reviews, for example), is to give hardly any idea of the book which one is supposed to be writing about, and to look upon it simply as a pretext for the promulgation of new considerations, more or less appropriate, and of new essays; the original author, on whom one's arguments are based, disappears; it is the critic who becomes the principal, the real author. These are books written about books. Grimm's method lies between the two and is perfectly balanced.

"What is a 'literary correspondent'?" inquired Abbé Morellet one day, who had been criticised right merrily by Grimm, and, in his old age, had had the vexation of seeing that gentle raillery printed; and Morellet answered his own question thus: "He is a man who, for a little money, undertakes to entertain a foreign prince every week, at the expense of whom it may concern, and, generally speaking, of every literary production that sees the light, and of the man who happens to be the author." Abbé Morellet spoke thus because he was prejudiced; but Grimm, despite a few inevitable inadvertences and hasty judgments, does not belong in the inferior class to which the abbé-economist would like to relegate him. As a general rule, he aims to instruct the princes, his correspondents, much more than to amuse them; and when one was read by Frederick the Great or by Catherine, one certainly had a constituency which was equal to many another, and which demanded solid substance in its entertainment. Such minds as those it was really honourable to entertain.

Grimm, in respect to inspiration, may boldly be likened to the school of the masters in criticism, of the Horaces, the Popes, and the Boileaus; he has their keen, enthusiastic, irritable sensitiveness in the matter of taste. His severity is in proportion to his very faculty of admiration. Having to discuss the tragedy of *Philoctète* by Châteaubrun (March, 1755), he notes all its defects, especially its unnaturalness, its utter lack of genius. According to him there are three deadly things: a tragedy in which the speeches are false, a picture in which the colouring is false, an operatic air in which the enunciation is false.

"And the man who can stand such things," he declares, "may follow his own bent in his pleasures and his tastes; he will never be keenly affected by what is truly beautiful and sublime. When you are in a position to feel beauty and to grasp its nature, frankly you are no longer content with mediocrity, and whatever is ugly distresses and annoys you in the same degree that you are enchanted with the beautiful. It is therefore false to say that one should not have an exclusive taste, if the meaning is that one must put up with mediocrity in works of art, and even make the best of what is ugly. People who are so accommodating have never known the joy of feeling the enthusiasm inspired by the masterpieces of the great geniuses, and it was not for them that Homer, Sophocles [I omit Richardson, whom Grimm places in company that is too good for him], Raphael and Pergolese worked. If such indulgence for poets, painters, and musicians should ever become general among the public, it would be a sign that taste had utterly vanished. . . . People who admire ugly things so readily are not in a frame of mind to appreciate beautiful ones."

When nature has once endowed a person with such acuteness of tact and such sensitiveness to impressions, if these qualities are not joined with a creative imagination, that person is a born critic, that is to say, an admirer and judge of the creations of others.

When we open Grimm's volumes to-day, let us not forget that his pages were originally written for foreigners. Byron or Goethe, on reading him, would acquire a just and complete idea of the literature and the mode of life of that time; and Byron bestowed the greatest praise on him when he wrote carelessly in his journal, or " Memorandum," at Ravenna, these words: " All in all, he is a great man in his kind."

We Frenchmen, who know beforehand and by tradition a multitude of things that are found in Grimm, ought not to read him through, but to take him up here and there, in the significant passages. An excellent index is a sufficient guide for that purpose.

What does Grimm think, for example, I will not say
of Homer, Sophocles, Molière (he speaks of them
only incidentally), but of Shakespeare, of Montaigne,
and of all the men of the eighteenth century — Fontenelle, Montesquieu, Buffon, Voltaire, Jean-Jacques,
Duclos, and the rest? By questioning him concerning them, we shall very soon come to know him in
the quality of his intellect and the excellence of his
judgment.

Concerning Shakespeare he is the most advanced
and the most perspicuous of the French men of letters
of his day. His opinion has the more weight in that
he has a more profound realisation of the genius of
the masters of our stage, and considers them more
in harmony with the genius of French society. He
never advises the French to abandon their own type
of tragedy in order to imitate foreign beauties. "On
the contrary he will say: 'Frenchmen, cherish your
tragedies carefully, and remember that, if they have
not the sublime beauties which we admire in Shakespeare, neither have they the gross faults which mar
those beauties.'" When passing judgment upon
the French tragedy of his time, he is fully aware of
all its weaknesses and dulness; he indulges in some
reflections on this subject, which are suggested to
him by La Harpe's *Timoléon,* but which go farther
back and aim higher. These four or five pages of
Grimm (January 1, 1765) establish the real similarities
and the fundamental distinctions between the tragedy

of the ancients and our own.   Shakespeare, despite
his faults, often seems to him nearer to the ancients
than ourselves.   He recognises him as being in the
first rank with respect to the luminous progression of
the *ensemble,* the power of the plot, and the principal
effects which the stage aims to achieve—with respect
to "that great hoard of interest of which he seems
to interrupt the flow at his pleasure, and which he is
always sure to set in motion again with the same
energy."   But where he finds him incomparable is
in the art of drawing character and of imparting to all
his characters an air of reality.

> "What genius ever penetrated more profoundly into all the pe-
> culiarities, all the passions of human nature ?   It is evident from his
> works themselves that he had but an imperfect acquaintance with an-
> tiquity; if he had been familiar with its great models, doubtless the
> arrangements of his plays would have been improved; but, even if he
> had studied the ancients with as much care as our greatest masters
> have done, even if he had lived on familiar terms with the heroes
> whom he strove to depict, could he have represented their characters
> with greater truth to life?   His ' Julius Cæsar ' is as full of Plutarch as
> ' Britannicus ' is of Tacitus; and if he did not learn history more thor-
> oughly than any one, it must be said that he divined it, at all events
> so far as men's characters are concerned, better than any one ever
> learned it."

After this, it is not surprising that the English critics,
and notably the judicious Jeffrey in the *Edinburgh
Review,* attributed great weight to the testimony of
Grimm, as a useful auxiliary in the war which they
were then (1813) preparing to renew against the
dramatic authors of the continent.   But, we repeat,
although he admits its shortcomings, Grimm does not

sacrifice French tragedy to that of our neighbours; he
recognises the fact that each is adapted to the nation
and the class which it moves and interests. "One
[the English stage] seems to be intent solely upon
strengthening the character and morals of the nation,
the other [the French stage] solely upon enervating
them." Grimm goes farther; he thinks that the same
tableaux which one of the two nations has witnessed
without any risk, however terrible and terrifying their
truth to nature, could not well be exhibited without
inconvenience to the other, which would instantly
misuse them. "And might these not even result,"
he asks, "in something altogether opposed to the
moral purpose of the stage ?"

With Montaigne, Grimm is at the very heart of
France, and of old France; it is as if he were at home.
After all that has been written about the author of the
*Essais,* he finds things to say which no one has said
so well. He observes that, although there is in the
*Essais* an infinitude of facts, anecdotes, and quotations, Montaigne was not, properly speaking, a learned
man. "He had read almost nothing but a few Latin
poets, a few books of travel, and his Seneca and
his Plutarch,"—the latter especially; Plutarch, "is in
very truth the *Encyclopédie* of the ancients; Montaigne has given us the flower of his work, and he
has added to it the shrewdest reflections, and, above
all, the most secret results of his own experience."

The eight pages that Grimm devotes to Montaigne's

*Essais* form perhaps the most impartial, the most cogently reasoned, and the most elegantly expressed of French criticisms of that work. I might cite some of the bright sallies that are to be found there; but it is the sound sense and the logical coherency of that delightful passage which give it its value.

Grimm's philosophy is gloomy and barren; he is a sceptic, and on the days when he is sceptical on his own account, he is so without a smile; we will recur to this subject. But in speaking of Montaigne, he softens. Since the circle of human knowledge is so limited, and since one can hardly flatter oneself that one can extend the limits of the human intellect, what is a philosophical author to do who wishes still to interest his readers? According to Grimm, there are only two ways to go about it: either to exert oneself to point out as clearly as possible how small a number of truths one may know (which was what Locke did); or else to *paint in vivid colours the particular impression* one receives from these same truths, which serves at all events to multiply one's points of view; and this is what Montaigne did. The majority of so-called authors content themselves with working over the ideas of other men, which they twist and turn, and adapt to the taste of the moment; nothing is more rare than that vivacity and that courage to describe his own thought and his own feelings, which make the original author. Montaigne is original, even in his erudition; he is original even in the ideas which he borrows from others, "because he makes use of them only when he has found an idea of his own, or when he has been impressed by them in some novel and strange way."

To excuse Montaigne's self-love, Grimm invents an argument of great acumen and shrewdness; observing that self-love is less offensive when it shows itself without concealment and with good-nature, he adds: "Far from excluding feeling for others, it is often the surest token and measure thereof. A man is interested in his fellow men only in proportion to the interest which he takes in himself and which he dares not expect from them." And he quotes on this subject a remark of Rousseau, who, having unbosomed himself one day to a friend, observed that that friend (perhaps it was Grimm himself) received his confidence without reciprocating. "Can it be that you don't love me?" cried Rousseau: "you have never told me any good of yourself."

Concerning Montesquieu Grimm expresses himself with admiration and respect, but in few words; he proclaims him a genius abounding in virtue, and salutes him at his obsequies. All of Montesquieu's great works had appeared when Grimm began his *Correspondance*. If he had been called upon to give his views of the historical method adopted in those works, he would have raised some objections.

"I do not like," he says, apropos of some book treating of political considerations, "I do not like overmuch these outlines of *a priori* political theories, although they have in their favour the authority of Président de Montesquieu, who is particularly addicted to them. It always seems to me that, if the author who proceeds by that method had no knowledge of historical events *a posteriori,* the principles from which he claims to deduce them would not enable him to divine a single one, an evident proof that these principles are made by hand and after the event, that they are rather ingenious than solid, and that they are not the true sources of the action that is attributed to them. . . . In politics nothing ever happens twice in the same way."

Grimm's politics are gloomy, sceptical, or readily become negative like his philosophy. He has little belief in the general progress of the time; progress, when it does take place, or the arrests of decadence, seem to him mainly due to exceptional individuals, great geniuses, great legislators, or princes, who cause mankind to take unhoped-for steps forward, or spare it backward steps that are inevitable sooner or later. His ideas concerning the origin of society differ little from those of Hobbes, Lucretius, Horace, and the Epicureans of old. Profoundly impressed by the difficulty of the social conception in so far as it rises above a primitive sort of gathering, altogether instinctive and rude, and arrives at genuine civilisation, he believes it to have been impossible except by force of miraculous passions in some individuals, and of the heroic power of genius. "It must be," he thinks, "that the first legislators of the primitive societies, even the most imperfect, were men of supernatural powers or demigods." Thus, in politics, Grimm resembles Machiavelli more than he does Montesquieu, who gave more credit to the genius of mankind itself.

Concerning Buffon, Grimm gives us some profound reasoning and some excellent judgments. Taking up the general discussions which Buffon has placed at the beginning of several volumes of his *Histoire Naturelle*, he estimates them from a literary standpoint, as a man born under the French constellation of Malherbe, Pascal, and Despreaux would do. "One is justly surprised," he says, "to read discourses of a hundred pages written, from the first line to the last, always with the same nobility of style and the same fire, adorned with the most brilliant and the most natural colouring." Surely he was no longer a foreigner who could thus appreciate the consistent and constant beauty of a Frenchman's style. As for the substance of his ideas, he ventures more than once to raise objections. There is one especially of a moral and literary order: "M. de Buffon has always surprised me," says Grimm, "by the intimate conviction which he seems to have of the certainty of his theory concerning the earth. If it were among the small number of manifest truths as to which there cannot be two opinions, he could not speak of it more confidently." Rousseau seemed to him to stand in the same position with respect to his theory concerning the wild state of mankind, that alleged golden age of felicity and virtue. While marvelling at the confidence in their respective theories of those men of powerful talents, "who do not abound in ideas," Grimm does not fail to reflect sometimes that that prepossession is necessary perhaps to give to their writings that fervour and that force which are so noticeable in them, whereas "the modest and humble sceptic is almost always silent."

Voltaire is nowhere better described, as to his works and as to his character, than by the detail of the anecdotes and the *ensemble* of the judgments which are set down in Grimm's pages. There are some passages (such as those on the death of Voltaire) which seem to me too emphatic to be by Grimm, and which are, at all events, a tribute paid to the public opinion of the moment. The shrewd and accurate judgments, the interesting revelations, are found on a hundred other pages. Grimm explains very clearly how and why Voltaire is not comic in his comedies; in his *Ecossaise*, for example, he has not succeeded in making of his Frélon, who tells himself all sorts of truths, a comic character. "We see in this comedy, and, generally speaking, in all of M. Voltaire's humorous works, that he never realised the difference between the ridicule that one heaps upon oneself and the ridicule that is heaped upon one by other people." And it is the latter that is truly comic. He is equally alive to Voltaire's lack of certain qualities of a genuine historian:

"In general the writing of history requires a serious and profound genius. Lightness of touch, facility, charm, all those things which make of M. Voltaire so seductive a philosopher and the first *bel-esprit* of the age—all these are but ill-adapted to the dignity of history. The very rapidity of his style, which may be invaluable in the description of a battle or the sketch of a picture, is sure to offend ere long."

In philosophy he treats him with the scorn of a
man who has not stopped half way, and whose un-
belief is not, at all events, inconsistent. Voltaire, on
the other hand, does stop half way, and while con-
tinuing to do harm, takes fright now and then at his
own audacity. " He reasons thereupon like a child,"
says Grimm, "but like the pretty child that he is."
After *Tancrède* everything that Voltaire writes for the
stage seems to him to be stamped with the seal of old
age; but, on his death, he resumes his scrutiny of
him in his entirety, and with the admiration which
such a career inspires; he sets forth very clearly his
opinion of the literary decadence, which, according to
his view, Voltaire retarded, and which then resumed
its headlong course. "Since Voltaire's death a vast
silence reigns in these regions and reminds us every
instant of our losses and our poverty." He wrote this
to Frederick in January, 1784.

Grimm is classic in this sense, that, with respect to
imagination and the arts, he believes that there is a
single great age in the life of a nation. Without
claiming to understand the causes of this fact, it seems
to him that constant experience has sufficiently demonstrated it.

" When that age has passed, great geniuses are lacking; but as the
taste for art still exists in the nation, men seek to do by dint of wit
what their masters have done by dint of genius, and, wit having become more general, everybody makes pretensions to it before long ;
hence sound wit becomes rare, and mere piquancy, false *bel-esprit,*
and pretension take its place."

Thus in France he hails as incomparable the age of Louis XIV, and he finds in the eighteenth century only a single class of superior men and of a special type: "I will call them *philosophers of genius;* such are M. de Montesquieu, M. de Buffon, etc." Voltaire is the only man of letters pure and simple, the only poet, who sustains genuine taste by his charms of style, his imagination, and his natural fertility; but, according to Grimm, he simply supports what was already tottering.

Rousseau is not maltreated in Grimm's letters, as one might imagine; he is constantly spoken of with appreciation for his talents, at the same time that his theories are refuted. Grimm lays hold at the outset of the *Discours sur Inégalité,* in which Rousseau's theory may be found in its entirety, and from which all the rest will flow. In a most judicious and most respectful discussion, he strives to grasp the point at which the eloquent and extravagant writer takes the wrong road, and at which his doctrine becomes extreme; he labours to refute and set right his idea. Rousseau for ever prates of leading mankind back to some vague primitive age of gold at which he regrets that the human race did not halt in its progress.

"Let us suppose with M. Rousseau," says Grimm, "that the human race is now at the age which corresponds to sixty or seventy years in the individual,—is it not evident that it cannot be charged to a man as a crime that he is sixty years old? And is it not as natural to be sixty as to be fifteen? Now, the race cannot be blamed for that for which an individual cannot be blamed."

I commend as a most excellent moral chapter to set in opposition to Rousseau's assertions the chapter which begins the year 1756 with these words: "I have often marvelled at the vain pride of man." Sometimes Grimm begins the year with some general reflections which are grand in their solemnity. In the species of biography of Rousseau which he writes on the publication of *Émile* (June 15, 1762), Grimm checks himself in his reminiscences at what would be an indiscreet disclosure and a violation of their former friendship; and after going over the principal periods of Rousseau's life, his first more or less freakish efforts, he adds: "His private and domestic life would be no less interesting; but it is written in the memory of two or three of his former friends, who have maintained their self-respect by not writing of it anywhere." If Grimm had been a perfidious traitor, as Rousseau believed, what an excellent opportunity he had there, to tell secretly, by way of contrast to *Émile,* what Rousseau did with his own children, and a mass of other details which have since become known only through the *Confessions!* Instead of that, he maintained a dignified reserve; he confined himself to giving the main features of the man's character, while he discussed his writings minutely. When, about 1780, there appeared that extraordinary work entitled *Rousseau, Juge de Jean-Jacques,* wherein is seen "the most amazing medley of vigour of style and weakness of mind, all the confusion of a deeply wounded sensitiveness, inconceivable absurdity, and madness the most serious and most deserving of pity," Grimm found therein a subject of reflections, noteworthy for their moderation and humility, upon the unfortunate human intellect.   "Generally speaking," said the English critic Jeffrey, discussing a portion of this *Correspondance* of Grimm, "all that he has to say about Rousseau is frank and judicious."

There is between Grimm and Diderot, despite their close intimacy and their reciprocal admiration, this essential difference: Diderot is a teacher also, and Grimm is not.  A very interesting conversation between them brings out clearly the point of divergence. Grimm and Diderot were talking together one evening—January 3, 1757; Diderot was in one of those periods of philosophic excitement and prediction which were frequent with him: he saw the world in bright colours, and the future governed by reason and by what he called light *(lumières)*; he lauded his epoch as the grandest that mankind had seen thus far. Grimm doubted, and recalled the enthusiast to reality.

"We are for ever boasting of our epoch," he said to him, "and therein we do nothing new.  In all ages men have preferred the instant at which they lived to that boundless expanse of time which preceded their existence.  By some miracle, the illusion of which is handed down from generation to generation, we look upon the period of our own lives as a time most favourable to the human race, and distinguished in the annals of the world.  .  .  .  It seems to me that the eighteenth century has surpassed all others in the eulogiums that it has heaped upon itself.  .  .  .  A little more and the best minds will persuade themselves that the mild and peaceful empire of

philosophy is about to succeed the long tempests of unreason, and to
establish for ever the repose, the tranquillity and the happiness of mankind. . . . But unluckily the true philosopher has less consoling
but more accurate notions. . . . I am therefore a long way
from believing that we are approaching the age of reason, and I
lack but little of believing that Europe is threatened by some fatal
revolution."

I abridge, but I give the tenor of the conversation as
it was written down by Grimm in January, 1757.
Diderot combated these objections on his friend's part;
he waxed excited and declaimed in his most eloquent
style: "the age of philosophy was indubitably destined to regenerate the world." The door opens, a
servant enters with a horrified air. " The king is assas-
sinated!" he exclaims. He referred to the murderous
assault of Damiens. Grimm and Diderot exchanged
glances in silence, and Diderot made no further reply
at that time.

Grimm, at about the age of fifty, became a courtier:
appreciated at his true value by the distinguished or
eminent princes who then reigned in Germany, and
by the Empress of Russia, he did not feel called upon
to decline their favours or their benefactions. Therein
he became once more to some extent a German. The
Duke of Saxe-Gotha appointed him his minister to the
French Court; the Court of Vienna conferred upon
him the diploma of a baron of the Holy Empire, and
the Court of St. Petersburg made him a colonel, then
councillor of State, and grand knight of the second
class of the Order of St. Vladimir.

We have a portion of his correspondence with Frederick the Great; that which he carried on with the Empress Catherine, and especially the letters that he received from her, would be of the deepest interest. Catherine had the highest opinion of him and of his intellect.  She wrote to Voltaire in September, 1773: "I had the pleasure of seeing M. Grimm appear in the suite of the Hereditary Prince of Darmstadt.  His conversation is a delight to me; but we have so many things to say to each other that thus far our interviews have been marked by more eagerness than order or sequence."  In the midst of these conversations, in which she wholly forgot herself, she would suddenly rise and say laughingly that she must attend to a *gagne-pain;* that was her name for business of state and the trade of royalty.

There remains one aspect of Grimm's character which may be revealed some day, and which it will be interesting to know.  Such intimate relations with the powers placed him in a position where he could often assist merit; and if we find him at times severe or slightly satirical in his judgments, those persons who knew him best assure us that he could be amiable in private; he took pleasure in directing the attention of his august correspondents to the talents of men of letters and artists who were worthy to be honoured or patronised.

Among the benefactions which Catherine bestowed at his recommendation, there is one which seems to me to be touching. Madame d'Épinay, in the last years of her life, had found herself in distress financially; the reforms which M. Necker had introduced in the administration of the farmers-general had reduced her income materially. Catherine, being informed by Grimm, desired to repair the misfortunes of a woman of intellect, and she herself displayed in the matter a woman's delicacy combined with the grandeur of a sovereign. On this occasion Grimm in his gratitude exclaims: "Ah! who ever carried farther than Catherine the great art of kings—that of taking and of giving!" In the way of exquisite flattery Voltaire could have done no better.

A biographer tells us that Grimm in his youth, while a student at the University of Leipsic, was especially struck by his reading of Cicero's treatise *De Officiis,* as interpreted by the learned Ernesti, and that he carried away from the university a profound impression of that work. Between that time and the day when he addressed these thanks and this praise to Catherine, Grimm had travelled far,—we may say that he had traversed the whole circle of moral experience.

The French Revolution impressed Grimm but did not surprise him. We already know what his politics were. From the first day, he opposed to that immense, almost universal uprising, reasonable and dispassionate arguments, which touched upon every illusory feature in the vertigo of the moment, but which did not make enough account of the gravity

of the issues at stake.   His constitution was all contained in these lines of Pope: "Let fools contend
over forms of government; that which is best ad-
ministered, whatever it may be, is the best."   The
events which followed were only too well adapted to
confirm him in his favourite idea, that "the cause of
the human race was beyond hope," and that the
sole resource was at best in some great and good
prince, here and there, of the type which fate bestows
upon the earth; in "one of those privileged souls who
repair for a time the ills of the world."   It was many
years since, writing to Mademoiselle Voland, Diderot's
friend, and speaking of truth and virtue as two great
statues which Diderot loved to fancy towering above
the earth's surface, immovable amid ruins and destruction, he cried :   "And I too see them ; but
what does it avail that those statues are eternal and
immovable, if there is no one to gaze upon them, or
if the fate of him who sees them does not differ from
the fate of the blind man who walks in darkness?"
In his essentially aristocratic doctrine he still thought
that virtue and liberty, as he understood them, had no
place in this world, except for a small number, an
elect few, and only "on the express condition that
they enjoy them without overmuch boasting."

These gloomy ideas, which he had always cherished, and in which he held the majority of mankind
very cheap, became more habitual to him and more
constantly present in the years of his unhappy old

age, after he had lost all his friends, and when society, apparently turned topsy-turvy, returned to life in such strange fashion.

Almost blind, having survived his friends and himself, and vegetating in retirement at Gotha, Grimm died on December 19, 1807, at the age of eighty-four. His mind, already asleep, did not awake at the roar of the cannon of Jena. We have few details concerning the close of his life, and it may be that there were none of interest. He had missed, as he used sometimes to say, "the moment to have himself buried."

# Madame d'Épinay.

1725–1783.

# Madame d'Épinay.

THERE is no book which depicts more faithfully the eighteenth century, its society and morals than the *Mémoires* of Madame d'Épinay. When they were first published, in 1818, there was a great outcry. We were still so near to the principal characters; they had hardly disappeared, and their descendants were only of the first generation. In society and in families people showed that they were sensitive to such publicity, as they were sure to be; they blushed and suffered. There was some idiot or other who, on the pretext that he was half-related by marriage to somebody, began to raise a riot in every direction and addressed petition after petition to the king's ministers. Nor did literature, on its side, remain unmoved. The blind admirers of Jean-Jacques Rousseau took up the cudgels for him against the new witnesses who accused him and convicted him of madness and perhaps of falsehood. Even Duclos had his defenders. The lapse of thirty years has sufficed to let many rumours fall into oblivion and to allay much excitement. The disadvantages attendant upon so sudden and so vivid a revelation have disappeared;

the slight errors or infidelities of the pencil, the inaccuracies in detail, have lost their importance. What remains is the general view of the morals of the time, the background of the picture, and nothing could seem more true or more alive. The *Mémoires* of Madame d'Épinay is not a book, it is an epoch.

It was not exactly Madame d'Épinay's intention to compose memoirs; but at an early age she loved to write, to keep her journal, to trace *the history of her soul*. That was the fashionable mania of that time. The journal that one keeps of one's life is also a sort of mirror. Jean-Jacques Rousseau used that mirror freely, and passed it on to the women of his time. Every woman of wit and sensibility, following his example, kept a record of her impressions, her memories, her dreams; she wrote her "confessions" *in petto,* even though they were the most innocent in the world. And when she became a mother she nursed her child if she could; at all events she set about superintending its education, not only in detail and in the good old way, by maternal fondling, kisses, and smiles, but also theoretically; she would discuss methods and discourse thereupon without end. It was the time of the Genlis, of those wanton or frivolous women who became at a certain point Mentors and Minervas, and composed moral treatises on education during the brief intervals of leisure which their lovers left them.

Madame d'Épinay, who wrote treatises on educa-

MADAME D'ÉPINAY
*From a portrait by Liotard*

tion (and treatises crowned by the Académie) and who had lovers, was of finer grain than the women to whom I refer.  But, being only a very amiable, very clever person, and not of superior endowments, she fell under the influences of her time.  At the beginning of her liaison with Grimm, pining for him during his campaign in Westphalia on the staff of Maréchal d'Estrées (1757), and inspired by hearing the letters of *La Nouvelle Héloïse* read aloud about the same time, she conceived the idea of writing, herself, a sort of romance, which should be the story of her own life, and in which she would disguise nothing but the names.  That was one way of informing her friends of many things which she was not sorry that they should know if she need not tell them *viva voce*. She sent Grimm two huge packages of manuscript. Grimm was delighted with it, and, although in love, he was not enough so to disturb his critical sense. "On my word," he said of this composition, "it is fascinating.  I was very tired when it was handed to me; I ran my eye over it, and I could not put it down; at two o'clock in the morning I was still reading; if you go on in the same style, you will surely produce a unique work."

Grimm was right, and Madame d'Épinay's work is really unique in its kind.  "But do not work at it," added the excellent critic, "except when you really feel an inclination to do so, and above all things never remember that you are writing a book; it will be easy to supply the connecting links; *the air of verity is the thing that cannot be acquired when it is not present in the first outflow,* and the happiest imagination does not take its place."

Madame d'Épinay follows her friend's advice rather closely. She does not run after imagination, which in truth is not her forte. There is no air of pretension, no positiveness apparent in her narrative. Only in a few passages, when she is pleased to indulge in pure sentiment, when she tries to exalt her style, does she fall in some slight degree into declamation and invocation, which is permitted only to Jean-Jacques; but everywhere else we find familiar letters, earnest, natural, dramatic conversations, reproduced with an appearance of absolute verity. Grimm must have been satisfied.

However, the bulky romance which Madame d'Épinay left to him was never published by him, and it was in danger of remaining unknown for ever when it fell into the hands of that scholarly publisher, M. Brunet, who was able to discover behind the masks of the characters all the interesting historical material which it contained. The principal names were supplied without question; digressions and superfluous passages were omitted, and the three volumes prepared which appeared in 1818, and which proved so popular that there were three editions in less than six months.

In the present condition of the work, the novel

form is hardly perceptible; it is of no importance except in one point: it is an imaginary guardian,—Madame d'Épinay's guardian,—who is supposed to tell the story of his ward, but who generally does it by yielding the floor to herself and the other characters, whose letters, journals, and conversations he quotes at length. This guardian is the machinery of the romance—machinery too perceptible, too unskilfully concealed, to endanger the reality of the whole work. Strike out the fictitious guardian and all the rest is true.

Mademoiselle Louise - Florence - Pétronille Tardieu d'Esclavelles, who, in the romance, calls herself by the pretty name of Émilie, was the daughter of an officer who died in the king's service, and was born about 1725. At the age of twenty, on December 23, 1745, she married her cousin, M. d'Épinay, the oldest son of M. de La Live de Bellegarde, farmer-general. Her husband and she believed themselves to be very deeply in love with each other at first, but the illusion lasted only a short time; she alone loved, and that with the first love of a boarding-school miss. As for him, he was simply a man of pleasure, a dissipated spendthrift, abominably indelicate in all his conduct toward his young wife; he treated her in such wise that it is impossible to go into details here, and we must refer the reader to what she herself says about it.[1]

---

[1] Somebody asked Diderot what sort of man M. d'Épinay was: "He is a man," was the reply, "who has spent two millions without making a *bon mot* or doing a good deed (*bonne action*).

At this time Madame d'Épinay was a clever, pretty young woman, "impressible and interesting," as was said. Nature had made her very shy, and it was long before she freed herself from the influence and promptings of others—before she was herself. Three portraits might be drawn of Madame d'Épinay: one at twenty years of age, another at thirty (she has drawn this one for us, about the time that she began to know Grimm); and a third after a few years of that acquaintance, when, thanks to him, she had acquired more confidence in herself, and when, being still a most attractive person, she was becoming a woman of real merit, which she eventually became altogether.

At twenty she was ardent, emotional, trustful, and slightly credulous, affectionate, with a pure and modest brow, hair well placed about it, a freshness of colouring which soon vanished, and with tears of emotion ready to suffuse her lovely eyes.

At thirty she herself tells us:

"I am not pretty, and yet I am not ugly. I am short, thin, with a very good figure. I have an air of youth, but without bloom,—a noble, gentle, ardent, intellectual and interesting air. My wit is slow, impartial, deliberate, and inconsequent. I have in my heart vivacity, courage, firmness, elevation of sentiment, and extreme shyness.

"I am genuine but not unreserved. [*The remark is Rousseau's, who had made it to her in person.*] My shyness has often given me the appearance of dissimulation and insincerity; but I have always had the courage to acknowledge my weakness, in order to demolish the suspicion of a vice which I had not.

"I have shrewdness enough to attain my end and to put aside obstacles; but I have none to detect the plans of other people.

"I was born affectionate and sensitive, constant and not coquettish.

"I love retirement, the simple, private life; however, I have almost always led a life opposed to my tastes.

"Ill health, and keen and repeated disappointments, have transformed my naturally cheerful disposition into one of great gravity.

"It is hardly a year since I began to know myself well."

Rousseau speaks of her in his *Confessions* with much injustice, even in respect to the matter of beauty; he insists upon certain points, essential in his judgment, which, he claims, were lacking in Madame d'Épinay; in short, he speaks of her as a lover might to whom she would not listen. Diderot is more just, and he describes Madame d'Épinay in charming fashion at that age of second youth, one day when he was at La Chevrette, while he and she were having their portraits painted.

"Madame d'Épinay is being painted sitting opposite me," he writes to Mademoiselle Voland; "she is leaning on a table, with her arms loosely folded and her head turned a little as if she were looking to one side; her long black hair is held in place by a ribbon that encircles her brow. A few locks have escaped beneath the ribbon; some are falling over her neck, others over her shoulders, and heighten its whiteness. Her costume is simple and *négligé*."

And recurring to the same portrait a few days later, he says, still with a charming turn of phrase:

"Madame d'Épinay's portrait is finished; she is represented with her breast half uncovered; a stray lock or two scattered about her neck and shoulders, the rest held in place by a blue ribbon which encircles her brow; her lips are parted, she is breathing, and her eyes are heavy with languor. She is the image of tenderness and sensuality."

Behold her, then, at thirty years past, flattered a little, if you choose, or at least viewed by friendly eyes, on a beautiful day of sunshine. What she was in those same years of plenitude and decline, but on a day of illness and suffering, we will let, not Diderot, nor Jean-Jacques, but Voltaire tell us. She went to see him during a trip that she took to Geneva for her health. Her frail machine was already in a fair way to break down and go to pieces. Voltaire, however, who looked especially to the mind, to the general appearance, and who, in respect to women, was less material than Rousseau, found her much to his liking. He was more amiable with her, more lively and more extravagant than he was at fifteen; he made her all sorts of declarations, the most amusing that can be imagined. One day when she was writing at his house to her friend Grimm, he insisted on remaining in the room while she composed her letter.

" He expressed a desire to stay so that he could see what my two big black eyes say when I am writing. He has seated himself in front of me, and is poking the fire and joking; he says that I am making fun of him and that I look as if I were criticising him. I tell him that I am writing everything that he says, because it is worth quite as much as all my thoughts."

### Voltaire said of her to Doctor Tronchin:

"Your patient is truly philosophical; she has discovered the great art of putting the best possible face on her condition; I would like to be her pupil; but the ply is made. What am I to do? Ah! my philosopher! she is an eagle in a cage of gauze. If I were not dying," he added looking at her, "I would have said all this to you in verse."

With all due allowance for gallantry and poetic verbiage, that "eagle in a cage of gauze" proves at least that Madame d'Épinay had fine eyes, and a very warm heart in its transparent envelope.

I have chosen to describe her, first of all, with the pen of the eminent men whose names are connected with hers; it is well to know people by sight before listening to their romance or their history. Madame d'Épinay's romance is decidedly involved, although it resembles those of many women. She was in the mood to love her husband, when she discovered by signs that were too unequivocal that he was by no means a lovable person and was even contemptible. She had just become a mother; but maternal affection, although in her case it was a very active sentiment, was not enough for her. She strove to make her conjugal duties a law; she suffered, she mused, she had tears in her eyes for she knew not what, when on a day she received a visit from M. de Francueil, an agreeable young man, of refined manners, powdered as fashion required, fond of music like herself—the type of a first lover of the day. She was touched, she fought against the feeling, but she recurred to it. She did not lack the advice of kindly souls.

Among the kindly souls whom she had about her there was one who was assuredly the slyest insect, the most treacherous and cunning confidante that one can imagine. She was a Mademoiselle d'Ette, a maiden of more than thirty years, "once as beautiful as an angel and with nothing left save the craft of a demon." But such a demon! Diderot, who paints in the style of Rubens, said of her: "She is a Fleming, and that is evident from her skin and her colouring. Her face is like a great pan of milk on which some one has thrown rose-leaves." I omit the rest of Diderot's description.   This Mademoiselle d'Ette, who was the Chevalier de Valory's mistress, is introduced to Madame d'Épinay; she worms herself into her confidence, gives her bold, positive, selfish advice. The shrewd, crafty creature has remarked Francueil's love and thinks that she can detect that it is returned; she tries to learn all about it, to assist it, to have a hand in it, to make herself useful and necessary, and all to her own advantage.   She claims to have become the mistress of that wealthy household, to hold the key to all its secrets, and to make twofold use of them at need.

This character of Mademoiselle d'Ette is admirably grasped and described; it is by virtue of the depiction of character, the coherence and naturalness of the conversations reported, that Madame d'Épinay's *Mémoires* is a unique book.   The amorous Francueil, and later the amorous Grimm, resemble all lovers more or less, —the former, the lover of one's first youth, the latter, him of one's second youth, who is less handsome, less seductive, less fascinating, but often more reliable, and who heals the wounds left by the first.

This part of Madame d'Épinay's *Mémoires* is true,

but is not otherwise original. Their peculiar originality consists in the candid and absolutely lifelike delineation of the characters of other people; in the description of Mademoiselle d'Ette, that domestic pest; in that of Duclos, her worthy pendant, as he reveals himself in these pages; in the confidences of Madame de Jully, who bluntly avows to her sister-in-law her love for the singer Jelyotte and asks service for service. This originality is even more apparent in the scenes at the two dinner-parties at Mademoiselle Quinault's, in the inconceivable orgies of conversation which are indulged in there by the *beaux-esprits,* Madame d'Épinay being present as an eye-witness, who says her little word, and who, above all, knows how to listen. By virtue of this quality Madame d'Épinay, whose purpose was simply to write a romance, has proved to be the authentic chronicler of the manners of her age. Her book belongs between that of Duclos, *Les Confessions du Conte de* ——, and that of Laclos, *Les Liaisons Dangereuses;* but it has more of the atmosphere of the time than either of the others, and it gives us a more lifelike and more complete picture of it, and one which expresses more truly, if I may use the phrase, its average corruption.

In the eighteenth century the type of this feminine corruption, respectable in outward appearance, is presented to us in the person of Mademoiselle d'Ette.

All the scenes in which she appears are excellent and drawn from nature; but the first, in which she extorts the young woman's secret, and incites her to go farther, surpasses all the others. The precise situation is this: young Émilie, just up from her lying-in, grieving over her husband's infidelities, already despising him, and with perfect justice, has met the attractive Francueil and feels a vague interest in him, but dares not declare herself as yet, and sees her desire only through a mist. At this juncture the obsequious and insidious counsellor appears.

" Mademoiselle d'Ette came to pass the day with me," writes Émilie. " After dinner I lay in my long chair ; I had a feeling of heaviness, of ennui ; I yawned constantly, and fearing that she might think that her presence incommoded me or was disagreeable to me, I pretended to be sleepy, hoping that my indisposition would finally pass away. But no, it grew worse ; melancholy took possession of me and I felt that I must admit that I was depressed. Tears came to my eyes, I could stand it no longer."

In this state of vague discomfort and languor, the young woman apologises to her friend:

" ' I believe that it is the vapours ; I feel very uncomfortable.'
" ' Don't stand on ceremony,' she replied. ' Yes, you certainly have the vapours, and to-day is not the first time ; but I have been careful not to say anything about it to you, for I should have added to your trouble.' "

And after a little dissertation upon the vapours and their effect, she said:

" ' Let us come to the cause of yours. Come, be honest, don't conceal anything from me ; it is ennui, and nothing else.' "

And as the young woman attempted to enter into some explanation,

" ' Oh, yes ! ' Mademoiselle d'Ette interrupted, ' all this confirms
me in what I tell you ; for it is ennui of the heart that I suspect in your
case, not of the mind.'   Seeing that I did not reply,  she added :
' Yes, your heart is solitary ; it no longer cares for anything ;  you
no longer love your husband, you cannot love him.'   I attempted
to make a gesture of denial, but she continued in a tone which imposed
silence on me : ' No, you cannot love him, for you no longer esteem
him.'   I felt relieved because she had said the words that I dared not
utter.   I burst into tears.   ' Weep freely,' she said,  throwing her
arms about me ;  ' tell me all that is going on in that pretty head.   I
am your friend and will be all my life ; keep nothing from me of what
you have in your heart ; may I be fortunate enough to console you !
But first of all let me know what you are thinking about, and what
your ideas are concerning your situation.'   ' Alas ! ' I replied, ' I don't
know myself what I am thinking about.' "

And the young woman lays bare the conflicting
sentiments of her own heart: that she has for a long
time believed herself to be severed from her husband
and indifferent to him, and yet that she cannot think
of him without shedding tears, and that at times she
dreads his return almost as if she hated him.

" ' Ah, yes ! ' replied Mademoiselle d'Ette, laughing, ' one hates only
as much as one loves.   Your hatred is nothing more than love humiliated and disgusted; you will never be cured of this deplorable disease
except by loving some object more worthy of you.'—' Oh ! never !
never ! ' I cried, drawing away from her arms, as if I dreaded to see her
opinion verified.   ' I shall love none but M. d'Épinay.'—' You will
love other men,' she said, still holding me, ' and you will do well;
only find some one who is attractive enough to please you, and '—
' In the first place,' said I, ' that is what I shall never find.   I swear
to you in all sincerity that never since I was born have I seen any
other man than my husband who seemed to me worthy to be distinguished.'—' I can well believe it,' she rejoined; ' you have never
known anybody but old dotards and coxcombs; it is not much to be
wondered at that no one has ever succeeded in attracting you.   In all
those who come to your house, I do not know a single person who is
capable of making a sensible woman happy.   A man of about thirty,

past the age of folly, is what I should prefer; a man in a position to
advise you, to guide you, and with sufficient affection for you to have
no other aim than to make you happy.'—' Yes,' I replied, ' that would
be delightful; but where does one find a man of intelligence, agreeable,—in short, such a man as you describe,—who will sacrifice
himself for one and be content to be a friend without carrying his pretensions to the point of seeking to be a lover ? '—' Why, I do not
expect that, either,' replied Mademoiselle d'Ette; ' I propose, in his behalf, that he shall be your lover.'

" My first impulse was to be shocked, the second to be very glad
that an unmarried woman of good reputation, like Mademoiselle d'Ette,
could think that one might have a lover without committing a crime;
not that I felt any inclination to follow her advice, *far from it,* but at
all events I need no longer in her presence appear so distressed by my
husband's indifference."

And the scene continues in this vein, Madame
d'Épinay vowing that she will never have a lover,
yet flattered that the other should discuss the subject
with her, and, in effect, having one already; and
Mademoiselle d'Ette, in order to make her speak and
to obtain the mastery over her, applying herself skilfully to the task of inciting, frightening, reassuring,
and emboldening that youthful heart, and of bending
it toward the ends at which she is aiming. Mademoiselle d'Ette's favourite maxim, which is that of
the whole eighteenth century as well, is: "Only a
woman's inconstancy in her tastes, or a bad choice,
or the publicity that she gives to it, can injure her
reputation. *The essential thing is the choice.*" And
as for what the world may say, what does it matter ?
" People will talk about it for a week; or perhaps not
at all; and then they will think no more about it unless it be to say: ' She was right.' "

Madame d'Épinay's choice was already made at that time more definitely than she dared acknowledge to Mademoiselle d'Ette, for an instinctive sense of delicacy warned her that she must conceal something from that pretended friend, who placed her hand so boldly on these incipient and timid sentiments.

The sequel is varied with incidents of which I can mention only a few. Francueil at first appears in a flattering light: the love between him and Madame d'Épinay is genuine love *à la française,* of the sort that may exist in a polished, refined society,—a love devoid of violent tempests and of thunderbolts, of fits of frenzy *à la Phèdre* and *à la Lespinasse,* but with youth and affection and charm. They act in theatricals with wild enthusiasm; but the theatricals are only a pretext for isolating themselves, for being together constantly. "The people here are a flock of lovers," Mademoiselle d'Ette writes to her chevalier. "Upon my word, this company is like a living novel. Francueil and the little woman are as intoxicated as they were the first day."

But intoxication has its limits. Francueil grows cold, or, rather, he wanders from the fold; he goes to supper-parties, he gets intoxicated in good earnest, he is no longer so punctual or so attentive to his friend; the bad manners of the time have infected him. Then it is that Duclos tries to supplant him and to invade the citadel in his place. He despised Francueil, whom he considered a man of small brains, and whom he always called the cockchafer. "You are not happy, poor woman!" he cries, "and it is your own fault. *Mordieu!* why attach yourself to the leg of a cockchafer? You were deceived; La d'Ette is a hussy, I have always told you."

Older by at least twenty years than Madame d'Épinay, Duclos, caustic and bitter, carrying frankness to the point of brutality, and employing his brutality with rare adroitness, was very ready to make up to that clever, playful, and vivacious young woman; he passed all his evenings at her house, and thought that he did her honour by acquiring influence over her and training her. His whole plan is set forth in Madame d'Épinay's *Mémoires,* in his own words to her, with a brusque and picturesque crudity which she may have exaggerated sometimes, but which she certainly did not invent; a sweet and refined woman is incapable of inventing such manners and such remarks if she has not actually experienced them. Before the publication of these *Mémoires* Duclos enjoyed a good reputation, that of a man of original disposition and character, free of speech,—straightforward and adroit [*droit et adroit*]. Henceforth his name will convey only the idea of a dangerous friend, a sneering despot, cynical, and deceptively gruff. Whatever any one may say or do, the false *bonhomme* in him is unmasked, he will never be rehabilitated.

However, if he is the loser in respect to character, he loses nothing intellectually. The conversations re-

ported by Madame d'Épinay in which he took part
are most comical and entertaining, seasoned with the
most piquant of spices, and coloured with a Breton
*verve* which is not apparent in the same degree in
any of his writings. The best scene, and one of the
most respectable, in which he figures, is that in which
he goes one day to the college with Madame d'Épinay, and subjects to an inquisitorial examination the
tutor of young d'Épinay, that poor and grotesque M.
Linant, of whom it is said in one place: "The poor
man is more stupid than ever." While Duclos sends
the child to write a theme in an adjoining room, he
takes the tutor aside and puts him to the question in
a most entertaining way—in a most sensible way, I
would say, except that it was humiliating and far too
harsh. For we must not forget that in the midst of
these memoirs, amid the medley of gallantries and
love intrigues which fill them and in which the principal character is painted at more than half-length,
the prepossession, I had almost said the chimera, of
a systematic moral education occupies a large place,
and in the vicissitudes of her two affectionate foibles,
Émilie is constantly in competition with the author of
*Émile*.

There was one critical moment in the life of poor
Madame d'Épinay, when her reputation was subjected
to a terrible attack. It was at the death of Madame de
Jully, her sister-in-law, a charming woman who, beneath her affectation of indolence, was herself imbued

with the philosophy of the age in all its essence, and practised it in all its audacity and charm. Taken away suddenly, in her prime, she had barely time, as she breathed her last, to intrust a key to Madame d'Épinay; it was the key of a secretary which contained letters to be destroyed. Madame d'Épinay, who was apprised of everything, understood and instantly carried out her wish. But an important paper, bearing upon certain matters in which her husband and M. de Jully were interested, not being found at once, she was suspected of having burned it with the other papers, the ashes of which were found in the fireplace, and odious reports, sanctioned by the family itself, gained currency. These reports acquired such consistency in society that one day, at a supper-party given by the Comte de Friesen, Grimm, who had known Madame d'Épinay only a short time, felt called upon to defend her openly, and provoked a duel in which he was slightly wounded. This was beginning like a *preux chevalier,* and Madame d'Épinay, in her gratitude, gave him that title and accepted him as such.

It was high time: in the clutches of the detestable Mademoiselle d'Ette, of the unworthy Duclos, of a husband who was more extravagant than ever, and who was involving Francueil in his dissipated and extravagant courses, Madame d'Épinay was fighting against too great odds, and her frail constitution was on the point of giving way. For a moment she had the idea of a religious life and of taking God as a makeshift; but an excellent ecclesiastic whom she introduces, and whom she represents as speaking very sagely, had no difficulty in proving to her that she misinterpreted her own heart.  It was to Grimm that the task fell of setting her right and of curing her.  Let us say to his honour that he applied all his energies to it, and that he succeeded.

Grimm loved Madame d'Épinay, and he was from the first useful to her as a guide.  She had the good sense to form her judgment of him at once from that essential quality, and to realise that she had gained a genuine friend.  In the early days of their intimacy she writes: "We talked till midnight.  I am filled with esteem and affection for him.  His ideas are so just!  His advice is so impartial!"  Thus we find the critic with all his merits even in the lover.  He was immeasurably kind and helpful to her; he first gave her confidence in herself, a realisation of her own worth; he set her free.  "Oh! how happily endowed you are by nature!" he wrote to her.  "In Heaven's name, do not be false to your vocation; it depends only on yourself to be the happiest and most adorable creature on earth, provided that you no longer set others' opinions above your own, and that you learn to be sufficient unto yourself."  And when he is not speaking to her, with what just appreciation he still speaks of her, emphasised and quickened by affection! *"Bon Dieu!"* he writes to Diderot, "how that woman is to be pitied!  I should not be troubled about her, if she were as strong as she is courageous. She is gentle and confiding; she is placid and loves repose above everything; but her situation constantly demands unnatural conduct. entirely foreign to her nature; nothing so wears out and destroys a person as a naturally frail organism."

Only after she knew Grimm did Madame d'Épinay became her real self. Through him that mind, instinct with grace and refinement, acquired its true temper; he liberated and gave its value to the trait which particularly distinguished her,—" a delicate and profound uprightness of sentiment." Madame d'Épinay, compromised as she was by the incidents of her early life, and slandered by her former friends, was on the way to become a better woman at the very time when she was being painted in the darkest colours; and she was able to reply one day, in a strain no less witty than touching, to a man from Paris who called upon her at Geneva, and who rather awkwardly showed to her face his surprise at finding her so different from the conception of her that people had chosen to give him : "Understand, monsieur, that I am not so good as my Geneva reputation, but better than my Paris reputation."

Grimm was thirty-three years old when he first knew Madame d'Épinay, and during the twenty-seven years that their liaison lasted, his attachment did not waver for a single day. After a certain time, however, he found himself imperceptibly more attracted by literature, by the labours and duties imposed upon him by honourable obligations, and by the ambition natural to one of mature years.   That judicious person felt that he must seek new motives for living as he lost his youth.   He advised his friend on the same theory.   When he left Paris it was she who held the pen in his place, and, under the guidance of Diderot, carried on his literary correspondence with the sovereigns of the North.   She wrote books, which did not interfere with her making knots, tapestry, and songs. "Go on with your work," Abbé Galiani wrote to her; "it is a proof of attachment to life to compose books."

With enfeebled body and ruined health she had the talent to live thus to the end, to dispute foot by foot what was left of her distressing existence, and to make the best of it, with affection and rare charm, for the benefit of those about her.

She died April 17, 1783, at the age of fifty-eight. We find her and all her circle, during the last four years of her life, depicted in her correspondence with Abbé Galiani, which would be well worth the trouble of an examination by itself.   My only purpose at this time is to dwell upon these interesting and almost ingenuous memoirs of an epoch of sophistry, this curious monument of the morals of a century, and also to recall attention to a woman of whom we may say, in her praise, that in all her failings, as in all her good qualities, she was and always remained a true woman; and they are becoming rare.

# Buffon.

## 1707–1788.

# Buffon.

BUFFON, the last to disappear of the four great men[1] of the eighteenth century, closed that century, so to speak, on the day of his death, April 16, 1788. Born at Montbar in Bourgogne, in September, 1707, he was five years older than Jean-Jacques Rousseau; he was thirteen years younger than Voltaire and eighteen younger than Montesquieu. His father, M. Le Clerc, was counsellor in the Parliament of Dijon, which then contained many studious and learned men, many a one of good stock in whom the old sap had not run dry. Buffon, however, used to say that he took especially after his mother, of whom he always spoke affectionately and with pleasure. He was educated at the Collége of Dijon, and displayed at the outset a great inclination for work and for amusement. Nature had given him all the advantages of face, figure, bearing, and strength, and an intense ardour in every direction, which good sense and will finally succeeded in mastering. "The body of an athlete and the mind of a sage"; thus Voltaire described him later, in his hours of justice and fair dealing.

[1][Montesquieu, Voltaire, Rousseau, Buffon.—Tr.]

Buffon, however, became a philosopher and sage only by degrees. His youth seems to have been decidedly tempestuous and boisterous; but, no matter how he had employed his evening, he always ordered that he be roused at a stated hour in the morning, to apply himself to his studies. Geometry had deeply interested him from his school-days, and from the zeal with which he applied himself to it, it seemed almost to be his vocation. It may more properly be said that, in his soaring and unbounded curiosity, he cultivated all branches of knowledge simultaneously, from his early youth. "He was not willing that anybody else should understand what he did not understand himself"; he would have felt humiliated as a man to have it so, and that noble pride, upheld by an obstinate will and served by an admirable intelligence, carried him to the very summit of the sublime sciences. Nature perfected all these gifts by clothing them with eloquence.

As a young man he became intimate with the tutor of a young English nobleman who was living at Dijon, and that intimacy led him to make a journey to Italy, and another to England; these are the only journeys that he ever made. That man who had covered such vast spaces and so many epochs, and had described so many living forms, was able to say: "I have passed fifty years at my desk." Buffon was short-sighted; that was his only infirmity. On that account he developed the more thoroughly his power to see every-

COMTE DE BUFFON
*From a portrait by Drouais*

thing with the eyes of the mind, to form a mental image of everything by means of absorbed meditation.

This early intimacy with an Englishman was very useful to Buffon; it put him in the way of being informed betimes of every great scientific discovery in England. He entered without hesitation into the theory of Newton and that of the great physicists of his school. His first published works were two translations from the English. He translated Hales's "Vegetable Statics (1735), and Newton's "Method of Fluxions and Infinite Results" (1740). In his preface to this last he expresses himself like one who is altogether master of his subject, and sets forth in a succinct, superior, and almost entertaining way, the disputes that had arisen apropos of the invention of this method of reckoning infinity. In the preface to his translation of Hales, he extols the experimental method in physics and declaims against "systems" so earnestly that we wonder whether he can be the man who is destined to construct such excellent systems.

"The system of nature," he says, "depends, it may be, upon several principles; these principles are unknown to us, and their combination no less so. How dare we flatter ourselves that we can unveil these mysteries with no other guide than our imagination? and how do we make out to forget that the effect is the only means of ascertaining the cause? It is only by subtle, well-considered and persistent experiments that we can force Nature to disclose her secret to us; no other method has ever succeeded, and true physicists cannot help looking on the old systems as old-fashioned visions, and are reduced to reading most of the new ones as one reads novels. Collections of experiments and observations are therefore the only books capable of adding to our knowledge."

This first Buffon, at once geometrician and experimenter, gave no promise as yet of what the second Buffon would be—a bold generaliser, by no means eager to subordinate facts to ideas. Every one knows the reply that he made one day to the chemist, Guyton de Morveau, who wanted to subject a body to the crucible in order to make sure of the fact which Buffon deduced from some theory: "The best crucible is the mind," said Buffon. A decidedly risky remark when it is a question of pronouncing upon the works of nature!

But the explanation is that there was in Buffon a genius which was soon to set itself free and to demand satisfaction in its turn. At the beginning of the twelfth volume of his *Histoire Naturelle*, he avows with a sort of artless candour that imperious craving of his nature which beseeches him to introduce in his history some general dissertation wherein he can develope his theories, treat nature on a large scale, and compensate himself for the tedium of the details. "Then we shall return to our details with better courage," he says, "for I confess that one requires courage to devote one's energies constantly to little objects the examination of which demands the most apathetic patience, and gives genius no chance."

Appointed in 1739 superintendent of the Jardin-du-Roi, and in the same year an associate of the Académie des Sciences, Buffon was as yet known only by one of the translations that I have mentioned, and by a

number of memoirs on certain special subjects. It
was then that he conceived the plan of turning his
positition in the Jardin-du-Roi to the very best account and of becoming the historian of nature. He
was thirty-two years old.

The title "Natural History" was a little vague at that
time. It was so to Buffon, who, viewing his subject in
its most general aspect, proposed to try to define it,
but only on condition of never limiting it. After ten
years of preliminary labour, during which he had
taken Daubenton as a collaborator for the descriptive
and anatomical part of the work, he published in 1749
the first quarto volumes of his *Histoire Naturelle*.
It was one of the events of the century. From that
time the successive volumes of that monumental
work continued to be published regularly until the
author's death (1749–1788). A serious illness, which
interrupted his labours for nearly two years, caused
no appreciable delay in publication. During the execution of this long undertaking Buffon took on several
collaborators. When Daubenton, the man of the
scalpel, left him, he left a great, an irreparable void;
his place was never filled. But so far as literary collaborators are concerned, Buffon was well supplied
with them, and he had at hand his descriptive school
in the Gueneaus de Montbelliard, husband and wife,
and Abbé Bexon. M. Flourens, the editor of Buffon's
works, and the correspondence published in 1860,
afford us some interesting information on this subject.

Beware of admiring too warmly the "Birds" in Buffon's work; do not be led into exclaiming that the great delineator never wrote anything finer; a most amusing error ! You would, in that case, do just what all Paris did when it complimented M. de Chateaubriand on an unsigned article which was attributed to him, and which was written by M. de Salvaudy. For the "Birds" are by another pen than Buffon's; the "Peacock" is Gueneau's, and the "Nightingale"; the "Swan," that much-belauded "Swan," may well be pure Bexon; it is certain that the little abbé did a good deal to it before it passed under the hand of the master, who simply gave it the final polish. We have the documentary evidence, the canvas in manuscript (not of the *Swan,* but of the other birds); we have the rough drafts; the emendations can be counted and measured.

But all the greatest and most important portions of the work are Buffon's; each volume bears his stamp and his imprint by virtue of some immortal page; the last volumes are not to be distinguished from the earlier ones, and are especially noteworthy only by reason of their more exact arrangement. The one containing *Les Époques de la Nature,* published in 1778, is considered to be Buffon's masterpiece.

His life did not vary during these fifty years of toil. Each year he passed a few months in Paris to fulfil the duties and obligations of his post, to attend to the interests of the institution over which he presided, and which, thanks to him, became of greater importance every day. Then he returned to Montbar, where he lived the greater part of the year, engrossed in study and composition. He has often been represented in that rural and feudal abode, in his tower, where he shut himself up in the morning, to meditate and to write. I regret that in some of our French writers more or less inclination to jest is mingled with the sentiment of respect and veneration which such an existence ought to inspire above all else. Amid the tumultuous, dissipated, and agitated life of the eighteenth century, Buffon stands alone; he finds in the strength of his character, in his exalted love of glory, and in the powerful interest of the boundless studies to which he has consecrated himself, the means of resisting all the allurements, all the paltry temptations of his surroundings. Observe how all yield to them more or less and succumb, except him; I say all, and I am speaking of the greatest. Voltaire, as is only too well known, lives on nothing but battles and quarrels; poor Jean-Jacques is at death's door with them for twenty years, and his brain goes astray by dint of trying to reply to unkind remarks and to slanders. Even Montesquieu does not retain his tranquillity if any one takes him to task. His *Esprit des Lois* appeared at the same time with Buffon's first volumes. The Jansenist Gazetier attacked the two works sharply, and Montesquieu even more violently than Buffon. Instantly Montesquieu took up the pen. "He has replied by quite a thick pamphlet in his best style," Buffon wrote to a friend (March 21, 1750); "his reply has been perfectly successful. Despite his example, I think that I shall take a different course and shall not answer a single word. Every one has his own refinements of self-esteem; mine goes so far as to believe that certain people cannot even insult me." [1] Such was constantly the principle on which Buffon acted—to allow calumny to react upon itself. And twenty-eight years later, when he recurred to the same subject of attack, upon resuming in his *Époques de la Nature* this same general system of ideas and of work,

"Let us try, nevertheless," he said, "to make the truth more palpable; let us increase the number of probabilities; let us make the verisimilitude greater; let us heap knowledge upon knowledge by assembling facts, by accumulating proofs; and then let us pass judgment without anxiety and without appeal; for I have always thought that a man who writes should give his attention solely to his subject and in no wise to himself; that it is unbecoming to try to interest others in himself, and that, consequently, personal criticisms should be left unanswered."

This lofty sense of personal dignity governs Buffon's whole life. He never allowed himself to be turned

[1] Letter to Abbé Le Blanc in the *Mélanges de la Société des Bibliophiles,* 1822.—The articles in question may be read in the *Nouvelles Ecclésiastiques,* a Jansenist sheet, in the issues of February 6 and 13, 1750; they were a formal denunciation of the book and led the Sorbonne to censure it. (See the same sheet for June 26, 1754.) Amid a multitude of narrow views and bitter sneers, there is one point in which the critic is not mistaken, and that is the non-Christian tendency of Buffon's book. As I have remarked elsewhere *(Port Royal,* iii., p. 332), Pascal's greatest adversary in the eighteenth century, his most eminent refuter (although he does not seem to be so) is Buffon.

aside or diverted a single day from this contemplation and description of nature, for which the longest mortal existence was still too brief. Let us consider him as he was at Montbar, but let us not enter, as Hérault-Séchelles did, as a frivolous, disloyal, and mocking spy; let us enter rather with that exalted and reverential feeling which led Jean-Jacques, when he passed through Montbar in 1770, to express a wish to see that study which has been called the cradle of natural history, and to kiss the threshold on his knees.

The pavilion in which Buffon worked was at the farther end of his gardens, and it was reached by going up from terrace to terrace. He went thither every morning at six o'clock. In midsummer he worked in a very lofty study, the arched ceiling of which resembled those of churches and ancient chapels. " M. de Buffon," said Madame Necker, " thinks better and more readily in the great elevation of his tower, at Montbar, where the air is purer; that is a remark that he has often made." There, in a bare room, seated at a wooden desk, he meditated and wrote. There were no papers before him, no pile of books; all such display of that erudition and old paper simply embarrassed Buffon. A subject profoundly considered, contemplation, silence, and solitude—these were his materials and his tools. In another room, not quite so high or so cool as the first, where also he sometimes worked, there was no other ornament on the walls than an engraving of Newton, the great interpreter of nature.

Some one has chosen to make merry over the toilette that Buffon was wont to make before sitting down to write. When he rose each morning he was accustomed to be dressed and to have his hair dressed according to the fashion of the time; he thought that the man's garb formed a part of his personality. Apart from that, everything in his study indicated the utmost simplicity. Hume described the impression that Buffon produced on him by saying that in gait and carriage he corresponded to one's idea of a marshal of France rather than to that of a man of letters. His countenance bore the stamp of the loftiest ideas. "Black eyebrows, shadowing very lively black eyes," stood out even more noticeably beneath his lovely white hair. Elevation of thought, tranquillity, dignity, consciousness of his strength,—these were the characteristics that were manifest in his whole person.

"Buffon lives absolutely as a philosopher," one judicious observer has said; "he is just without being generous, and his whole conduct is founded on common sense. He loves order and enforces it everywhere." With this perfect sense of justice and the kindliness due to a regular life and to his natural disposition, he constantly did good in his neighbourhood, and the people of Montbar adored him.

Such an attitude, so unusual, so unwavering, and so imperturbable, was well adapted to stir up and incite the satirists; Buffon found them even in the camp of the *philosophes*. Voltaire tried sometimes to bite

him and to turn him to ridicule, but was checked by
an involuntary sentiment of respect. D'Alembert,
with less delicate instincts than Voltaire, and less
quick to obey the sentiment cf the beautiful, gave
himself full licence concerning Buffon. He liked neither his personality nor his talents; he persistently
called him "the phrase-maker," "the king of phrase-
makers"; he mimicked him (d'Alembert had the unfortunate talent of mimicking people). Buffon was
told of it; he was moved to pity to see the great
geometrician playing the monkey, and he paid no heed.

The publication of the first three volumes of the
*Histoire Naturelle* (1749) made a great sensation and
a great noise. There were expressions of admiration,
and there were exclamations of dissent. It was not
the theologians alone who dissented, but the scientists
as well. We have the critical *Observations* which
those volumes caused M. de Malesherbes to write.
When he entered upon that vast subject, even after
ten years of study, Buffon was still not fully prepared.
The botanists especially were able to detect him *in
flagrante delicto* of inaccuracy, and of carelessness in
his manner of passing judgment on Linnæus, whose
methods he criticised. Buffon knew little of botany;
"I am short-sighted," he said; "I have learned botany
three times and forgotten it as many; if I had good
eyes, every step that I take would refresh my knowledge in that subject." It seemed that, being built on
a large scale by nature, it was hard for him to stoop

to study small things: the cedar of Lebanon he con-
templated with pleasure, but the hyssop seemed to
him too trivial.  Thus it was that he knew nothing
about insects and maligned the bees, although Réaumur had already appeared.  It required all the charms
and prettiness of the humming-bird to reconcile him
to the tiny creature.  When he speaks of animals, it
is always of those animals that are more or less analogous to man, vertebrates of the higher order.  In his
*Histoire Naturelle,* he conceives at first no other
method than that which consists in treating creatures
according to their relations to man in respect to proximity and utility.  He imagines a man wholly un-
learned and without any ideas, in a field where the
animals, fishes, birds, plants, and stones appear, one
after another, before his eyes.  After the preliminary
straightening out of things, this man will distinguish
animate matter from inanimate.  Having reached this
first great division, *animal, vegetable,* and *mineral,* he
will go on to distinguish animals that live on *land*
from those that live in the *water,* or those that fly
through the *air.*

" Then let us put ourselves in this man's place," says Buffon, " or let
us suppose that he has acquired as much knowledge or had as much
experience as we have: he will proceed to judge the objects of natural
history by their relations to him: those that are the most *necessary,* the
most *useful,* to him, will hold the first place; for instance, among
animals he will give preference to the horse, the dog, the ox, etc.
Then he will turn his attention to those which, while they are not do-
mesticated, always live in the same regions, the same climate, as stags,
hares, etc."

In this arrangement, then, which he calls the most natural of all, and which is only provisional, Buffon proceeds, in the first place, to classify animals and other living things solely according to their degree of *utility* to man, and not according to the essential characteristics which distinguish them and which may bring together some that appear to be very far apart. To conclude upon this branch of the subject, I will say that it was only after a considerable number of volumes had appeared that Buffon, learning gradually by practical experience and by Daubenton's supplementary descriptions, finally prepared classifications more in accordance with the facts and based upon comparative observation of the creatures among themselves. His professional brethren observed his progress in this direction in his work on the gazelles, published in 1764 (volume xii), and above all in his nomenclature of the monkeys (volumes xiv and xv, 1766 and 1767).

But if this detail and this scientific method left much to be desired in Buffon for a long while, in the view of a small number of advanced observers, he impressed men's minds at the very beginning by his broad views, the broadest that can be suggested for the meditation of the natural philosopher. In a discourse on the theory of the earth, he sought to determine, first of all, the structure and method of formation of this terrestrial globe, the stage upon which animals live and plants grow; he attempted, in accordance with the important geological facts then known, to establish its

successive revolutions from the beginning to its grad-
ual hardening and its present composition.    Thence
he passed to certain conjectures concerning the birth
and reproduction of living beings.    When he came to
man, these slightly mystical elucidations were heightened by remarks no less shrewd than judicious concerning the various stages of childhood, puberty,
virility, and old age; concerning the acquirements
and the sphere of action of the various senses.    The
third volume was crowned by the well-known admirable passage, in which the first man is described
as he may have been on the first day of the Creation;
awaking to life an entire stranger to himself and to
everything about him, and telling the story of his first
thoughts.    Here Buffon became the rival of Milton
himself, a physicist Milton, minus the piety and adoration.    Later, Condillac, seeking to rebuke Buffon
and to convict him of inaccuracy, imagined, in his
*Traité des Sensations,* that strange statue, which he
endowed with life little by little, giving it first one
sense, then another.    Buffon made much sport of that
colourless and frigid statue, and when Condillac came
to ask him for his vote for the Académie Française, it
is said that he received him with a smile, promised
him what he wished, and said as he embraced him:
"You have made a statue talk, my dear abbé; I embrace you because you still have some warmth, but,
my dear abbé, your statue has none."

The fourth volume of the *Histoire Naturelle* ap-

peared in 1753. Faithful to the method that he had
announced, Buffon gave therein the history of the
principal domestic animals,—the horse, ass, and ox,—
and prefaced it with an excellent discourse on the
nature of animals compared with that of man. He
represents good triumphing over evil as a general rule,
and pleasure over pain, in the physical nature of every
sentient being. The thing that disturbs the equilibrium in man is his imagination, which corrupts the
good, and, by anticipating evil, often produces it.
Buffon would not reduce mankind to the stupid well-
being of the animal, but would exalt him, through
the reasoning power, to a state of superior felicity.
He would convince us that "happiness lies within
ourselves; that the peaceful felicity of our heart is our
sole genuine blessing." He would turn mankind
away from the insane passions which put force upon
nature and bring in their train ennui and disgust.
From the way in which he speaks of "that horrible
disgust with oneself, which leaves one no other desire
than that he may cease to exist," we see that, if that
placid and superior mind was never afflicted with the
malady of the Rousseaus and the Werthers and the
Renés of the future, he did not fail to recognise that
malady and to denounce it at its fountainhead. "In
that state of illusion and of darkness," he says, "we
would fain change the very nature of our mind; it
was given us only to gain knowledge, and we would
employ it only to feel." The really wise man, in his

judgment, is the man who has the power to overcome these false assumptions and false desires.

"Content with his fate, he does not wish to be other than he has always been, to live otherwise than he has always lived; sufficient unto himself, he has but little need of others, he cannot bear to be a burden to them; constantly intent upon employing the powers of his mind, he perfects his understanding, cultivates his intelligence, acquires new knowledge, and satisfies his own needs at every instant, without remorse, without repugnance; he enjoys the whole universe while enjoying himself. Such a man is, beyond doubt, the happiest being in all nature."

Give to this wise man a motive, an additional stimulus, give him "glory, that mighty incentive of all great minds," and you will have Buffon himself,—Buffon, who, in order to describe the noblest type of mankind, had only to grasp its characteristic features in himself. But to all that he says against the passions, we may offer a single suggestion in reply. "But would you yourself," we may say to him, "have escaped that ennui, that listlessness of mind which follows the age of passions, had you not been upheld and possessed by this unwavering passion for renown?"

The point that Buffon was most particular about in writing was continuity, connection between the parts of the discourse, each leading up to the next. He could not endure what was detached and jerky, and that was a fault for which he reproved Montesquieu. He ascribed genius to continuity of thought on the same subject, and he insisted that the words should

flow like a river that spreads out and bathes everything
with its ample limpid stream. " He did not put in his
works a single word which he could not explain."
Clearness no less than continuity was his constant
preoccupation. When his secretary was reading his
manuscript to him, at the faintest sign of faltering or
hesitation he would make a cross, and would return
to the passage and correct it until he had made it
smooth and luminous. For all that, I do not find in
his writings anything novel or any expressions of his
invention so terse and vigorous as we might imagine
to-day; in that respect Chateaubriand, and even Bernardin de Saint-Pierre left him far behind. There are
some delightful examples in Buffon of a new and
genuinely original language, but they are rare. His
great charm consists rather in the constant flow and
the plentitude of the current. His expression, at least,
is never marked by that restlessness and writhing
which in some other authors accompanies an extreme craving for novelty. In certain bits of description, there are light and charming touches which affect
me more than the passages more frequently cited.

There was in Buffon's day a man of his own age,
but illustrious before him, a man born a naturalist, as
other men are born musicians, painters, or geometri-
cians, a man whose name has become synonymous
with that of science itself—the Swede Linnæus. Born
in the same year with Buffon (1707), of a family of
peasants and country ministers or vicars, he conceived

a fondness for plants while playing in the garden of the paternal parsonage. His father employed his leisure in horticulture, and it is said that Linnæus's mother, during her pregnancy, never lost her interest in her husband's labours. When her child was born, and the moment he began to cry, it sufficed to quiet him, they say, that his mother should put a flower in his little hands ; and she was not surprised. A charming legend of Linnæus's childhood, which recalls the tales of the ancient bucolics concerning young Daphnis. However, Linnæus's youth and his beginnings were arduous in the extreme; he had to triumph over the vexations and obstacles of poverty, as Buffon had to rescue himself from the perils of dissipation and wealth. Linnæus's life, of which he has told more than once himself, is full of artless and innocent details. Betrothed to the daughter of a physician, early in 1735, after assuring himself of the young woman's heart, he started on his travels in foreign lands. He lived at least three years in Holland, then passed some time in Paris, where the Jussieus welcomed him; Buffon had not as yet been heard of. His absence being thus prolonged, Linnæus learned, not without surprise, that a faithless friend was endeavouring to take advantage of it to steal his fiancée's heart. He returned, without undue haste, but still in time to defeat this anti-conjugal scheme, and found the maiden true.

In every respect Linnæus, the man of regularity and

method, a fresh, ingenious, inventive observer, with
the eye of a lynx, a concise and eloquent writer, a
poet even in his Latin, which was strewn with metaphors and carved into aphorisms,—Linnæus forms an
absolute contrast to Buffon, the painter of development and of expansive views, whose sentences, with
their numerous distinct members, bound together by
flexible punctuation, cannot without difficulty decide
to come to an end. In 1748, a year before the publication of the first volume of Buffon's *Histoire Naturelle,*
Linnæus, already at the pinnacle of renown, took
several hundred pupils into the country about Upsala.
"We made frequent excursions in search of plants,
insects, and birds. On Wednesday and Saturday of
each week we herborised from dawn till dark. The
pupils, wearing flowers in their hats, returned to the
town and escorted their professor to his garden, preceded by rustic musicians. That was the last degree
of magnificence in our pleasant science." Thus
Linnæus ; and, by way of contrast, we must once
more observe Buffon at Montbar, alone at six o'clock
in the morning in summer, going up from terrace to
terrace, opening the gates at the foot of each flight of
steps, and thus, at a lordly gait, attaining his study at
the far end of his gardens, whence he comes forth
only to walk slowly about, with his head full of ideas,
in the elevated paths, where no one dared disturb
him. His thoughts alone served him as escort.

Linnæus and Buffon were rivals; they were even

unjust to each other. Buffon, with superb disdain, attacked Linnæus first, concerning his artificial methods, and even when he had come to acknowledge the necessity of classifications, he never did him full and entire justice. "Buffon, the antagonist of Linnæus," Linnæus himself tells us in his fragmentary memoirs, "was compelled, *nolens volens*, to have the plants in the Jardin-du-Roi arranged according to the sexual system." But Buffon did not give way on this point so readily as Linnæus thought; he never consented, so Blainville tells us, to allow Linnæus's method and nomenclature to enter the Botanical Garden with flags flying; "he simply allowed the names given by Linnæus to be written on the tags used to label the plants, but only on condition (an incredible thing if genius were not human!) that they should be written on the under side." However, Linnæus, who rewarded his friends by giving their names to the prettiest plants, revenged himself innocently enough on his enemies by giving their names to rough or thorny ones. It was said that he had an idea of such reprisals in his mind when he bestowed the name of *Bufonia* on a most unattractive plant; but the accuracy of the fact and the real purpose of the allusion have been contested. "Buffon," said Linnæus, toward the end of his life, "did not extend the boundaries of science, but he knew how to make it popular; and that too is a way of serving it to advantage." To be sure this praise does not go far enough; but let us at least see therein a sort of reparation accorded by the prince of botanists, by the naturalist who was a naturalist by birth and by pure genius, to him who had become one by force of will, and who also reigned by right of genius and of power.

Buffon, at the beginning, was no more just to Réaumur than to Linnæus. Réaumur held the sceptre of natural history in France when Buffon appeared, and, the better to wrest it from him, Buffon took delight in fighting him, in harassing him even, and in lowering him little by little in public opinion. Buffon, who on account of his defective sight did not use the microscope, so that he did not examine plants closely, was inclined to despise insects. He was amazed at what seemed to him the excessive pains which some naturalists took to describe their habits at such length, and, above all, to arouse admiration of their industry. "For," he said, "a fly ought not to occupy any more room in a naturalist's head than it occupies in nature." It seems that Buffon, confining himself to the point of view of man, and placed between the two infinities, infinite greatness and infinite littleness, was sensible only of the first. He was rather fond of arranging things and creatures in order of height, if one may say so, and of physical size; so it was that he thought it fitting to begin the history of birds with that of the Ostrich, which is the elephant of that order of creatures.

However that may be, he loses no opportunity to criticise Réaumur, both as to the substance and as to

the form of his ideas; he rebukes him for drowning
himself in "an immensity of words"; and in truth,
compared with Buffon's, Réaumur's style is very diffuse and very prolix; it is perspicuous and natural,
however, and when he speaks of the bees he becomes
charming.  Severe to the point of injustice with these
men of positive science, Buffon, who is susceptible
to talent, to the imposing, has a much higher regard
for a Pliny, "with his proud, melancholy, and sublime intellect"; although he always decries man to
exalt nature, he never refers to that ancient writer
save in a tone of respect, passing over his numerous
failings in silence.

I have seen positive scholars, observers of merit,
albeit their horizon was somewhat confined and depressed, who, when they were questioned about
Buffon, would scarcely reply; and one of them said
to me one day : " There is Bernardin de Saint-Pierre,
too, who composed some fine pictures in that style."
Evidently these professional scientists, failing to find
in Buffon the exact detail of observation which they
prize above everything, detecting in his work generalisations or vagueness (which they confuse), having
discovered errors therein, and not appreciating the
elevation and prime originality of some of his luminous conceptions and his perspectives, are paying him
back for the contempt that he felt for their predecessors of the same race; they wreak upon him the vengeance of the positive naturalist, the anatomist, the

observer with the microscope, upon the man of talent who has been too much inclined to keep them at a distance; they are proud because they are more advanced to-day than he was; and by coupling him so closely with Bernardin de Saint-Pierre, whom they read very seldom, they relegate him to a place among the pure men of letters, forgetting that Buffon was a genius capable of a scientific education, which Bernardin de Saint-Pierre never was.

There is another class of scientists, as positive and more philosophical (Cuvier at their head), who seem, on the contrary, to have discovered in Buffon all that is worthy of being praised, and to have taken account of the real progress for which science is indebted to him. I have often talked with modest scholars who cling to this method of observation and experiment, and after each conversation, I have always come away overflowing with respect for Buffon the scientist, to say nothing of that other admiration which one naturally entertains for the painter and the writer.

As I have already said, Buffon's most perfect work is his discourse or tableau of the *Époques de la Nature*, which he published in 1778, at the age of seventy-one, and which he had had copied, we are assured, *as many as eighteen times* (strike off as many as you please) before he brought it to the degree of perfection which satisfied him. He recurred then to the ideas of his first volume on the theory of the earth, and presented

them in a more complete light and in new combina-
tions—I dare not say with more verisimilitude. For
this is the way in which Buffon corrected his work:
in the amplitude of his style, he was opposed to re-
vision; like a great artist, he deemed it the simpler
way, when a work was once published, to correct his
errors in a new work, a new picture, by beginning
entirely anew, as Nature does. In the *Époques* he nar-
rates and describes in seven tableaux the revolutions
of the terrestrial globe from the time when he assumes
it to have been in a fluid state, down to the time
when man appears, to reign. Buffon does not put
forward his hypothesis as actual fact, but simply as a
means of imagining what was likely to have taken
place, in a manner bearing more or less analogy to the
fact, and of fixing one's ideas upon the most important subjects of natural philosophy. This precaution
once taken, he describes with a continuity, a precision,
and a sense of reality which surprise us and create an
illusion at the same time, those immense and terrifying scenes of disentanglement, those awe-inspiring
spectacles which had no human witness.

It is said that Buffon was very fond of the English
novelist Richardson, "because of his great truth, and
because he had seen at close quarters all the objects
that he described." We might apply the same praise
to him apropos of the *Époques de la Nature;* he
knows and sees those things that happened before
the creation of man, because he has examined them at

close quarters. In truth Richardson is no more familiar with the domestic life of the Harlowe family than
Buffon seems to be with those for ever unknown and
vanished epochs which he brings before our eyes,
that internal life of the universe to which he introduces us. Never, in all that vast field of circumstan-
tial details, does the smile of doubt play about his
lips. He treats that sublime romance with the finished precision which he would have employed in
a description of real, existing nature. "Where were
you," said God to Job, "when I laid the foundations of
the earth?" M. de Buffon seems to say to us without
excitement: "*I was there!*" He exalts the mind, he
dignifies it, disturbs it, and confounds it as well, by
this audacity, which consists in so resolutely putting
himself, a simple mortal, in the stead and place of God,
of Infinite Power. It would seem that such an act of
temerity, or sublimity, as you choose to call it,—such
an act of usurpation could be expiated only by falling
to his knees immediately after and humbling himself
in the most submissive of prayers.

Milton and Bossuet would have done it and their
picture would have seemed all the greater for it. Buffon did not do it, and did not even think of it. The
moral sense is a little offended, amid all the wonder
that that noble work arouses, to find it so dumb and
so barren on the subject of Heaven.

In no other of his writings did Buffon manifest more
clearly than in this work of his septuagenarian period

the full value of his perspicuity and plenitude of expression, of the boundless and flexible current of his speech applied to the greatest and most solemn subjects. Thus, as he grew old, he never ceased to mature and develop, acquiring new knowledge slowly each day, adding to his ideas, and finding a sort of freshness and rejuvenation even in the very profundity of his reflections.

Montesquieu when he grew old was fatigued, and showed it; Buffon was not. A comparison of the two men would be profitable and would definitively fix the characteristic features of Buffon's idea of nature and of the processes of his talent. Buffon acknowledged Montesquieu's genius, but he denied that he had style: he considered that, especially in the *Esprit des Lois,* there were too many sections and divisions; and this fault, for which he blamed the general plan of the book, he found repeated in the details,—in the thoughts and sentences; he criticised the over-refined style and the lack of connection. "I knew Montesquieu well," said he, "and this fault was due to his physical condition. The President was almost blind, and he was so quick that most of the time he forgot what he intended to dictate, so that he was obliged to confine himself within the least possible space." This is how he explained what sometimes seems like curtailment in Montesquieu's language. Buffon, on the other hand, had the faculty of retaining his voluminous writings in his memory, and he could display them at will in all their vast extent,—ideas as well as the mode of expression.

In revenge, Montesquieu's conversation overflowed with flashes of wit, bright sallies, and metaphors, and resembled his writings. It was abrupt, like his style, impulsive, full of surprises, of sudden outbursts and apt retorts; he never missed the ball when it came in his direction. On the other hand, Buffon's conversation was laughed at a good deal as being far below the level of his style. I should think so! after working so many hours a day, after such incessant application of the mind that had borne and upheld so many things, he needed to relax, and his tongue moved as it could, in his family circle and among friends. And yet Madame Necker, who is such an excellent guide in everything relating to Buffon, speaks of the piquancy and instructiveness of his conversation, and cites more than one example. It would, in truth, be very strange if it had been otherwise. A mind rich in such stores of knowledge and of ideas could not be commonplace except by forgetfulness. But it was necessary to wait, to seize him at the right moment, and to know how to listen to him. In conversation Buffon liked neither contradictions nor interruptions; he would hold his peace and remain silent at the first objection that was made. "I cannot make up my mind," he would say, "to continue to converse with a man who deems himself justified, upon considering a subject for the first time, to contradict one who has thought about it all his life." This led him to have intimates and admirers in his household, who never contradicted him; he could easily endure them. He allowed them to talk of him and his genius to his face, and talked of them himself good-humouredly, as his own age was already talking of him and as posterity was destined to do.

Let us try to view men as they are, without exaggerating them in all sorts of ways. Some superficial minds persist in seeing in Buffon the writer with powdered hair and lace cuffs; they are never tired of anecdotes about Montbar, and so far as he is concerned they do not go beyond the jests of d'Alembert or Rivarol; they blame him for the "Peacock," as if the "Peacock" were his; they berate him to this day for taking Gueneau de Montbelliard for an associate and Lacépède for his successor. But let us leave these frivolous critics. Another danger, which is that of serious and elevated minds, is the propensity to make Buffon more of a thinker and a prophet than he really was, to fancy that he had our present-day systems in his mind, and to place a halo about his brow. We should always ask ourselves, when we admire so profoundly a genius of the past: "What would he say to this way of being admired?" I do not know what Buffon would think of the various theories now contending with one another in natural history; I consider it hazardous to attempt to conjecture what he would think. God forbid that the temple of nature which he so majestically reared should end by becoming a little church, where, on the pretence of bowing before him, people proceed to praise one another, as I see that they invariably do in many of the writings that I have mentioned.

The other day I was looking at Augustin Pajou's bust of Buffon, in the Musée du Louvre; he is there represented in his old age; the circle of the eye, the wrinkled and slightly wasted temples tell the story; but it is a fine head, dignified, erect, and nobly carried. The distance from the nose to the upper lip is considerable, and seems to indicate more or less arrogance and haughtiness. I find little of the lion, whatever Madame de Genlis may have said. The face is fine, however; it might well belong to the "amiable great man," as Gibbon called him. One divines a something sweet in its glance. The lofty forehead is not in the least bulging or Olympian, as our sculptors never fail to make it in all the heads carved for encyclopædias. I made the same reflection just before as I looked at the bust of Bossuet; there is no touch of exaggeration in all those sublime heads, and that of Buffon bears the imprint of his human character.

# Bernardin de Saint-Pierre.

1737–1814.

## Bernardin de Saint=Pierre.

THE disciple and biographer of Bernardin de Saint-Pierre, M. Aimé Martin, who married his widow, has rendered more than one service to his memory; but he has carried his zeal and enthusiasm so far as to draw a romantic portrait of him and to write one of those impossible biographies which put a sensible reader on his guard at the beginning. Having to defend Bernardin against a number of accusations which affected his character, M. Martin plunges into an unqualified apology in terms that keep no bounds. A single passage will suffice as a specimen: "How many times," he cries, "I have found myself a better man on leaving him! Then virtue seemed natural and easy to me. A divine flame consumed me; I was like those disciples of Jesus Christ, who, on recalling the impression produced by his discourses, said one to another: ' Our hearts burned on listening to him.' " We must get away from this high-flown sort of thing as quickly as possible in order to find the real Bernardin.

Born at Havre on January 19, 1737, of a family originally of Lorraine, which would have liked to claim

descent from Eustache de Saint-Pierre of Calais, and
which, in everything, had more claims than proofs,
Bernardin de Saint-Pierre received a very informal and
irregular and decidedly spasmodic education, in which
nature, the ocean, and the country played a large part
from the first day. At the age of eight he cultivated
a little garden and did his share in raising flowers, as
befitted the future author of the *Fraisier*. At the age
of nine, having read several volumes of the "Fathers
of the Desert," he left the house one morning, with
his breakfast in his little basket, to take up the life
of a hermit in the neighbourhood. He displayed an
almost fraternal sympathy for various sorts of animals.
There is a story of a cat which, when he told it to
Jean-Jacques later, brought tears to the eyes of the
man who, following Pythagoras, expressed his indignation that mankind should have reached the point of
eating the flesh of beasts. One day he shook his fist
threateningly at a carter who was abusing a horse.

His father having taken him to Rouen, young Bernardin, when they bade him look up at the towers of
the cathedral, exclaimed: "*Mon Dieu!* how high they
fly!" And everybody laughed. He had seen nothing
but the swallows which had their nests in the towers.
There again was manifested the predominant instinct
of one whom none but natural beauties ever captivated
and whom all art born of man touched hardly at all,
nay, even offended, and who, in *Paul et Virginie* (the
only blemish perhaps in that masterpiece), went so

far as to declaim in four passages, very close together, against the monuments of kings as opposed to those of nature.

The perusal of "Robinson Crusoe" was a great event in his life; he too sought in imagination his island; but it soon ceased to be a solitary island,—he provided himself with companions and peopled it at his pleasure with a select company of whom he constituted himself the pacific lawmaker; for he was ambitious, and his inclination led him naturally either to isolate himself or to play a noble rôle.

Judicious persons who knew him have explained to me his failings and his irritable character by saying that he had no bringing-up, that he was never subjected and broken to discipline. Perhaps he was not of a nature to bend to it. He was one of those mortals with a sweet and noble countenance, with fine blue eyes and a benevolent smile, who are endowed at birth with an unconquerable instinct. Speaking somewhere of the various instincts of animals, and likening them to those secret, innate affections which are allotted to every man destined to make his way or to suffer, he says:

"Our whole life is simply the development of these affections. It is they which, when our condition is antipathetic to them, inspire us with unwavering constancy, and involve us, in the midst of the multitude, in never-ending, deplorable battles against others and against ourselves. But when they develop under favourable circumstances, then they cause unfamiliar arts and extraordinary talents to manifest themselves."

And he cites Homer, Raphael, Columbus, Herschel, as having been endowed, one and all, with a characteristic genius which ruled them and which they could not avoid. Bernardin de Saint-Pierre had his genius as well as they. His ideal marked itself out betimes, and through all his disappointments he never turned aside from it. This ideal was to found a colony which should be an idyllic affair and in which he would reign over docile and happy subjects, not without some notes of the antique flute. In Russia one day, when the Empress Catherine seemed to smile, Bernardin smiled only upon his cherished plan of founding a colony on the shores of Lake Aral,—a cosmopolitan colony for the benefit of all poor and virtuous strangers. Later, he went on, in imagination, to attempt to transplant something of the same dream to the shores of Madagascar, then to Corsica, and still later to that undefined expanse in the western part of America, north of California. He conceived in his brain and carried with him wherever he went a world where all was order and harmony, a sort of Eden or age of gold, which he absolutely refused to lay aside, and persisted in treating as real amid the discords of all sorts which were so repugnant to him. It was only at the end, despairing of success, that he abandoned the idea of carrying out his projects in distant lands and made up his mind " to draw water from his own well," that is to say, instead of trying to do things, to take his paper and describe them.

The Utopian, at the end of his rope, seized the pen and became a painter. Those harmonies which he could not realise on earth, in political and civil life, he sought in the study of nature, and he narrated with a sense of consolation, and with delight, what he saw there. " All my ideas are simply shadows of nature, gathered by another shadow." But with these shadows his brush blended softness and light; that is sufficient for his glory.

Thus Bernardin de Saint-Pierre's life is divided quite distinctly into two parts: in the first he roams about the world at random, passing from disappointment to disappointment; young, handsome, full of charm at first sight, and generally well received, he fails in everything because he does not in reality apply himself seriously to any occupation; and because, in whatever he undertakes, he always has his secret *arrière-pensée* of becoming a semi-mythological coloniser, his chimera of being an Orpheus or an Amphion. In the second part of his life, which he does not enter upon until late, too late, and after much suffering and bitterness of spirit, he is simply an author and man of letters, aspiring, under a roof of his own, to dislodge his Minerva, as he says, from her rustic throne, and to put a globe at her feet, if he can; his real vocation is found. These two periods of his life are separated by a sort of crisis and moral illness, which is interesting to watch and which gives us the key to his nature.

After some elementary studies in mathematics, Bernardin, who had entered the School of Roads and Bridges as a pupil, conceived the idea of serving in the engineer corps of the army; he was admitted to that corps in pursuance of this first blunder, but he was never successful in his efforts to be received on a footing of equality. He made a campaign in Hesse in 1760, and got into trouble with his superior officers. Shortly after, he repeated the same blunder in a journey to the island of Malta, then threatened with a siege; he went without his commission as geographical engineer, could not manage to be received on a suitable footing, and returned home angry and dissatisfied. He encountered new difficulties on his return to France. It fell out with him then as with all imaginative men, who soar the higher the more you refuse them. Being unable to obtain his rehabilitation and a commission in the French service as quickly as he wished, he reverted to the idea of becoming a legislator on a great scale, and he determined to offer his services in Russia where Catherine had just seized the Empire.

He betook himself thither by slow stages, through Holland and Lubeck, making friends along the road; for he was an attractive youth, with much charm of manner and a touching artlessness, and with rich stores of delicate feeling and affection when his sensitive self-esteem was not involved. In this Russian trip, however, he again found a way to make his position embarrassing by calling himself the *Chevalier* de Saint-Pierre, and assuming a coat of arms of his own manufacture. Very often, when he was presented to some person of note, he was asked if he belonged to the noble family of Saint-Pierre, which was then very much in evidence at Versailles; he was obliged to answer "No," and it made him wince.

His adventures in Russia, and, after leaving there, in Poland, have been strangely doctored and *romancified* by his biographer, M. Aimé Martin; a simple narrative would have served the purpose much better than his always sentimental descriptions. Bernardin's imitator and disciple has put on two or three layers of moonlight where Bernardin himself would have introduced only a single beam.

A published correspondence shows us Bernardin *au naturel* after his sojourn at Warsaw in the summer of 1764 (he was then twenty-seven years old); it is his correspondence with M. Hennin, then French resident at Warsaw, and afterward chief clerk in the Department of Foreign Affairs. This series of letters was intrusted by M. Hennin's son, a distinguished antiquary, to Bernardin de Saint-Pierre's widow and M. Aimé Martin, who had them printed in 1826. The editors considered it their duty, however, to suppress some passages, and Bernardin's widow in particular besought the owner of the letters, most urgently and with tears, to permit her to destroy five

or six, which revealed the great writer's moral position
in too distressing a light.

At the very beginning, which corresponds to the
climax of the young officer's love-affair with the beautiful Princess Miesnik, at Warsaw, we find him describing the fêtes and balls of that luxurious life of
which he is a part. On leaving these festivities and
returning home, at three in the morning, he dreams,
he says, of nothing but Lignon and Arcadie. But the
man of sense adds these words, which show that in
Bernardin the romantic did not strangle the actual:

" All these fêtes do not amuse me so much as you imagine. When
I return home I naturally compare my position with all those about
me, and I see that I am nobody, and that I must soon have done with
it all; a substantial and influential friend would be much better suited
to my character and my means; I shall have found such an one in
you if your friendship may be won by friendship."

Racine's tragedy, *Iphigénie,* is given by amateur
actors and actresses, who are all princes and daughters or nieces of palatines; the Chevalier de Saint-
Pierre plays Achille. On leaving these gorgeous
functions, he must needs return to a little room which
he has hired for five ducats. These material details
reveal the weak side of his precarious situation, and it
is a side that Bernardin never lost sight of.

After making an attempt to throw himself into the
faction opposed to the new King of Poland, Stanislas
Poniatowski, he is received by him with distinction;
but the place in the artillery that is offered him is

worth only forty ducats a year. " This offer *humili-ates* me," he writes to M. Hennin ( January 2, 1765), " and distresses me to a degree that I cannot express. I have made up my mind, and I propose to return to France." In M. Hennin's reply to this letter, which the editors were so ill-advised as to omit, we find that sensible man combating Bernardin's determina-tion and representing to him that there is nothing humiliating in the offer that was made him; that the first step is the essential thing, and that the rest cannot fail to follow. M. Hennin, having assisted Bernardin with his purse, is entitled to give him this good advice; he speaks the language of a judicious mind which assumes in its correspondent a genuine desire to establish his fortune and his destiny. He speaks one language, but Bernardin speaks another; at that very moment he is listening involuntarily to the inward voice of that genius which has hitherto deluded him with promises and will continue to de-lude him for a long while, but which nevertheless does not lie to him when it says: " It is not in that direction that glory lies for you."

As he sincerely wishes to oblige his young friend, M. Hennin makes inquiries at the departments in Paris, and he is told that Bernardin de Saint-Pierre is not a chevalier, and that there is some question about the other titles and qualifications that he has assumed. Bernardin takes umbrage at this result of the inquiry, and, as M. Hennin has accommodated him none the

less without first telling him what he knew, he says
to him:

> " You gave me at Vienna, monsieur, a strong proof of your friend-
> ship; but the silence that you have maintained does not prove your
> esteem for me. That does not at all diminish my gratitude, how-
> ever, and gives me the highest opinion of you, since you accommo-
> dated me when I must have been an object of suspicion to you."

Here we detect the germ of that tone and those sentiments *à la Jean-Jacques* of which Bernardin was
destined to be an additional example in the critical
period of his life, and which constituted in his case, as
in that of the Genevese philosopher, a genuine disease
of misanthropy.

Returning to France (1766) without resources, and
burdened with debts, he becomes a more urgent so-
licitor than ever to the ministers and their satellites.
He seems, at certain times, to hesitate between his
first wandering vocation, and his second and final one,
which was the pen. Taking up his abode with the
curé of Ville-d'Avray, he arranges his observations
and his reminiscences of travel; he writes his *Mémoires* concerning Holland, Prussia, Saxony, Poland,
and Russia. His plan expands as he applies himself
to it. His structure would easily become immense,
were it not that time, materials, and tranquillity of
mind are lacking. "Thus do I spin my silk," he
says; "I shall see the end of it with the end of my
strength."

This life, although rather depressing, would suit

him well enough if it could only last.  He is even
beginning to carry his plans farther; his systematic
mind leads him on to physical speculations.

"I have collected," he says, "my observations on the movement
of the earth, and I have formed a theory so bold, so novel, and so
plausible that I dare not communicate it to anybody.  I let it sleep in
peace, for I distrust my solitude, in which one may unsuspectingly
familiarise oneself with the most absurd ideas.  You can see from this,"
he adds, "that I grasp at everything, and that I leave threads floating
about here and there, like the spider, until I can spin my web."

And we see, as he goes on, the talent of writing
come to life of itself under his pen, and metaphors
burst into bloom.

Meanwhile he succeeds in obtaining an assignment
as captain of engineers in the Île de France,[1] and he
decides to go thither.  He is thirty-one years old; he
has not yet exhausted all his spirit of adventure and
his youthful vigour, and it is well that he should go
to that unfamiliar hemisphere to mix his colours and
finish his painter's palette.  We have the narrative of
his journey, which he published in 1773:  *Voyage à
l'Île de France, à l'Île de Bourbon, au Cap de Bonne
Espérance, par un Officier du Roi*.  To be a king's
officer,—that was always his ambition, his hope, and
it was never fully satisfied.

In this first effort of Bernardin we can detect already
the substance and the principal lines of his talent; it is

[1] [More familiarly known to us as Mauritius, the scene of *Paul et
Virginie*.—Tr.]

less fully developed, less ideal, but for that very reason, more real in places, and in a certain sense more
true, than what he will say later in the *Études* and the
*Harmonies*.   The work was noticed by only a few;
in order that men shall pay any heed to a new talent
or genius, it must needs appear to them with plenitude and superabundance, and give them always a
little too much.

There is, then, sobriety of expression and a very
clean-cut turn of phrase in the *Voyage*, written in the
form of letters to a friend ; they are sketches instinct
with life, rather than pictures.   The emotional painter
can be recognised, however, in the very first lines;
the descriptions are not dry; the landscape is introduced only to be brought into relations with the living
characters.   "A landscape," he says, "is the background of the picture of human life."

When he reaches the Île de France he describes its
soil and vegetation in detail and with interest, but
without pleasure,—rather with a sort of melancholy.
"There is not a flower in the fields, which indeed are
strewn with stones and covered with a grass as tough
as hemp.   There is no flowering plant with a pleasant
odour.   Of all the shrubs not one comes up to our
whitethorn.   The wild vines have not the charm of
the honeysuckle or the ivy.   *There are no violets in
all the woods.''*   But when he goes farther into the
island, when he approaches one of those little dwell-
ings lost in the densest woods and on the slopes

of the mountains, and finds there the unlooked-for
image of plenty, of peace, and of family life, he is
touched, and he finds some very harmonious colours
with which to depict his emotion.

"I saw but a single room in the whole house: in the centre, the
kitchen; at one end the storerooms and servants' beds; at the other
end the conjugal bed, covered with a sheet, on which a hen was setting; under the bed were ducks; pigeons in the arbour, and three
great dogs at the door.   On the walls were hanging all the utensils
used in housekeeping or the work in the fields.   I was really surprised
to find in that wretched abode a very pretty woman.   She was a
Frenchwoman, and of a respectable family, as was her husband.   They
had come there several years before in search of fortune;  they had left
kindred, friends, fatherland, to pass their days in an uncivilised spot,
where they can see naught save the sea and the awful declivities of
Brabant Mountain;  but that young matron's air of contentment and
kindliness seemed to make every one happy who approached her.   She
was nursing one of her children;  the other four were playing about
her, merry and contented.

" When night came, everything eatable that the house contained
was served with perfect cleanliness.   That supper seemed very delicious to me.   I was never tired of watching the pigeons fly about the
table, the kids playing with the children, and so many animals assembled about that charming family.   Their peaceful games, the solitude
of the place, and the murmur of the sea afforded an image of those
first days when the daughters of Noah, set down upon a new earth,
shared with the gentle domestic beasts their roof, their table, and their
bed."

That man was already a great painter who, without
applying himself to the task, thus described what he
saw.   But despite such happy touches, the *Voyage*
still fell short of entire exactitude in that it lacked that
intimate, magical life which Bernardin, after a second
visit to the Île de France, was able to impart to these

same scenes when he saw them again in the distance, no longer in the tedium of exile, but with the fondness of regret and with the vividness of absence.

Many pages of *Paul et Virginie* are simply a poetic and coloured painting of the sketch that we have in the *Voyage*. To cite but a single example: the journey of Virginie and her brother to the Rivière-Noire is made, in the *Voyage*, by Bernardin, accompanied by his negro attendant; and where, on his return, before reaching the mountain of the Trois-Mamelles, he has to ford a river, and the negro takes his master across on his back, in the romance it is Paul who takes Virginie on his back. Thus the imagination, with its facile and powerful touch, transfigures and glorifies everything in retrospect.

After undergoing much suffering and finding himself so cramped in that island which he was destined to immortalise, Bernardin, once more in France (May, 1771), set about tempting and wearying fortune anew. He busied himself in writing his *Voyage;* he saw some men of letters,—Rousseau and d'Alembert; for some little time he was popular in the Encyclopedist circle. Condorcet became interested in him and wrote to Turgot about him. Turgot was Minister of Marine, and Bernardin had been for some time petitioning to be sent overland to the Indies, on a mission of observation and discovery.

It was with Rousseau that Bernardin de Saint-Pierre had most to do, and with him he formed as close a friendship as the wretched philosopher's mental state permitted. The pages that Bernardin wrote about him afford perhaps the simplest and most natural idea of the man and his character; for it seems to me that by dint of writing about Rousseau, people end by drawing him out terribly thin and putting him to the torture.

At the time when he was seeing Rousseau frequently and trying to lighten his gloomy moods, Bernardin himself was, or was on the point of being, afflicted in some degree with the same malady. He confesses it in the Preamble to his *Arcadie;* and even if he did not confess it, his correspondence with M. Hennin makes it impossible to doubt it. M. Hennin had become, in March, 1778, chief clerk in the Department of Foreign Affairs, under M. de Vergennes. Bernardin, in his readiness to be deluded, instantly made up his mind that he had found in him a powerful patron, whereas he really found in him, as before, simply a judicious, loyal, steadfast friend, trying to serve him step by step, but being himself, with respect to the ministers, in a subordinate and secondary position only. The correspondence between them that has been published would give only an imperfect and too one-sided idea of their relations, if we were not aware that many of M. Hennin's answers have been suppressed; that this excellent friend who does not always reply, acts more than he talks; and that there are times when the letters he receives from

Bernardin in rapid succession find him in the midst of an overwhelming press of work. "Your third letter," he wrote (November 18, 1780), "is the *seventy-ninth* that I ought to answer to-day, and there are some among them that relate to matters of great urgency." And in a postscript: "I had written *nine hours* last evening when I finished the draft of this letter. I actually could not see. I gave it to my copyist, who was unable to despatch it until this morning."

Bernardin, who lives in solitude, whose nerves are excited, and who has no rest until he receives a reply, falls into the error of thinking that he has rights where he can ask only favours. He conceives that the government owes him reparation and an indemnity for his adventures in Poland, and for his various abortive enterprises,—even for the memorials that he has sent to several ministers without being asked for them. One day, after many attempts, M. Hennin obtains for him from M. de Vergennes (November 29, 1780) a gratuity of three hundred livres on the fund set aside for men of letters. "It's a trifle, but the thing is to make a beginning." Moreover, these gratuities on the literary fund are annual and equivalent to pensions for life, although that is not stated in terms. Bernardin, who has petitioned *ad nauseam,* takes offence at the form of the grant and at the fund on which it is charged: it is as an officer in the king's service, as a captain of engineers, that he wishes to be indemnified, or as having served French diplomacy in Poland. He

writes to the minister that "it is impossible for him
to accept alms from his department." I have before
me a long letter from M. Hennin in which he urges in
reply the most sensible arguments imaginable. "I will
even confess," he adds, "that I was just starting, when
I received your letter, to ask M. le Marquis de Castries
for a like annual sum for you in the shape of a pension
on the Marine establishment, with the hope of succeeding sooner or later." In conclusion he gives him
counsel inspired by affection: "My friend, you are
too much sequestered from the world; you know nothing of men or of the progress of affairs. How do
you expect to extricate yourself from a plight which
causes you distress, if you spurn the hands that would
help you out of it?"

This sensitiveness of Bernardin's manifests itself in
the most trivial matters: he is displeased if letters are
sent to him from Versailles with the title of "Engineer in the Navy"; he says that he never was that.
He takes offence likewise if any one, in writing to him,
gives him his baptismal name, Bernardin, in conjunction
with Saint-Pierre. "M. Panckoucke," he says in one
place, "is the first and only man who ever called me
*Bernardin.*" We, ourselves, while using that name
so often and so familiarly to designate the great writer,
almost feel that we must apologise to his ashes. This
remark about M. Panckoucke is connected with another outbreak of sensitiveness on Bernardin's part,
which did not take place till later. He received notice

one day that the king had granted him a gratuity on the *Mercure,* and that all he had to do to obtain it was to go to the treasury. But as the notice came to him from the treasurer, and without a letter from the minister, M. de Breteuil, he declined it at first and took umbrage as he did in the case of M. de Vergennes' gratuity. Whereupon M. Hennin, whom he was near driving frantic, wrote to him this line, which sums up our whole opinion: "You are good-tempered, simple, and modest, and yet there are times when you seem to have taken for a model your friend Jean-Jacques, the vainest of mortals." [1]

Meanwhile, amid these freaks and spasms of an ever so slightly diseased brain, Bernardin never ceases to petition all the departments, and thanks to good friends, among whom M. Hennin is always numbered, he succeeds in securing a modest competence with the various odds and ends and gratuities that he extorts. Let us speak out the whole of our thought: if Bernardin had thus solicited aid only in those years when he was absolutely in need of it, when he was like a father or a mother striving to bring forth the unknown fruit of his genius or the child of her womb; if he had not retained that habit of lamentation and begging

---

[1] [M. Sainte-Beuve prints in full these two letters of M. Hennin (December 3, 1780, and August 13, 1785), which, according to him, "throw a bright light upon Bernardin de Saint-Pierre's mental peculiarity, without, however, exaggerating it in the least. . . . Need I say," he adds, "that these two refusals on Bernardin's part were simply for form and did not hold good?"—Tr.]

even in his most fortunate days, and alternated constantly between the idyll and the account book,—it
would be simply touching, it would be worthy of respect and sacred.

There are many delightful passages in these letters.
This man of genius, more than forty years old, so
poor that, when he wants to see M. Hennin, he is
compelled to walk from Paris to Versailles and to return the same way, selecting in advance nights when
there is a moon, which sometimes leaves him in the
lurch,—this man writes words worthy of an Eastern
sage or of an ancient.

> " At last I have sought water in my own well; in the last six years
> I have put on paper many thoughts which need to be arranged in
> order.  Amid much sand there are, I hope, a few grains of gold."
> " Hopes are the nerves of life; in a state of tension they are pain-
> ful; cut them and they no longer hurt."
> " We are always too old to do good, but always young enough to
> advise it.  What care I !  I shall have produced some beautiful pic-
> tures; I shall have comforted, strengthened, and encouraged man in
> the swift passing of life."
> " I have to arrange some most interesting materials, and I can recover
> my strength only where I can see the sky.  I should prefer a charcoal
> burner's cabin to a château.  Procure a rabbit's burrow for me, in
> which I can pass the summer in the country."

The ancients said "a lizard's hole."

In order to work more independently, he has lodgings
in Faubourg Saint-Marceau, on Rue Neuve - Saint-
Étienne, at the very top of a house, where he over-
looks the garden of the Dames Anglaises.  This is not
the acme of his desires, for he aspires to a garden of

his own and a cottage, to live near the ground and not
so high in the air.  However, while he is finishing
there his *Études,* a sort of rustic poem, or concert,
which he dedicates to Nature, he has some pleasur-
able emotions, forerunners of the joys of paternity.
On February 7, 1781, he writes to M. Hennin these
words, which are like a burst of song; there is in the
depths of Bernardin's being a pastoral soul, which, in
the midst of his sorrows, awakes at the slightest excuse and begins to sing:

"I shall come to see you with the first violet; I shall have nearly
five leagues to walk, but I shall come gaily, and I propose to give you
such a description of my retreat that I shall arouse a desire to come to
see me here and take a little collation.  Horace invited Mæcenas to come
to his little house at Tivoli and eat a quarter of lamb and drink Faler-
nian.  As my fortune falls far short of equalling his golden mediocrity, I
shall give you only strawberries and cream in earthen dishes; but you
will have the pleasure of hearing the nightingales sing among the
shrubbery of the Dames Anglaises, and of seeing their scholars and
their young novices play about in their garden."

I have been unable to fix the precise moment of
Bernardin's great nervous crisis, when he reveals himself to us (in the Preamble to *Arcadie*) stricken by a
strange malady, subject to sudden flashes which dis-
tort his sight, seeing everything double and in motion,
and fancying that he is surrounded by enemies and ill-
wishers whenever he meets a number of people in the
public gardens or in the streets.  I imagine that the date
of this curious attack was not far from that on which he
wrote M. Hennin the charming letter that we have just

read; that is to say, it was during the months immediately preceding the publication of the *Études.* He frequently repeated this proverb of the Persians: "The
narrowest part of the mountain pass is where it enters
the plain." He passed the whole winter of 1783–1784
in copying his work, adding to it, and cutting it. "The
bear does not lick her cub with more care. I am
afraid that I shall end by wearing away the muzzle of
mine by dint of licking it. I do not propose to touch
it any more."

It is in such moments of exhaustion that he writes:
"Sedentary work is a noiseless file. It was high time
that I finished mine; my eyesight is blurred at night; I
see things double, especially anything in the air or on the
horizon; but my trust is in Him who makes the light
and the eye." He is seized with enthusiasm as he reads
over his work, and he is the first to enjoy the beauties
that he is about to disclose: "There are moments,"
he cries, "when I have glimpses of heaven, while I
suffer in this world, if the truth be told, indescribable
tortures." He feels that he has the power to charm;
the old theological censor who is assigned to his work
is himself fascinated, and cannot help saying that it is
"divine, delightful." "I know how much I must dis-
count such praise, but it pleases me. In order to be
useful, one must be agreeable, and I venture to hope
that the tribute which I owed to God and to man will
give pleasure to my epoch."

And in very truth the *Études de la Nature,* which

were published in 1784, were expressly adapted to
that very period and to the very hour when they appeared; to that brilliant and placid portion of the reign
of Louis XVI, after the American war and before the
Assembly of the Notables, when an effeminate and
corrupt society dreamed of all sorts of perfection and
easily managed regeneration, with no purpose to renounce any of its luxuries. Bernardin de Saint-Pierre,
whose plan included "seeking our pleasures in nature
and our ills in society," attacked this *beau monde*
on its weak side, and flattered it even while he
criticised it.

His book was not a conventional work; he had at
first, he said in opening, had the idea of writing a
general history of nature; but ere long, abandoning a
too extensive plan, he had confined himself to bringing together some portions of it,—ruins he called
them,—leaving only the façade standing.   These ruins
of his original work resembled those which are scattered over a landscape and which embellish it; he had
covered them with flowers and verdure.   There were
too many flowers, there was too much verdure, but
the age wanted a good supply of them, especially in
books.   The theories which Bernardin had mingled
with his descriptions did no harm.   Ignorant people,
the semi-learned, were very fond of arguing about all
sorts of things, divine and worldly, after the publication of the *Encyclopédie*.   After Buffon, Bernardin appeared in those avenues of nature in the guise of a

gentler, more attractive high priest, who introduced in
his plausible explanations something of the unctuous-
ness and of the smile of Fénelon.  He began by giving the history of his strawberry-vine, and every one
who could duplicate it on his window-sill was won
over to a science so readily acquired.  He spoke against
methods, against libraries, schools, and academies; he
protested against the abuse, even against the use,
of analysis.  "In order to judge fittingly the magnificent spectacle of nature we must leave every object
in its place, and ourselves remain where nature has
placed us."  He insisted therefore that we should accustom ourselves to consider living things in their natural and harmonious situations, and not isolated and
dissected in the cabinets and collections of scientists.
However, this recommendation was very vague; one
kind of study does not exclude the other; we examine the plant on its stalk, and we preserve what we
can of it in our herbariums.

These objections, and many others which any judicious mind might offer, did not prevent the success
due to novelty, fascination, and elegance; moreover,
the increasing influence of Rousseau and of discussions
concerning susceptibility and religion had prepared
men's minds to seize eagerly upon such prospects.
The women, the young people, all that ever-swelling
crowd of followers of Émile and Saint-Preux, hailed with
cries of joy this new apostle, of the fascinating speech.
People became innocent by reading the *Études* on the

morrow of the *Mariage de Figaro*. Grimm, the clever
literary chargé d'affaires of eight sovereigns of the
North, wrote in vain to his patrons that the work
was simply "a long series of eclogues, hymns and
madrigals in honour of Providence"; fashion in this
case was in accord with eternal morality.

Bernardin was a painter who declared that he knew
nothing, while really believing himself to be better informed than the scholars, and whose whole system re-
sulted simply in describing his natural impressions to
himself in a thousand different ways. If one would
form an idea at the outset of his type of talent, let him
read, in the first *Étude,* the picture of a landscape at the
mouth of a river. How well he draws it! how he arranges everything in order! how he clothes it with
plants and trees, happily combined or contrasted! how
he sheds light upon it, and the impression of peace, of
silence! and how skilfully he introduces a moral sentiment as well! Therein lies the secret of Bernardin de
Saint-Pierre's triumph. In landscape he has the moral
force of Poussin, the light of Claude; and in describing
those objects which others before him had deemed hor-
rifying or inanimate, he has the soft outlines and purity
of Guido.

Bernardin is not simply pious and affecting, he
is inclined to preach; he sins by the over-suscepti-
bility of his time, and there is a certain severity of
taste which he does not observe. Because of this excess, he is always inferior to Poussin. In the compo-

sition of this first landscape, on an island at the mouth
of a river, seeking to give his work a moral imprint,
he imagines a tomb there, and at first he selects the
tomb which was then classic and fashionable, that
of Jean-Jacques Rousseau.   Then he rejects or modifies this first idea.

"Do you wish," he says, "to magnify the impression produced
by this picture without, however, changing the nature of its subject?   If so, remove the place, the time, and the monument to a
greater distance.   Let the island be Lemnos, let the trees be the thick-
ets of laurel and wild olive, and the tomb that of Philoctetes.   Let
us see there the cavern in which that great man lived, abandoned by
the Greeks whom he had served, his wooden jar, and the bow and
arrows of Hercules."

And thus he produces an effect wholly moral, which
becomes more imposing at a distance, "because,"
he says, "to confer benefits on men, and to be
out of their reach, is to resemble Divinity in some
measure."

That is a fine conception.   But in a somewhat analogous picture, which he offers us in the thirteenth
*Étude,* and in which he shows us a traveller ship-
wrecked on an unknown island, which proves to
be Naxos, he has overshot the mark; applying the
same idealising process to the story of Ariadne, he
represents that young daughter of Minos, in the
legendary tale of a shepherd, bewailing the faithless
Theseus night and day, and refusing to be comforted
even by the young women of Naxos who offer her
wine in golden cups.   The shepherd, pointing to the

tomb which tradition designates as Ariadne's, adds:
" This monument, like all those in this country, has
been defaced by the years, and even more by the bar-
barians; but the memory of unfortunate virtue is not
in the power of tyrants on earth." And Bernardin,
having completed his picture, adds in his turn: "I
doubt whether an *atheist* even, who recognises nothing
in nature but the laws of matter and of motion, could
be insensible to the sentiment evoked by these present-
day morals and these memories of the olden time."
What is there in common, I pray to know, between
an *atheist* and the natural ideas suggested by the story
of Ariadne, after Catullus, as told by a shepherd ?
And what has Ariadne, a fugitive lover, afterward
abandoned, who tries to drown her sorrow in wine, in
common with the idea of *unfortunate virtue* ?   It is
these touches of the eighteenth century and of the
age of Louis XVI which spoil Greece for me in Bernardin's pages, and which mar, in my eyes, the descriptions due to his pure talent.   There is always
room for a virtuous Duc de Penthièvre in some part
of his landscapes.

The first part of the *Études de la Nature* is directed
wholly against the atheists.   In the eighteenth century
the atheist was a genus apart, a condition; men said
of such an one, pointing the finger at him: " He is an
*atheist*"; and, consequently, of another: "He is a
*deist.*"   These two categories stood face to face.
Bernardin, who was religious at heart, became a deist

by profession, and he never ceased to contend, by every conceivable argument, against his adversaries. He pleaded the regularity and harmony of nature against the partisans of disorder and chance, and he found in this controversy, which it delighted him to prolong, admirable subjects and openings for his talent, together with pretexts for his well-meaning subtleties and for the infinite variations of his reveries. He improved upon the *Vicaire Savoyard,* and seemed to have taken it upon himself to develop him in innumerable new ways in which there was mingled the charm of mystery.

About the tenth *Étude* he begins to set forth more directly his views and his conception of the harmonies of nature, the play of contrasts and consonances, of reflections and echoes in everything; there are some very nice distinctions, but it is very subtle, and in his old age, as he becomes more and more fixed in his views, he accentuates all his faults, which his final work, *Les Harmonies,* displays in immeasurable profusion.

Unknown, looked down upon, and indigent but yesterday, the author became in a few days a great man and a favourite of public opinion. Letters from admirers began to pour upon him in his solitude from all directions.

"Susceptible souls write me letters overflowing with enthusiasm; women offer me prescriptions for my diseases ; rich men, dinners ; landed proprietors, houses in the country ; authors, copies of their works ; society folk, their good offices, their patronage, and even money. I accept none of all these things except the simple testimony of their good will."

And Bernardin added artlessly: "If the clergy offer me a pension I will accept it with gratitude, I who have lived hitherto solely on the king's benefactions." There was, in truth, a time when the clergy entertained the curious scheme of adopting Bernardin as an opponent of Buffon and the Encyclopedist party, and of paying him a pension as their advocate. It was a mere notion which a little reflection cut short. But the favour of society went on increasing, and infected all classes, even the highest. Queen Marie Antoinette, dining with Madame de Polignac, quoted the *Études,* apropos of the East Indian birds, "some of which have red breasts in the mating season, as if they were arrayed in dress clothes supplied by nature only for the honeymoon." That was a remark calculated to impress a young and beautiful queen.

Madame de Coislin, one of the most considerable and most refined women of the old Court, invited the author to call upon her. While he enjoyed these tardy but sincere testimonials, he was not seduced by them; he withdrew more and more out of reach of the whirlpool, and bought a little hermitage near the Barrière du Jardin-du-Roi, on Rue de la Reine-Blanche. "He has gone to live," said Chamfort (who was then quartered at the Hôtel de Vaudreuil), "in a quarter so out of the way and inhabited by such a low class of people, that those who are interested in him are alarmed for his safety." "I do not know," Bernardin retorted, "whether M. de Chamfort knows anybody who is interested in me. When I came to live in the quarter of the poor, I put myself in the place in which I had long been classified." [1] His wound was not yet healed despite the sweets of success and the public recompense of his labours. "You see only the flower"; he said to those who congratulated him; "the thorn has remained in my nerves." Nevertheless, in the midst of this half-assuaged suffering, he pursued his course, and in 1788 he published the fourth volume of the *Études,* which contained *Paul et Virginie.* [2]

[1] Bernardin never went into society except against his will. He was always sensitive and constrained there. Here is an anecdote which I had at first hand, and which probably belongs to a somewhat later date; in it we see how eagerly the fair sex sought the author of so many delightful pages and failed to find him. I allow the witness of the incident to use his own words:

" Bernardin de Saint-Pierre was at Malmaison, at Madame Lecoulteux du Moley's; he exhibited himself in as unamiable a light as Abbé Delille was amiable; he made disagreeable remarks to the ladies and about them. He had brought a dog with him that was taken sick. Madame Lecoulteux was troubled about him and had him nursed and drugged; but the beast died. One morning, as Bernardin did not come down at the breakfast hour, the mistress of the house sent to his room to make inquiries. They found no one in his room,—only a short note in which he said that they had killed his dog and he had gone. Thereupon that amiable and sentimental company was deeply moved; they conceived the idea of having a funeral for the cherished dog and interring him in a little grave, with a branch of weeping willow *à la Jean-Jacques*. They wrote all this to the sulky boor, to appease him; they got no reply."

[2] It was published separately, immediately after, in innumerable editions.

That simple tale is Bernardin's really immortal work;
one cannot reread it without tears, and that is true of
so few books that are popular at their birth.[1]  I will
not repeat here an analysis that has been made so
many times; let us shun commentaries longer than
the poem itself.  Here everything—almost everything
—is perfect; simple, modest and affecting, tranquil and
enchanting.  The metaphors blend with the narrative
and crown each portion of it with perfect judgment,
with no appearance of effort, and no attempt to compel
admiration.  All the harmonies, all the contrasts, all
the reflections, of which he had so much to say in the
*Études,* and of which he drew a somewhat vague poetic description,—all these are made real here, in an
appropriate frame, where, at the outset, the location,
the names of places, the varied aspects of the landscape are calculated to arouse presentiments and to
contribute to the emotion evoked by the ensemble.
The thing that sets this lovely pastoral apart for all
time is that it is true, with a human and palpable reality: the graces and sports of childhood are not succeeded by an imaginary and fabulous youth.  From
the moment that Virginie feels that she is excited by
an unfamiliar malady, and her lovely blue eyes are

---

[1] ["One day, at Madame Necker's," says Sainte-Beuve in another
place, "Bernardin de Saint-Pierre, then hardly known, tried to read
*Paul et Virginie;* it is a simple story and the reader's voice trembled;
everybody else yawned, and after quarter of an hour, M. de Buffon,
who had a loud voice, called out to the footman : ' Tell them to put
the horses to my carriage ! ' "—TR.]

"streaked with black," we are plunged in passion; and this fascinating little book, which Fontanes, a little too tritely, placed between *Télémaque* and the *Mort d'Abel,* I should place between *Daphnis and Chloe* and the immortal fourth book of the Æneid, in honour of Dido. The true Virgilian genius breathes therein. Toward the end, in the heartrending scene of the storm, Bernardin demonstrated that his brush had at its command, when he chose, strong and solemn colours, and that he knew how to depict nature in the sublimity of her horrors no less than in her beauties. For all analysis, then, let us read *Paul et Virginie* once more, and, if we wish to realise its worth more fully, let us try to read *Atala* immediately after; there is a complete lesson in natural rhetoric in the comparative impression that will result.

To a person who should have asked him if he himself were not the old colonist of *Paul et Virginie* (in whose mouth the tale is put), Bernardin might have made the same reply that Rousseau once made to him when he asked him if Saint-Preux were not himself: "No, he is not altogether what I was, but what I would have liked to be." In the whole speech of the colonist, " And so I pass my days far from mankind," etc., he drew his own ideal portrait and his dream of the happy close of life. But, apart from this somewhat too amiable portrait of himself, I think that there are no portraits in *Paul et Virginie;* the characters,

lifelike as they are, are wholly of the painter's creation.  Some far-off resemblances to persons whom
he had met in his earlier days have been noticed, but
it is in the names alone that the reminiscence, the
echo, so to speak, is perceptible.  In Russia Bernardin
might have married Mademoiselle de la Tour, niece of
General du Bosquet; in Berlin he might have married
Mademoiselle Virginie Taubenheim; pleasant remem-
brances led him to combine the two names in that of
the dearest creation of his fancy.[1]  Being too poor he
had thought that he ought not to accept the hand of
either.  Benign munificence! lo, in this single offering
he paid them both the marriage portion of genius.
The name of Paul, too, not without design, happens
to have belonged to an excellent monk, whose life he
determined, in his childhood, to imitate, and whom
he used to accompany in alms-seeking expeditions.

The Revolution, sweeping through his life and subjecting it to new tests just when he thought that he
was safely in port, did not prevent Bernardin from
dreaming, or from pursuing the peaceful development
of his theories.  He continued to listen to the harmony of the spheres, to believe and to say that "the
human race is progressing toward perfection; that our
forefathers passed through the age of iron, and that
the age of gold lies before us."  His pen and his imagination concurred in these views, and the reality did

---

[1] [It will be remembered that Virginie is the daughter of Madame de
la Tour.—Tr.]

not embarrass him. He formed very accurate judgments, however, on particular facts; he remarks somewhere that "the majority of men obey fear alone." But in his study he reverted to the theory of universal benevolence and love.

In 1792, when he was fifty-five years of age, he married a young woman of twenty-two, Mademoiselle Félicité Didot, and in his correspondence with her we find him exclusively intent, as always, upon realising his project of a lonely island and a cabin. He was for some time superintendent of the Jardin-du-Roi; but he was not allowed to retain that post.[1] Appointed professor of morals at the École Normale, which was hurriedly instituted in the year III, he appeared two or three times in his chair, and was applauded for the least word he spoke. He deemed himself fortunate, however, when the approaching close of the school set him free from that duty of public speech, for which he was little fitted. Established at Essone, he there lost his first wife, who left him two children, named as of right Paul and Virginie, and who also bequeathed to him some unpleasant quarrels with her family.

Married a second time, at the age of sixty-three, to Mademoiselle Désirée de Pellepore, a young and attractive person who readily adapted herself to his

---

[1] [In 1791 his name was included by the National Assembly in a list from which a governor of the Prince Royal was to be chosen.— Tr.]

tastes, Bernardin de Saint-Pierre had a happy old age.
His letters, even to the very end, bear witness to his
joyous imagination. "I am an old tree," he said,
"that bears young twigs." He had exchanged his
hermitage at Essone for another retreat at Eragny, on
the banks of the Oise; there he lost himself in the
pleasing speculations with which he filled his *Harmonies*. He flattered himself that we should go some
day to the sun, where, as the reward of a virtuous
life, we should enjoy the marvellous spectacle of all
creation; he saw in his Paradise the plenitude and
triumph of his physical system.

There are some very pretty passages in Bernardin's
letters to his second wife; a sincere love of the country breathes in every line. Speaking of a change of
the moon and of violent rains in the month of May,
he writes to her: "This abundance of rain hastens
the growth of the vegetation; it is essential to its
progress and its needs; the month of May is a child
that wants the breast all the time. I embrace you,
my love, my joy, my month of May." Is not this
"month of May always wanting the breast," a most
charming and most eloquent image, especially when
addressed to a young wife and mother?

When he comes to Paris for the sessions of the Insti-
tute, Bernardin is always less contented. One day he
was present when they were discussing, as usual, the
Dictionary, that Penelope's web of the language.
Under the word *Appartenir* they had put as an ex-

ample: *Il appartient au père de châtier ses enfants.*[1]
At that Bernardin protests, he rebels, and thinks it
most surprising that when there are so many cherished ties between a father and his children, they must
needs choose the most hateful of all,—the one by virtue
of which he chastises them.

"Thereupon Morellet the stern, Suard the pallid, Parny the erotic,
Naigeon the atheist, and others, all quoting Scripture and all shouting
at once, attacked me with quotations and joined forces against me,
according to their custom. Then I got excited in my turn, and told
them that their quotations were worthy of pedants and school-teach-
ers, and that, even if I were alone in my opinion, I would maintain it
against them all. They took a vote, all raising their hands in the air,
and, when they applauded their very large majority, I told them that
I challenged their competency because they were all bachelors."

To be a bachelor was, in his eyes, a vice, and of the
greatest detriment; he had by instinct the morals of
the Patriarchs. Even when he is most kindly treated
and made much of on his trips to Paris, when every
one caresses him and tries to detain him, Bernardin
sighs none the less for his country solitude. He feels
that life is flying, that the last pages that he has to
write are calling him away, and he writes ingenuously
to his young wife:

"I am like the beetle in the grain-field, living happily with his
family in the shadow of the harvest; but if a ray of the rising sun
makes the emerald and gold of his wings glisten, then the children
spy him out, lay hands on him, shut him up in a little cage, and suf-
focate him with sweets and flowers, thinking to make him happier by
their caresses han he was in nature's bosom."

Thus Bernardin lived and grew old, not unhappily,

[1] "It is the father's place to chastise his children."

in his retirement at Eragny.   There he put the finishing touches to his last book, *Les Harmonies,* which
was not published until after his death, in 1814.   He
ceased to live on January 21st of that year.   *Les
Harmonies* presents some very beautiful pictures, as
beautiful as in any of his earlier works, but it is marked
also by all the exaggerations of theory and style natural to the author, in which his old age took especial
delight.   He rejects no dream, provided that it coin-
cides ever so little with his views, and he abandons
himself to it thenceforth, with method and at the
same time with a sort of frenzy; we find ourselves in
the very heart of the mysticism of nature.   For instance, among other astounding enormities, he says
this, without a quaver, on the subject of the sun:

"If it were permissible for a being of such limited powers as myself to venture to extend his speculations to a planet which I have not
even had the good fortune to look at through a telescope, I should say
*that its substance must be gold,* in the first place because gold is the
heaviest of all known substances, which is most appropriate for the
sun, occupying the centre of our universe."

The perusal of *Les Harmonies,* if prolonged, produces a singular effect, which I cannot express better
than by saying that it is enervating and that it turns
the stomach.   The best reading after laying this book
aside, the most direct antidote to take, is Pascal, who
causes the eternal spirit of contradiction in man to cry
aloud at every instant, and who, in his powerful and
unadorned language, is the least Asiatic of writers.

From this very imperfect study, which, however, is based upon more reading and more comparisons than I have been able to adduce here, it seems to me to result that Bernardin de Saint-Pierre, in his life, was only half a sage, and that, in his writings, he went astray almost as often as he hit the mark. But on one occasion he had a simple and perfect inspiration, he followed it with docility and produced it in its entirety, as if under the sun's rays; therein he deserved that his memory should remain for ever distinct and be constantly renewed, and that around that masterpiece, *Paul et Virginie,* literary interest should collect every one of the widely dispersed charms of the writer.

# Frederick the Great.

1712–1786.

# Frederick the Great.

T HE writings of Frederick have not heretofore[1] obtained the high esteem that they deserve. It has been the fashion to make sport of some wretched verses written by that poetry-mad prince, which are no worse, after all, than much verse of the same time which was considered delightful then, and which cannot be read to-day; and too little attention has been paid to the serious works of the great man, who would not resemble other great men if he had not actually affixed his seal to the numerous pages of politics and history which he wrote, and which form an immense whole. As for Frederick's letters, more justice has been done them; on reading in Voltaire's correspondence those which the king addressed to him mingled with those that he received in reply, we find not only that they bear the proximity quite well, but that, in all fairness, they are marked by a superiority of insight and of sense which is due to strength of mind and of character. To-day it behooves us to lay aside once for all these petty ideas of a rhetoric far too literary in its essence, in order that we

[1] [Written in 1850.—Tr.]

may recognise the king and the man in the writer, and salute in him one of the best historians that we possess.

I say "we," for Frederick wrote in French, he thought in French, his mind was often upon the French people, and it was to them that he applied, to be read, even when he penned opinions and narratives of events which were so unlikely to be pleasant reading to them. As a prose writer Frederick is a disciple of our best authors, and in history he is a pupil, and assuredly a unique and original pupil, of the historian of the *Siècle de Louis XIV*.

Despite the injury that he inflicted upon himself by certain of his rhapsodies and his speeches, by the ostentatious cynicism of his impiety and his ill-timed pleasantry, and by the mania for versifying that always arouses a smile, Frederick was a truly great man, one of those rare geniuses who are manifestly born to be the leaders and guides of nations. When we divest his personality of all the anecdotic nonsense which is the favourite feast of frivolous minds, and go straight to the man and his character, we pause with a sentiment of admiration and respect; we recognise instantly and at every step that we take in his company a superior and a master, steadfast, sensible, practical, active, and unwearying; with sufficient originality to keep pace with his needs; discerning, never deceived, deceiving as little as possible, constant in all sorts of fortune, overcoming his private affections and his

FREDERICK THE GREAT
*After the painting by Pesne*

passions by his ardent patriotism and his zeal for the grandeur and usefulness of his nation; enamoured of glory while estimating it at its true value; careful and vigilant, and desirous of the betterment, the honour, and the well-being of the peoples intrusted to his care, although he has little esteem for mankind in general.

As a captain it is not for me to judge him; but if I rightly understand Napoleon's remarks upon Frederick's campaigns, and the simple narrative of Frederick himself, it seems to me that he was not a warrior before all else. In that respect there is nothing resplendent, nothing captivating about him at first sight. Often beaten, often at fault, his grandeur consisted in learning by dint of schooling, and above all in repairing his errors, or those of fortune, by coolness, tenacity, and an imperturbable equanimity. However warmly good judges may praise his battle of Leuthen, and some of his great manœuvres and operations, they find still more to criticise on many and many an occasion. "He was especially great at critical moments," said Napoleon; "that is the noblest praise that we can bestow upon his character."

This moral strength is what stands out in Frederick more distinctly than his soldierly abilities, and will always remain far superior to them; he was a finely tempered soul and a noble spirit, who applied himself to war because he was obliged to, and not because he was a born warrior. He had neither the rapid and overwhelming valour of a Gustavus Adolphus or a Condé, nor that transcendent geometrical talent which characterised Napoleon, and which that mighty genius applied to war with the same ease and the same amplitude of range with which Monge applied it to other subjects. Endowed with a superior mind, and with a temperament and a will in harmony with his mind, Frederick devoted himself to military science as he did to many other things; and he very soon excelled in it, mastered it, and perfected in his own hands its instruments and methods, although it was not perhaps in his case, at the outset, the vocation of a genius fully adapted to it, and although he was not at first quite in his element.

Nature had made him to reign, first of all, to be a king, with all the qualities which that lofty station demands; and military science being one of the most indispensable of those qualities, he gave his mind to it and mastered it. "One must acquire the spirit of his trade," he wrote jestingly to Voltaire, at the height of the Seven Years' War. That seems to be only a jest, but it is true. In Frederick the will and the temperament guided the mind in everything.

It has been attempted to establish a contradiction between Frederick's spoken and written words as an adept of philosophy, and his acts as king and conqueror. To my mind this contradiction is not so great as some have attempted to make it. I omit from consideration some early efforts and sallies of

Frederick when he was Crown Prince and a very
young man; but from the instant that he realised the
importance of his rôle as king, I find the whole man
in harmony with himself, and I find that he rings
true. For example, I cannot discover in his histories
a word that he did not justify in his conduct and in
his life.

" A prince," he said and thought, " is the first servitor and the first
magistrate of the State; he owes it an account of the use that he
makes of the taxes; he levies them so that he may be able to defend
the State by means of the troops that it maintains; that he may sustain the dignity with which he is invested, reward services and desert,
establish in some degree equilibrium between the rich and the debt-
ridden, and relieve the unfortunate in every class and of every sort;
that he may invest with splendour whatever interests the whole body
politic. If the sovereign has an enlightened mind and an upright
heart, he will turn all his outlay to the public benefit, and to the
greatest advantage of his people."

That is what Frederick really did, in peace, in war,
on almost every occasion, and he departed from it as
little as was possible. When we have discounted his
mistakes, his ambitions, and his personal failings, the
sum and substance of his policy are always what we
have just read, what he has so well marked out. To
judge him as a politician, it is proper to divest ourselves of the French point of view, of French illusions,
and of such influence as the Choiseul ministry may
still possess among us. Open Frederick's *Mémoires*
once more; in writing them he makes no attempt to
gloss over the truth. I know no man who is less of
a charlatan, with his pen in hand, than he; he gives

his reasons and does not colour them in the least.
" A borrowed rôle is difficult to sustain," he thought;
" one is never comfortable except in one's own proper
person." While writing the history of his family, under
the title of *Mémoires de Brandebourg,* he gives us the
first inspiration, the meaning, and the key of his acts.
Prussia did not really reach the point of counting for
anything in the world, and of putting, as he expresses
it, her *grain* in the political balance of Europe, until
the time of the Great Elector, the contemporary of
the glorious days of Louis XIV. In telling the story
of that clever and gallant sovereign, who "was gifted
with the power to combine the courage and the
meritorious qualities of a great king with the moderate fortune of an elector"; in what he says of that
prince, "the honour and glory of his family, the defender and restorer of the fatherland," who was far
greater than his surroundings, and from whom his
posterity date their beginnings, we feel that Frederick
has found his ideal and his model: what the Great
Elector was as a simple prince and member of the
Empire, he would fain be as king.

That title of king, which was first given to the
Great Elector's son, and only as a matter of favour,
seemed rather to have depressed the Prussian name
than to have exalted it. The first Frederick who bore
it, a slave of ceremonial and etiquette, had made the
title of Majesty almost ridiculous in his person; he
was crushed by it. This first King of Prussia, by his

whole life of vain pomp and ostentation, said unwittingly to his posterity: "I have acquired the title, and I am proud of it; it is for you to make yourselves worthy of it." Frederick's father, of whom his son, whom he so maltreated, spoke so admirably and in a tone, not filial, but truly royal and magnanimous,—that vulgar, saving, niggardly father, torturer of his own children, and idolatrous worshipper of discipline,—a man of merit nevertheless, with "a laborious mind in a robust body,"—had restored to the Prussian State the strength which the grandiloquence and vanity of the first king had caused it to lose. But this was not enough: Frederick's father, an estimable man near at hand in many respects, was not respected at a distance; his very moderation and the simplicity of his manners had injured him. His eighty thousand troops were considered to be kept merely for show, —a corporal's mania for empty ostentation. Prussia was not reckoned among the Powers, and when Frederick, at the age of twenty-eight (1740), ascended that throne which he was destined to occupy for forty-six years, he had everything to do for the nation's honour and his own; he had to create Prussian honour, he had to win his spurs as king.

His first thought was that "a prince must compel respect for his own person, and above all for his nation; that moderation is a virtue which statesmen should not always practise strictly, because of the corruption of the age; and that, upon a change of reign, it is more fitting to give proofs of firmness than of mildness." He thought also, and he tells us frankly, that

" Frederick I. [his grandfather], when he raised Prussia to a kingdom, had, by virtue of that empty grandeur, planted the seed of ambition in his posterity, which must germinate sooner or later. The monarchy that he left to his descendants was, if I may so express myself [it is still Frederick who is speaking], a sort of *hermaphrodite,* which had more of the character of an electorate than of a kingdom. There was glory to be won in deciding which it should be; and that feeling was surely one of those which strengthened the king in the great enterprises to which so many motives impelled him."

He tells us what those motives were, and why he anticipated the house of Austria, instead of waiting for it to act and allowing himself to be beaten or humbled. He explains later with the same clearness and frankness the reasons which led him to take the initiative in the Seven Years' War, and decided him to appear to be the aggressor when he was not. These reasons, all derived from the best interests of his cause and his people, contain nothing that seems inconsistent with Frederick's maxims and his favourite ideas, both as philosopher and as writer. Knowing, as he knew, the men and affairs of this world, he realised that it is not allowable to be a bit of a philo- sopher on the throne until one has demonstrated that he knows how to be something very different. He was not of a temperament to play the devil-may- care rôle of a Stanislas. In order to be in greater security the shepherd of his people, he began by showing other nations that he was a lion. Whatever he wished to do, he did; he defined boldly the position and functions of Prussia, created a counterpoise to the house of Austria, and made of Northern Germany a centre of civilisation, of culture, and of toleration. It is for his successors to maintain it, and to be loyal, if they can, to his spirit.

All those who have spoken in praise of Frederick have always made an exception of his conduct in respect to Poland and the partition of 1773, which he incited, and by which he profited. On this point I shall beg leave to be silent, the question of Poland not being one of those which can be treated comfortably and with entire impartiality. There is in the very name of Poland and in the misfortunes which are connected with it a remnant of magic which sets men's minds aflame. Frederick, by the way, never varied in his opinion of the character of the Poles as a nation; that opinion is forcibly expressed in a dozen passages of his histories, long before the idea of partition was born.

Under the circumstances, however, and however much truth there may have been in the motives which he himself set forth in all their nakedness, he violated what the ancients called " the conscience of the human race," and he took part in one of those scandalous deeds which always shake the confidence of peoples in the laws that protect society. He forgot his own maxim: " The reputation of a knave is as injurious to the prince himself as it is disadvantageous to his interests." But in this case the momentous interests of the present and the future, and the natural instinct of aggrandisement, carried him away. And therein he was not so inconsistent as one might think. His sense of delicacy as a philosopher was not so refined that it could not reconcile itself to such political measures. With comparatively equitable, and even humane sentiments, Frederick absolutely lacked idealism, as did his whole age; he did not believe in anything that was of superior worth to himself. He guided and overlooked most energetically the men who were intrusted to his care; he staked his honour and his dignity upon the performance of that duty; but he based it upon no higher motive. And there we touch upon the radical defect of this sagacity of Frederick's—I mean irreverence, *irreligion*. We are familiar with the cynical mockery of his conversation and his letters; he had the capital fault, for a king, of jesting and making sport of everything, even of God. Love of glory was the only theme upon which he never jested.[1]

[1] A most competent judge, one of M. Preuss's collaborators in editing Frederick's works, M. Charles de La Harpe, writes me on the subject of this sentence: " There are two other subjects on which he never jested,—love of the fatherland, and friendship. That quizzical hero was the most affectionate and most loyal of friends, and every one knows that his passionate love for his country was so intense that he deprived himself of everything in order to obtain the means of relieving the sufferings of his subjects and of endowing Prussia with beneficial institutions."

Strange inconsistency of a noble nature! for if the human race is so stupid and so deserving of contempt, and if there is nothing nor anybody above it, why devote oneself, body and soul, to the dream of glory, which is nothing else than desire and expectation of the highest esteem among men ? It is incredible that, viewing everything, as he did, from the higher standpoint of the State and of the interest of society, Frederick should have looked upon religion as one of those neutral grounds, where people can agree to meet for after-dinner recreation and persiflage. He forgot that he himself, writing to Voltaire, said: "Every man has a savage beast within himself; few know how to secure him, the majority let go the curb when fear of the laws does not restrain them." His nephew, William of Brunswick, ventured one day to call his attention to the inconsistency of relaxing thus the religious bonds which hold the savage beast in check. "Oh!" rejoined Frederick, "against criminals I have the hangman, and that is enough."

Even if we leave the interest of the sovereign out of the account, it is distasteful to see a great man debase himself by jests of this sort, aimed at objects that are venerable in the eyes of the great majority; it was in a certain sense a violation of that hospitable toleration upon which he prided himself, thus to express aloud his contempt for what he pretended to welcome and tolerate. It has a savour of innate lack of refinement and of northern vulgarity, and a critic

was justified in saying, with merited severity, of
Frederick's letters, "There are some vigorous and
noble thoughts, but beside them may be seen stains
of beer and tobacco-juice on these pages of Marcus
Aurelius."

I propose to say no more of Frederick to-day except
as a historian. His histories consist of the *Mémoires
de Brandebourg*, which contain all that it is important
to know of the annals of Prussia prior to his accession,
and of four other works which contain the history of
his times and his reign, from 1740 to 1778. The history of the Seven Years' War is one of these four, the
one by virtue of which he takes his place naturally between Napoleon and Cæsar.

The *Mémoires de Brandebourg* alone appeared in
his lifetime. From the preface it is apparent that we
have to do with a lofty and resolute mind, which has
the noblest and soundest ideas upon the subject treated.
"A man who does not believe that he has fallen from
the skies," he says, "who does not date the beginning
of the world from the day of his birth, should be curious to learn what has taken place in all times and in
all lands." Every man ought at least to be interested
in what has taken place before his time in the land
wherein he dwells. In order that this knowledge
should be of real benefit, one condition is indispensable, —truth. Frederick insists upon truth in history.
"A work written without perfect freedom can be only
mediocre or bad." So that he proposes to tell the truth

about people, about others' ancestors as well as his own. But he considers it his duty to record only what is memorable or useful on every subject. He has nothing to say upon matters of mere curious interest. He leaves it to professors in *us,* enamoured of the trivialities of erudition, to find out of what material the coat of Albert, surnamed Achilles, was made. He is decidedly of the opinion that "a thing does not deserve to be written except in so far as it deserves to be remembered."

He runs rapidly over the barbarous, barren days, and over those of his ancestors of whom we know only the names or some anecdotes devoid of significance. "These are some histories," he says, "like rivers, which become important only when they begin to be navigable." He chooses French in preference to any other language, because "it is," he says, "the most refined language in Europe and the most widely known, and because it seems to be in some measure made stable by the excellent authors of the reign of Louis XIV." He might have added,—"and because it is best adapted to express the thoughts of a lucid, sensible, and determined genius."

When he comes to the period of the Reformation, of the Thirty Years' War, the historian-king defines in a few words those momentous events by their general features and in their real essence; always and everywhere he distinguishes the substance from the mere accessories. When he falls in with the horrors of devastation which mark those depressing periods of history, he manifests sentiments of humanity and of orderly government, in which there is no affectation and which he afterwards put in practice.

I have said that the type that he sets before himself, the man from whom he justly dates the real grandeur of his house, is Frederick William, called the Great Elector,—the man who took Brandenburg in hand, at the end of the disastrous Thirty Years' War, "which had transformed the electorate into a ghastly desert, where the villages could be recognised only by the heaps of ashes which prevented the grass from growing there." He dilates upon that reign with pleasure; he even goes so far as to venture to draw a parallel between that princeling of the North and Louis XIV in his glory; aside from two or three rather ornate and too mythological passages, and aside from a slightly oratorical tone that is apparent here and there, this comparison constitutes a noble page of history, and a passage of genuine elevation of mind.

It is to be observed that Frederick, when he has his pen in hand, while he is always exact, is less grave than Cæsar, or even than Napoleon; he does not forbid himself the display of talent, properly so-called, especially in this first history, of which Gibbon was able to say that it was "well written." Having to describe the campaign of 1679, during which the Great Elector, in midwinter, drove out the Swedes who had invaded Prussia, he says: "The retreat of the

Swedes resembled a rout; of sixteen thousand scarcely three returned to Livonia. They entered Prussia like Romans, they went thence like Tartars."

His judgment of men is profound and decisive. He has an evident penchant for heroes; he speaks always with respect, and with an instinctive feeling of noble fraternity, of the Gustavus Adolphuses, the Marlboroughs, and the Eugenes; but he does not misapprehend real grandeur, and is never lavish of the word. Queen Christina, with her whimsical abdication, seems to him simply "odd"; the duel between Charles XII and Peter the Great at Pultowa seems to him a duel between "the two strongest men of their age." Foreigner as he is, he has the art to select his words with an accuracy which measures the language or bends it to his thought.

To depict the characters of statesmen, of ministers, he employs lofty and authoritative expressions of the sort that are historical in anticipation and that engrave themselves upon the memory. The portraits of people whom he has known and handled are dashed off with the hand of a master, and as if by one who was quick, or even predisposed, to seize upon vices or absurdities. To give an idea of General von Seckendorff, who served the Emperor and Saxony at the same time, he said: "He was sordidly selfish; his manners were vulgar and countrified; falsehood was so habitual to him that he had lost the use of the truth. He had the soul of a usurer, which passed sometimes into the body of a soldier, and again into that of a negotiator." And observe that this is not in the shape of a portrait, as in some histories, more or less literary, where the historian poses before his model; it is said *au courant,* as by a historian by profession who thinks aloud.

When he approaches the affairs of his own time, those in which he had a share, and which he directed, Frederick maintains the same tone, or, rather, he assumes an even simpler tone than in his history of Brandenburg. In speaking of himself he is neither overweening nor modest; he is true. In speaking of others, even his greatest enemies, he is just. At the beginning of his reign, in telling the story of the conquest of Silesia, which aroused so much wrath, and which succeeded so entirely to his satisfaction, he exposes his motives without disguise; he points out his mistakes, and his *schooling* in war. Side by side with the measures and schemes dictated by far-sighted audacity, he recognises what he owes to " opportunity, that fruitful mother of great events," and he is careful to assign on every occasion due credit to fortune.

" The thing that contributed most effectively to that conquest," he says, " was an army which had been trained for twenty-two years by admirable discipline, and was superior to all the rest of the soldiery of Europe [*observe the compliment to his father*] ; generals who were loyal citizens, wise and incorruptible ministers, and lastly a certain amount of good luck which often waits upon youth and denies itself to advanced age. If this great undertaking had failed, the king would have been looked upon as a reckless prince who had undertaken something beyond his strength; its success caused him to be looked upon

as no less skilful than lucky.   In reality it is luck alone that decides
a man's reputation; he whom it favours is applauded; he whom it
spurns is blamed."

The history of the Seven Years' War is admirable
in its simplicity and its fidelity to truth.   The author
does not confine himself to the general result of the
strategical operations, he includes a sketch of all the
Courts of Europe during that period.   In his narrative of the events of the war he is grave and ex-
peditious, passing over special details except in a small
number of cases where he cannot refrain from paying
a tribute of gratitude to his brave troops or to some
gallant comrade in arms.   I commend to the reader
the sixth chapter, which deals with the campaign of
1757, that campaign so replete with vicissitudes and
changes of fortune, in which Frederick, driven to bay,
won his easy and brilliant victory at Rosbach, and his
scientific and *classical* victory at Leuthen.   If we
supplement his noble and fluent narrative with the
letters that he wrote to Voltaire during the same time,
we shall be present at the most splendid moment of
Frederick's career, at the crisis from which he emerged
with the most heroic and glorious perseverance.   In
that crisis it is that we really recognise the philosopher
and the stoic in the man of war.   The most severe
criticism that he ever made upon the House of Austria
was that " it followed the brutish impulses of nature;
swollen with pride in prosperity and crawling in the
dust in adversity, it has never succeeded in attaining

that judicious moderation which makes man impassive to good and evil alike, as chance may decree."
For his own part he is determined never to yield,
even in the greatest extremity, to chance or to brute
nature, and so to persevere in the path marked out
by great souls as to make Fortune blush for shame at
last.

At the conclusion of that war in which so much
blood was shed, and after which everything in Germany was replaced on the same footing as before, devastation and ruin excepted, Frederick is pleased to
insist upon the feebleness and vanity of human plans.
"Does it not seem surprising," he says, "that the
most subtle human prudence, combined with force, is
so often deceived by unexpected events or strokes of
fortune; and does it not seem that there is a certain
indefinable something which scornfully makes sport
of the schemes of mankind?" We recognise in this a
reminiscence of Lucretius in some of his noblest lines:

" Usque adeo res humanas vis abdita quaedam."

I have tried thus far to exhibit Frederick, the king
and politician, in his highest and most impassioned
form,—the Frederick of history, not of anecdote. It
was so that he himself thought that great men should
be definitively judged, without wasting time over mere
accessories, but occupying a standpoint high enough
to overlook their contradictions and oddities. However, Frederick's domestic and private life is fully

known; every part of his character stands in the
light; we have his letters, his poetry, his pamphlets,
sallies and jests, his confidences of every sort; he did
nothing to suppress them, and it is impossible not to
discover in him another most essential personality,
which goes to the very heart of the man. We may
say that, if the great king was *lined* with a philosopher, his individuality was further complicated with
a man of letters.

The great Cardinal de Richelieu was of the same
type: to write a fine tragedy would have been almost
as sweet to his heart, and would have seemed almost
as glorious an achievement as triumphing over the
Spaniards and supporting the allies of France in Germany; the laurels of *Le Cid* kept him from sleeping.
After the Seven Years' War, when d'Alembert visited
Frederick at Potsdam and spoke to him of his glory,
"he said to me," writes d'Alembert, "with the
utmost simplicity, that there was a tremendous dis-
count to be made from that same glory; that chance
was responsible for almost everything, and that he
would have preferred to have written *Athalie* rather
than to have fought that war." There is certainly
something of the philosopher in this way of looking
upon military triumphs; but there is also something
of the man of letters in this preference for *Athalie*.
I am not sure that Frederick would not have taken it
back if some mischievous genie had taken him at his
word and he had been forced to choose between the

Seven Years' War and *Athalie;* or, rather, I am quite
sure that the king would, in the end, have carried the
day; but the heart of the poet would have bled in-
ternally, and it is enough for the purpose of our
interpretation of his character, that he might have
hesitated even for an instant.

When we study Frederick in his writings, in his
correspondence (especially in that with Voltaire), we
observe, it seems to me, one fact that rests on strong
evidence: there was in him a man of letters antedating all the rest, even the king. What he was by
nature before everything else, and, if one may so express it, most artlessly of all, was a man of letters, a
dilettante, a virtuoso, with an ardent love of the arts
and with a passionate adoration of intellect. He had
only to abandon himself to his own inclinations, to
expand in that direction.

His station as king, his love of eminent renown,
and the noble character with which he was endowed,
diverted his energies in other directions, which aimed
at achieving the social welfare and the grandeur of his
people; he considered that "a good mind is susceptible of all sorts of forms, that it brings to whatever it
undertakes a disposition to do its best. It is like a
Proteus, who changes his shape without difficulty
and seems to be in reality the object that he represents." Thus, he seems to have been born for all
that he would have to do as king; he was equal to
his task. "The strength of a State," he thought,

"consists in the great men whom Nature causes to be born therein at the opportune moment." He desired to be, and he was, one of those great men; he worthily performed his rôle of hero. The nation which the Great Elector had roughly sketched, he completed the construction of; he gave it a body and imprinted upon it unity of spirit; Prussia did not really exist until she came forth from his hands. Such was the rôle of Frederick the Great in history; but in reality, his secret taste (it can hardly be called secret), his real delight, was to argue on every subject, to follow out his philosophical ideas and also to put them on paper, sometimes seriously, sometimes in sport, as a rhymester and as a writer.

He was educated by a Frenchman, a man of merit, named Duhan, who implanted in him a love of our language and our literature. The thirst for glory, which Frederick's youthful heart cherished, naturally led him to turn his eyes toward France. The age of Louis XIV, now at an end, was gradually extending its influence over the whole of Europe. Brandenburg was lagging behind the other nations; there was nothing surprising in that, but Frederick felt humiliated, and said to himself that it was time for him to inaugurate the new era of regeneration in the North. So long as his father lived, this purely literary aspiration of Frederick prevailed over his other ideas and impelled him to measures, to overtures, wherein the future king forgot himself more or less.

As we have seen heretofore,[1] Frederick was twenty-eight years of age, and Crown Prince of Prussia, when he began his correspondence with Voltaire.

One delights to find, amid the insipidities and exaggerations, sometimes ridiculous enough, of the early part of this correspondence, more than one passage in which we may already detect the king that is to be, the man of superior mould, who, although he has the craze for rhyming and for publishing his first works, will be able to master it by means of a nobler passion, and who will never be a mere prattler on the throne. In everything, even in these diversions of the mind, Frederick always ends by giving the last word to action, to social utility, and the welfare of his fatherland; his genius is merely amusing itself while awaiting something better, and will continue to amuse itself and make merry in the intervals of sterner tasks; but will aspire, at all times, by dint of steadfast application, to make itself effective in practical and beneficial grandeur. There is a time for him to laugh, to play on the flute, to write poetry, and a time to reign. The man of letters may outweigh the king for some time and gambol before him, but only to give way to him whenever it is necessary, at the precise moment. We may say that no one of his talents, of his passions, or even of his manias, ever encroached upon one of his duties.

[1] [See vol. i., pp. 212-221, for Sainte-Beuve's discussion of the correspondence between Frederick and Voltaire.—Tr.]

From the standpoint of taste there are many things to be noticed. The rough and somewhat coarse nature of the Vandal makes itself felt in Frederick, even through the man of intellect and the dilettante eager to be instructed and to please. It is not alone that language and the fitting expression sometimes fail him,— often the refined touch is lacking. Whenever he mentions Madame du Châtelet to Voltaire, he has much difficulty in not appearing coarse or absurd. "I have too much respect for the bonds of friendship," he writes to him at Cirey, "to desire to tear you from *Émilie's arms.*" When he tries to be gallant, his conduct is marked by the same puerility. He can think of no more graceful compliment than to send Voltaire as a gift a bust of Socrates, the long-suffering sage *par excellence;* which might have seemed intended for an epigram, if he had known his poet better at the time. But Socrates reminds Frederick of Alcibiades, whence more than one equivocal and *risqué* allusion, into which, by the way, Voltaire does not disdain to enter. It required some time for that rough diamond to get rid of its dross.

However, Frederick speedily formed himself; he is taking shape perceptibly in this correspondence, and there comes a time when he has mastered his French prose and handles it in such fashion as really to hold his own with Voltaire. As for verse-writing, we must needs despair of him; in that direction his voice will always be raucous and harsh, and he will never

improve. Let us have done with the subject of poet-
ising. He was very well aware that the mania was a
weakness in him and almost an absurdity; that people
praised him to his face only to call him *Cotin* [1] behind
his back. " This man," said Voltaire one day, pointing
to a pile of papers belonging to the king, " this man,
do you see, is Cæsar and Abbé Cotin combined." An
eminent English historian, Lord Macaulay, improving
upon this conceit, has called Frederick a compound
of Mithridates and Trissotin.

Frederick knew or foresaw all this, and yet he
yielded to his ardour for making rhymes. When
he was very young, he fell madly in love with a
young woman who loved poetry, and it was then
that he was stung by the scorpion; and, although he
was thoroughly cured of one disease (that of loving
young women), he was never cured of the other. It
would be impossible to say anything to him by way
of remonstrance or reproach that he did not say to
himself a hundred times. " I am unfortunate enough
to love verses," he wrote, " and frequently to compose some execrable ones. The thing that ought to
disgust me with them, and that would repel any
sensible person, is the very spur that most incites me.
I say to myself, ' You poor little wretch! you have

---

[1] [Charles Cotin (1604-1682), a French ecclesiastic and author, and
member of the Académie. Having incurred the enmity of Boileau, he
was held up to ridicule by him, and especially by Molière, who satir-
ised him in *Les Femmes Savantes,* in the character of Trissotin.—
Tr.]

never succeeded as yet; courage!'" Elsewhere he says: "Whoever is not a poet at twenty will never become a poet as long as he lives. No man who was not born a Frenchman, or who has not lived in Paris for a long time, can possess the language in the degree of perfection that is necessary to write good poetry or elegant prose." He compares himself to the vines "which always smell of the earth in which they are planted." But, for all that, it amuses him, it diverts him and relaxes his mind in the intervals of momentous affairs; and so he will go on rhyming to the very end.

He also composed music in the Italian style,—solos by the hundred,—and he played the flute to perfection, it is said; which did not deter Diderot from saying, "It's a great pity that the mouthpiece of that beautiful flute is stopped up by grains of Brandenburg sand."

Frederick was an excellent judge of historians, who were his special material for study and meditation; but, when we find him lavishing the title of Thucydides on Rollin or even on Voltaire, we are compelled to admit that he seems to have no conception of the peculiar historical style which constitutes the originality of that great historian. He was better fitted to judge Polybius, in whom matter predominates over style. A critic of real merit (M. Egger) suggests to me that there are some genuine and quite striking similarities. The reflections with which Frederick brings to

a close his history of the Seven Years' War strongly
resemble a page of Polybius: "At a distance of two
thousand years there is the same method of viewing
human vicissitudes, and of explaining them as games
of skill blended with games of chance." But the historian-king is, generally speaking, more serious in his
reflections.

German literature is barely mentioned by Frederick;
he fully realises its failings, which were without compensation at that time,—heaviness, diffuseness, division into dialects,—and he points out some of the
remedies. He prophesies, however, the national literature of the glorious days that are drawing near:
"I announce their coming, they will soon appear."
He does not seem to suspect that they had, in truth,
begun to dawn toward the end of his life, and that
Goethe had already arrived. But can we wonder that
Frederick did not appreciate *Werther?*

Frederick's relations with d'Alembert were of an
entirely different character from his intimacy with
Voltaire; they were never so intense, but they were
enduring and stable. It was not simply a natural
predilection that drew Frederick toward d'Alembert.
"We princes," said the former, "are always led by
self-interest, and we never make acquaintances unless
we have some particular object in view, which tends
directly to our advantage." Frederick at an early day
conceived the project of inducing d'Alembert to come
to Berlin, in order to make him president of his Acad-

emy.   This project he considered more seriously after
the death of Maupertuis, and when he had seen
the last of the Seven Years' War.   I have before me the
unpublished manuscript collection of letters written
by d'Alembert to Mademoiselle de Lespinasse during his visit to the King of Prussia.   In June, 1763,
he joined Frederick, who was then in his province of
Westphalia, at Gueldres, and made the journey to
Potsdam in his suite.   D'Alembert had met the king
several years earlier; on seeing him again he was
amazed to find him superior even to his renown.
Frederick had the characteristic peculiar to great men,
that the first sight always exceeded anticipation.   He
began by talking with d'Alembert for four hours in
succession; he talked simply and modestly, of philosophy, literature, peace, war, and all sorts of things.
At that time, only three months after the conclusion of peace, Frederick had already rebuilt forty-five
hundred houses in ruined villages; two years later
(October, 1765), he had rebuilt no less than fourteen
thousand five hundred.

We remark first of all, as d'Alembert did, this ad-
ministrative and even pacific side in the man of war.
The amiable, familiar, and fascinating side is clearly
indicated in this narrative of our traveller: the sagacious and unassuming guest had neither the time nor
the desire to observe faults which often impaired that
groundwork of wisdom and charm.   Moreover, honours did not turn d'Alembert's head; he was touched,

but not intoxicated. When he passed through Brunswick, he dined at the table of the ducal family, and
they called him "Marquis"; he submitted to the
title after a faint remonstrance. Apparently, he said,
that was the etiquette. With Frederick there is no
etiquette, and everything goes off as with a private
individual who is also a genius. D'Alembert would
have had to exert himself very little to become necessary to Frederick by his conversation, just as Frederick
was to d'Alembert. It was no longer the period of
the brilliant supper-parties at Potsdam, the last fine
days of which Voltaire had seen and, indeed, been
instrumental in producing; the habitual guests of those
days, the friends of the king's youth, were dead or
very old at this second period. Not only was the
king the most attractive man in his realm; if we except Lord Marischal, he was the only one. "He is
almost the only person in the kingdom," says d'Alembert, "with whom one can converse,—at least in this
sort of conversation of which we know almost nothing
in France, and which becomes a necessity when one
is once familiar with it."

All Frederick's excellent qualities are made prominent in this narrative; and d'Alembert, always circumspect, is careful to see no others during his three
months' sojourn. He is able, however, to resist the
king's flattery and his delicate offers of service. One
day, when they were walking in the gardens of Sans-
Souci, Frederick plucked a rose and presented it to

him, saying: " I would be very glad to give you something better." This "something better" was the presidency of his Academy; it is curious to see the presidency of an academy and a rose thus brought into juxtaposition. D'Alembert retains his prudence, he remains the philosopher and friend to the end, and loyal to Mademoiselle de Lespinasse. He returns to France, grateful, won over to Frederick for ever, so far as his heart is concerned, but not conquered.

The whole truth must be told: several years later, Frederick was showing some verses of his one evening to Professor Thiébault, an excellent grammarian and academician whom d'Alembert had secured for him; and he carelessly allowed himself to produce a very pungent epigram which he had written against d'Alembert himself; the satirical monarch had been unable to deny himself the malign pleasure of commemorating some absurd foible that he had observed in that honourable character. That was a capital failing of Frederick's: he found it hard to refrain from making unpleasant remarks to people and from writing sharp things about them. In the present case he speedily repented of having shown Thiébault his epigram, and he enjoined silence upon him; the excellent d'Alembert never knew anything about it. But, surrounded as he was, in his intimate circle, by would-be clever courtiers, all more or less dull of wit, Frederick was less scrupulous with regard to them. As soon as he had discovered their weak

points, he thrust at them pitilessly through the loose
joints of their cuirass; he made them his butts, he
practised at displaying his contempt for mankind upon
them, and thus acquired a reputation for cruelty,
when it was, in reality, nothing more than scathing
criticism of society at large.

After his return to France d'Alembert continued to
correspond with Frederick; and, if we forget the epigram which was never made public, the correspondence on both sides gives evidence of sound sense, of
genuine philosophy, and even of friendship, so far as
friendship could exist in those days between a private
individual and a monarch.   D'Alembert, too, we must
not forget, had his failings; we know already that the
philosophers of the eighteenth century had little fondness for the liberty of the press except when it was at
their disposition.   One day d'Alembert was insulted by
some journalist or other who conducted the *Courrier
du Bas-Rhin,* in Frederick's own dominion.   He de-
nounced him to the King.   On this occasion it is
Frederick who is the true philosopher, the true citizen
of modern society, when he replies:

"I know that a Frenchman, a compatriot of yours, smears two
sheets of paper with ink at Clèves every week; I know that people
buy his sheet, and that an ass can always find a greater ass to read
him; but I have much difficulty in convincing myself that a writer of
that stamp can have any prejudicial effect on your reputation.   Ah!
my dear d'Alembert, if you were King of England, you would endure
many worse taunts with which your faithful subjects would supply
you, to test your patience.   If you knew what a multitude of infamous screeds your dear compatriots put forth against me during the

war, you would laugh at this wretched penny-a-liner. I did not
deign to read all the outpourings of my enemies' hatred and envy, but
I remembered Horace's fine ode: 'The wise man remains immovable.' " . . .

And he proceeds to paraphrase the *Justum ac tena-
cem.*

In this admirable lecture we recognise the disciple
of Bayle on the throne. Another day it will be the
disciple of Lucretius. D'Alembert is in distress, in
profound and perfectly natural distress: he has lost
Mademoiselle de Lespinasse, he is about to lose
Madame Geoffrin. That geometrician's heart, so susceptible of affection, does not hesitate to pour itself
out on Frederick's breast, to find a vent for its sorrows there, and almost to sob aloud; and the king
replies like a friend and like a wise man, with two
or three letters of philosophical consolation, which
should be quoted in full. An exalted and affectionate
epicureanism breathes therein, the epicureanism of a
Lucretius addressing his friend:

"I am sorry for the misfortune which has befallen you, of losing a
person to whom you were attached. The wounds of the heart are
the most sensitive of all wounds, and despite the fine maxims of the
philosophers, nothing but time can heal them. *Man is an animal
more sensitive than reasoning.* I have, to my misery, had only too
much experience of the suffering caused by such losses. The best
remedy is to put compulsion upon one's self in order to divert one's
mind from a painful vein of thought which is likely to take too deep
root. You should choose some geometrical investigation which demands constant application, in order to keep back, so far as it is pos-
ble to do so, the gloomy thoughts which incessantly recur to the mind.
I would suggest more effective remedies if I knew any such. Cicero,

to console himself for the death of his dear Tullia, threw himself into composition, and wrote several treatises, some of which have come down to us. Our reason is too weak to overcome the pain of a mortal wound; we must concede something to nature, and above all say to ourselves, that at your age and mine we should be the more readily consoled because we shall not long delay to join the objects of our regrets."

And he urges him to come and pass a few months with him as soon as he can. "We will philosophise together concerning the nothingness of life, concerning the philosophy of men, concerning the vanity of stoicism and of our whole existence." And he adds, with a mixture of warrior-king and philosopher which would seem contradictory if it were not so touching, that "he will feel as happy in allaying his grief as if he had won a battle."

Such letters surely redeem some asperities of style which may be found close beside them, and which remind us at intervals of the master's presence; they are a sufficient answer to those who, judging Frederick by his harsh sayings and his epigrams alone, deny that he ever, from beginning to end, felt any sentiment of affection, of humanity, or, I venture to say, of kindness, just as they deny that he formed any genuine and cordial friendships in his youth. For my part, from whatever side I view him, and even in the years when his failings manifest themselves most distinctly, I can come to no other than a favourable conclusion with respect to him, and I can only say, as Bolingbroke said of Marlborough, "He was such a great man that I have forgotten his vices."

In a select edition of Frederick's works, for the use of healthy minds and people of taste, I would include only his histories, two or three at most of his dissertations, and his correspondence; there would then be enough of his verses, which are scattered through his letters, without adding others. Thus we should have in all about ten volumes of strong, healthy, pleasant, and always instructive reading. Let us lay aside, as applied to Frederick, those names so often repeated, sometimes with insulting, sometimes with flattering intent,—the too equivocal names of the Emperor Julian and Marcus Aurelius. On the other hand, let us not seek out the names of Lucian, of whom he could offer only strange parodies and burlesques; but, if we would define him *classically,* let us define him as being in his best features a writer of the noblest character, whose nature is peculiar to himself, but who, in habits and cast of thought, resembles at the same time Polybius, Lucretius, and Bayle.

# Wilhelmina, Margravine of Baireuth.

1709–1758.

# Wilhelmina, Margravine of Baireuth.

THE Margravine of Baireuth, a princess of great intellect and worth, Frederick's older sister, and a true sister of his in thought and in heart, married to the Hereditary Prince of Baireuth and sadly out of place in that petty court, set out one day, in order to relieve the tedium of her existence, to write down all the sufferings, all the domestic persecutions, that she had known before, and even after, her marriage. She recurred at various times to this narrative told to herself, and continued it down to the day when she became margravine and when her brother ascended the throne. She had no well-defined design in devoting herself to this means of diverting her thoughts from her solitude.

"I write for my own amusement," she said, "and do not expect that these memoirs will ever be printed; perhaps I may sacrifice them to Vulcan some day, perhaps I shall give them to my daughter [1]; in fact I am a Pyrrhonian on that subject. I say again, I write solely for my own amusement, and I take pleasure in concealing nothing of all that has ever happened to me, even of my most secret thoughts."

---

[1] Her only daughter, who married the Duke of Würtemberg, and died without issue.

But, while writing down what has happened to hei,
she tells what others have done, what they have said
and plotted; she draws their pictures and shows them
without disguise in their intrigues, in their vices, in
their capricious or brutish dispositions, in the dense
and still uncivilised vulgarity which was the real
foundation of their natures. Side by side with the
wicked and corrupt ministers at whose hands she had
to suffer, she paints her kindred as well, whom she
prides herself upon holding in veneration,—the king
her father, the queen her mother, several of her sisters,
the king her brother, whom she loves devotedly, but
of whom she speaks with much bitterness in certain
passages, because the last part of her memoirs was
written when she was on ill terms with him.

When these memoirs were written, she confided them to a clever man, her physician, M. de
Superville, who did not remain in her service. Having given him the manuscript, she forgot it, no doubt;
momentous events supervened, which engrossed all
the last years of her life. The work slept fifty years
and more at the bottom of a casket; after which it
was printed (1810), and instantly became, in the eyes
of all men, one of those truthful, natural, and terrible
productions of the sort that is so dear to Posterity,
that great busybody and violator of seals, and of the
sort that families have great reason to dread.

The harm has been done, and let us make the most
of it. The Margravine of Baireuth, who had had a very

THE MARGRAVINE OF BAIREUTH
*After the painting by Sir Joshua Reynolds*

careful education, who knew the modern languages, history, and literature, and who could have written her memoirs in English as well as in German, wrote them in French, just as she always corresponded with her brother in French. Thus we have in her still another French writer, and a painter-writer altogether worthy of notice. It is interesting, by way of giving oneself the impression of an absolute contrast, but a contrast in which there is nothing offensive, to place her over against a Hamilton or a Caylus painting with malign delicacy the beauties of the Court of Charles II, or those of Marly or Versailles. We may also compare her in our minds to Madame de Staal de Launay, describing for us in her ingenious memoirs the trivialities and elegant crazes of the Court of Sceaux. The Margravine has to deal with a totally different subject-matter which she attacks with less ceremony. One who has not read the book can form no conception of the Gothic and Ostrogothic barbarity which she reveals in her *entourage ;* and, superior as she is to her subject, she has something of it in her style, and now and then it casts unpleasant reflections upon her and her manner. This young woman (for she began to write her memoirs at twenty-five) indulges in crudities of expression worthy of Saint-Simon when he is tearing people to tatters; and, from lack of opportunity no doubt, and because she does not know where to bestow it, she never atones by an act of grace.

And yet, if we succeed in mastering the disgust occasioned by the hideous nature of the characters introduced and their intrigues, and by that endless series of enormities and horrors, we shall realise with what raillery, what playfulness, and what happy turns of expression she writes. I will mention simply a portrait of the General-Minister Grumbkow, the hateful persecutor of Frederick and his sister: in his duel with the Prince of Anhalt, she shows him to us terrified and trembling, and recalls all the proofs that he had given of the same temperament, whether at the battle of Malplaquet, where he stayed in a ditch throughout the action, or at the siege of Stralsund, where he most opportunely dislocated a leg at the beginning of the campaign, which excused him from going into the trenches. "He had," she concludes, "the same misfortune as a certain king of France, who could not see a bare sword without falling in a swoon[1] ; but, with that exception, he was a very brave general." And elsewhere, describing the king, her father, who could not reconcile himself to the courteous and reserved manners of the Hereditary Prince of Baireuth, although he had selected him for her husband, "he wanted a son-in-law," she says, "who cared for nothing but the military, wine, and saving money."

[1] She was mistaken; no king of France ever had such a faint heart. She refers to James, King of England and Scotland, son of Mary Stuart, who owed that disposition, it is said, to the fact that the murder of Rizzio was done in the presence of his mother when she was pregnant.

Surely, in a society in which we imagine the Cay-
luses, the Hamiltons, the Grammonts, the Sévignés,
the Coulanges, the Saint-Simons, the Staal de Lau-
nays, and the Du Deffands gathered together, the
Margravine would not have been out of place or embarrassed; she would very soon have found a way to
pay her scot by many a shaft of wit and highly seasoned pleasantry, which would have been applauded
by all alike, men and women, just as her brother, in
conversation, could hold his own with Voltaire or
with anybody else in clever repartee. But to one who
reads her, having regard to the type and the nature of
her pictures, she retains her exotic colouring and
her foreign accent. Let us treat her, then, if not as a
Frenchwoman in a foreign land, at all events as a
friend of France, who, at the height of the Seven
Years' War, wrote to the same Voltaire, referring to
the French, then her declared foes: "I have a deuce of
an affection for them that prevents me from wishing
them ill."

But let us understand one thing: the correspondence between her and her brother, which Herr Preuss
has lately published, and the notes which that painstaking editor has supplied, prove that, although the
*Mémoires* of the Margravine of Baireuth may be sincere, they are not strictly accurate. She wrote them
in solitude, and sometimes in ill-humour. She con-
ceals some facts, she changes others, or rather they
become changed of themselves in her memory and her

mind, soured by ill-health and too constant disappointments. The system of checks which we are now able to establish between the Margravine's *Mémoires* and her authentic correspondence with Frederick enables us to judge some of her assertions more fairly. Frederick gains thereby, and she herself, although detected in misstatements, does not really lose. In fact, the elevation of heart and nobility of feeling which were inherent in her nature, and which are hidden in the *Mémoires* by the spirit of jesting and satire, make themselves more manifest in the letters: in them the Margravine puts her best and strongest qualities foremost, no longer as the sarcastic painter and caricaturist of her family, but rather as a passionate, loving, and, at need, heroic and noble-hearted woman, devoted to the honour of her house.

Born in 1709, and therefore her brother's senior by three years, she very soon came to love that brother above all things. Employed all day by her teachers, her only recreation was to be with him. " Never did affection equal ours," she says; " he was bright, but his disposition was gloomy; he would think a long while before replying, but, to make up for it, he always answered right. He learned with great difficulty, and we expected that as time went on he would have more good sense than wit." She protected him on all occasions; when the time came for him to study, she spurred him on by shaming him for neglecting his talents; she was his dearest confidante before he knew what evil was; she was his good genius.

Her own faculties seem to have been in no wise inferior to those of her so illustrious brother. She was of the race of "sisters of genius," who have a share of the same sacred fire from which the famous brother derives his flame, and who keep it pure and bright. Although most happily endowed intellectually, with a mind overflowing with knowledge and flashes of brilliancy, with a wonderful memory, with excellent and honourable principles, with a beautiful soul created for virtue; although she was pretty in her youth, before unhappiness wrecked her life, and adorned with all natural charms; she was nevertheless, from her childhood, one of the most unfortunate, the most cruelly maltreated persons to be found in any rank of society (I do not except the lowest), and she had, so long as she lived, a life of suffering and torment, with very few pleasant moments.

The discord that arose between her parents on the subject of her marriage and her brother's, the selfishness and unintelligence of the queen their mother, the unheard-of violence and credulousness of the king their father, as they led to shocking domestic scenes, compelled the Princess Wilhelmina at a very early age to give herself up to the most melancholy and most profound reflections, and matured her before her time. Destined according to all appearances to ascend a throne, that of England, she was very lukewarm in her desire for that arrangement and readily consoled herself when it fell through. She was philosophical in the best sense of the word, and, fully realising what she was, and being determined never to descend to anything unworthy of her, she desired before everything a calm and serious life,—study, fine arts and music, and the charms of companionship. After the hours which she employed in working with her estimable governess, Frau von Sonsfeld, whom a special Providence sent to her to replace the detestable Leti, her pleasantest moments, her only pleasant moments, were those that she passed with her brother; and if raillery, satire, and laughter at their neighbours' expense did engross them too frequently, we can but agree that it was a sort of vengeance most pardonable to superior natures surrounded by vulgar, despicable, or evil-minded persons, who persecuted them. In this raillery of the Princess Wilhelmina there was much more of merriment and of an irresistible sense of the ridiculous, than of bitter malice; she never tried to repay to anybody the injuries that she had received from them.

Married by a freak of her father to the Hereditary Prince of Baireuth, with whom she had no previous acquaintance, she always speaks of him with esteem and affection; she loved him, became devotedly attached to him, and had to make no effort to bring her heart into accord with her duties. She was deeply pained by his inconstancy and his infidelities. And yet this conjugal attachment had not the character of a passion; it was rather her affection for her brother which would have assumed that character and would have become adoration, had not Frederick dealt it more than one blow by his involuntary vehemence and roughness. That passionate affection endured without abatement and without a blemish until Frederick, carried away by the impetuosity of youth, and exasperated by domestic persecution, abandoned himself without restraint to his evil inclinations. She noted the evident changes in her brother's conduct towards her after his absences and his outbursts of wildness. He did her the justice to agree that she did her utmost to induce him to reform.

> " Le vice à son aspect n'osait jamais paraître;
> De mes sens mutinés elle m'a rendu maître;
> C'était par la vertu qu'on plaisait à ses yeux." [1]

These verses are Frederick's and not of his worst.

The letter that opens their correspondence is from Frederick, dated at Küstrin, where he was then confined (November 1, 1730), on the eve of the council of war which his father had convoked to try him. His head was at stake, and his father insisted that the Prussian law relating to deserters should be applied to him. It is a playful letter, calculated to bring a mournful smile to the lips of that courageous sister, who remained so faithful and devoted to him at such an awful crisis.

[1] " When she appeared, vice never dared appear; she taught me to control my unruly passions; only by virtue could one win favour in her sight."

Their father often seems to be in very poor health during the first years, and Frederick on the point of becoming king. The sentiments which they express to each other concerning that dreaded monarch who has caused them so much suffering, and concerning his approaching demise, are what we may expect from two sincere natures. They will feel little regret, they will speedily find consolation; and still they are distressed, nature speaks—"nature suffers," as they say; they are conscious of the affection of blood (*tendresse du sang*); and when Frederick at last informs his sister of that long-expected death, he does it in these words (June 1, 1740):

"MY DEAREST SISTER: God disposed of our dear father yesterday, at three o'clock. He died with angelic firmness, and without much suffering. I cannot make up for the loss that you have sustained except by the perfect and sincere affection with which," etc.

Prior to the demise of their father, there are some jesting allusions to his mad whims and to what is known of them elsewhere. The Margravine is ill (as she habitually was as a result of the sufferings which had already destroyed her health, and which shortened her life); she needs a skilful physician. Frederick tells her of one in Berlin, Herr von Superville, and bids her write to the king, to obtain leave to consult him. When she has obtained it, he suggests to her a sure means of keeping him in attendance on her as long as she wishes, and even of taking a journey if he prescribes it; that means is for the Margravine to send the king a few tall men for his pet regiment; by virtue of this "six-foot compliment" paid to the king, all will go well; "two or three tall men, dispatched at an opportune moment, will be unanswerable arguments."

After Frederick became king (1740), the tender and affectionate tone of the correspondence did not change at once. In the first year of his reign Frederick goes to visit his sister at the Hermitage, near Baireuth, and she returns the visit, at Berlin; affection, and an intense, passionate affection, does not cease to breathe in all that they write to each other. And herein the letters, and the facts, do not coincide with the last part of the Margravine's *Mémoires*. She would have us believe in a sudden cooling-off on the part of Frederick when he became king, and she complains of it as of inconstancy for which there was no cause. But it was she who was first blameworthy in what ensued, and this is how her conduct is explained. When the Margravine married, she desired to have with her the Fraüleins von Marwitz, nieces of Frau von Sonsfeld, her governess. Later, noticing that her husband seemed to distinguish one of them by his attentions, she became jealous and determined to find a husband for her. Now, she had obtained from the late king the favour of having this young woman attend her, only upon the express condition, and upon her word of honour, that she would not marry her outside of Prussia. Thinking that she was relieved from her promise by the death of the king her father, she disregarded that condition and united Fraülein von Marwitz to an officer of the imperial regiment which the Margrave commanded. Frederick, to whom his sister had not confided her special reasons, and who was a no less jealous guardian than his father of the interests of the Prussian fatherland, found cause for displeasure in this foreign marriage, as well as in other indications which the Court of Baireuth seemed to be giving of its leaning toward Austria, and he manifested his displeasure to his sister. The Margravine, having finished the writing of her *Mémoires* while this quarrel was at its height (1744), gave rein to the prejudice which then swayed her, and, while recalling the past, interjected into her reminiscences something of her present irritation; they take this colour or that at the whim of her moods.

The correspondence enables us to set all this right to-day, with absolute certainty. In it we find the princess coming speedily to her senses and making reparation to her brother for the vexation that she has caused him, and for the injustice toward him of which she has been guilty.

From that moment all trace of the first discord between them disappeared; their affection blazed up again from its ashes, brighter and more intense than ever; its bonds were renewed, and were thereafter indissoluble; brother and sister never again ceased to be "one heart in two bodies."

The nine years preceding the Seven Years' War are filled and enlivened by this correspondence, which is altogether pleasant reading and reflects honour on both. It was the brilliant period, and the most literary, of Frederick's reign; it was then that he endeavoured to gather about him the élite of the distinguished men of his time, and that he seemed for an instant to be on the point of succeeding.[1]

Among the men of letters who died at Berlin, there was one who was held in little esteem, and whose works have long since been thrown aside. Do not imagine that Frederick thought them good, but he draws a living and speaking portrait of the author, which tells the whole story in a few words:

"We have lost poor La Mettrie [November 21, 1751]. He died for the sake of a jest, by eating a whole pheasant pie ; he took it into his head to be bled, in order to prove to the German physicians that bleeding could safely be resorted to in indigestion; it succeeded ill with him. He is regretted by all who knew him. He was a jovial, good fellow, a good doctor, and a very wretched author; *but by not reading his books, it was possible to like him very well.*"

To know, of some people, only their books, and, for greater security, to shun their persons; of others, to know only the persons while carefully avoiding their books;—this is a good receipt to remember, and may still be found of useful application.

These various items of news which Frederick writes to his sister are only the accidents of their correspondence; its substance is made up of their sentiments, their thoughts, and of moral or metaphysical questions which the sister propounds to the brother, and

[1] See Vol. I, pp. 217, 218.

which he strives to solve; for instance: " What is the difference between constancy in esteem and constancy in love ?" She has plenty of leisure at Baireuth, and she lacks only subjects and intimates, to found there a Hôtel de Brancas or de Rambouillet on a small scale. She longs for conversation; there is emptiness and silence all about her. In default of conversation near at hand, she seeks it at a distance, and luckily she finds in her brother a correspondent who has time for everything. I am not sure whether it is true, as he says, that being king makes him feel like a slave, and that it is a trade which he follows solely from necessity and because his birth condemns him to it.

" Most people are ambitious to rise; for my part, I would like to descend if, as a reward of that sacrifice, which would not be a sacrifice for me because it would cost me nothing, I could obtain my liberty."

This liberty, if he had obtained it, might well have embarrassed him, considering his ambition and his eager activity. In a journey to Italy, undertaken by the Margravine for her health, she plucks at Naples a twig of Virgil's laurel and sends it to him as a gift from the shade of the poet to the hero who is Alexander's rival. Frederick does not enter into his sister's outbursts of enthusiasm, and although he has to his credit the five victories of his two Silesian wars, he seems really confused by the compliment.

" I confess that I had a shock when I received a laurel wreath from your hands. If anything could overturn this weak brain of mine the

complimentary words which you add would do it.  But, my dear
sister, when I examine myself, I find only a poor mortal composed of
a mixture of good and evil, who is often exceedingly ill-content with
himself and would be very glad to have more good qualities than he
has; who is fitted to live the life of a private individual, but compelled
to live in public; a philosopher by inclination, and a politician by
duty; who is, in a word, obliged to be everything that he is not, and
who has no other merit than religious devotion to his duties."

While feigning to belittle himself thus, by curtly
repelling all grandeur, and spurning everything that
savours of the demigod, Frederick looked carefully to
it that he resembled a very noble kingly ideal.  But in
this whole correspondence between the brother and
sister he reveals himself fully on one side of his nature,—the literary, artistic, virtuoso, *bel-esprit* side.
There is almost nothing of the king; he is a private
person talking of those things which are the delight of
his life.  And all this familiarity of an " old brother,"
as he calls himself, is heightened by his unfailing admiration for his sister, whom he evidently considers
superior to himself in talent, in beauty of intellect, and
in *genius*.  He lavishes attentions and little presents
upon her; he shares her suffering, he trembles for
her life; he shows her to us with " an indefinable
grace, an air of dignity tempered by affability," which
the Margravine's *Mémoires* do not reveal; in a word,
by the reverential affection which she inspires in him,
he arouses our interest in that fragile, rare creature, in
" that so feeble body and delicate constitution, con-
joined with such a noble soul."

The Seven Years' War, interrupting the flow of Frederick's prosperity and his fully occupied leisure, puts his sister's spirit to the test—that noble and sensitive spirit—and enables us to appreciate her in her most eminent qualities, in her truly historic attitude.

Frederick saw the war approaching from a long distance, although it surprised him a little at the last. His sister prophesied it and feared it in 1755, noting the collisions between England and France on the subject of the boundaries of Canada, and the maritime hostilities which followed.

" You tell me of your fear of war," he wrote to her (September 21, 1755), " but, my dear sister, it 's a long way from the Ohio River to the Spree, and from the fort of Beau-Séjour to Berlin.    I will wager that the Austrians will not move at once in Flanders.    War travels like a great lady: She began in America, now she has reached the ocean and the English Channel; she has n't landed yet, and if she does land next spring, she may perhaps, for greater comfort, travel in a litter, so that we shall see her coming a long way off.    And after all, one is exposed to so many risks in the regular course of life, that war adds to them only a trifle."

Ere long the two rival powers, realising that an open conflict was inevitable, laboured to involve the different continental powers in their quarrel: France formed an alliance with Austria, England joined hands with Prussia.    Having felt the pulse of Austria and satisfied himself of her unfriendly designs, Frederick determined to be beforehand with her and to take the field without a preliminary declaration of war.    That was his sister's advice.

The fateful year 1757 began; it was the year most fruitful in sudden changes of all sorts, when Frederick seemed to experience all possible contradictory freaks of fortune; in the following years he had to contend against repetitions simply, severe enough still, but less so than at first. The Margravine takes the most absorbing interest in his fate; she admires him as her hero, as the greatest of reigning princes, "and one of those phenomenal mortals who appear at most only once in a century." After his early successes, from which he does not perhaps reap all the advantage that he might have done, she beholds him on the point of being crushed between the three hostile powers; she burns to intervene in his behalf. Events urge him to consent. After his defeat at Kolin (June 18th), he seems disposed to allow her to move in his interest—this sister endowed with virile courage, who would be incapable of advising him to do anything unworthy. She offers to make an attempt at opening negotiations with France.

On July 7, 1757, Frederick writes to her these significant words which aptly define the delicate rôle that she had undertaken in that grave emergency.

"Since, my dear sister, you insist upon undertaking the great work of peace, I beg you to be good enough to send this M. de Mirabeau to France. I will gladly provide for his expenses; he may offer the favourite [Madame de Pompadour] as much as five hundred thousand crowns for peace, and he may increase his offer much beyond that sum if he can at the same time bind her to secure some advantages for us. You realise how discreetly this matter must be handled, and how little

I must appear in it; the least suspicion of anything of the sort in England might ruin everything. I think that your emissary would do well to apply also to his kinsman [Bernis] who has lately become minister, and whose influence is increasing day by day. However, I leave it all to you. To whom could I more fitly entrust the interests of a country whose welfare I seek, than to a sister whom I adore, and *who, although far more accomplished than I, is another myself?*"

It was shortly after this that the Margravine conceived the idea of making use of Voltaire for another essay of the same sort and with the same object, but which seems to be distinct from the preceding one.

She had never ceased to be on good terms with Voltaire, and had corresponded with him both before and after his fall from grace at Berlin. In her correspondence with him she called herself "Sister Wilhelmina," or "Sister Guillemette," of the same abbey as "Brother Voltaire."

I do not vouch for the perfect taste of all the pleasantry that we find in these early letters of the Margravine; she is eminently a person of the age in which she lived and, to some extent, of her native land. She suspects as much herself, and would like Voltaire to give to her little society a last touch, a final polish of civilisation, by making "a pilgrimage to Notre-Dame de Baireuth."

He always promises and never comes. "You impose upon me the fate of Tantalus; pray out-German the Germans in your resolutions and give me the pleasure of seeing you again." She implores the poet-philosopher "to guide her in the way of truth," and meanwhile she makes objections, but always in a more advanced, more radical direction.   But we have little concern with the Margravine's philosophy, which is little more than her brother's in a different form; we are especially concerned with the ardent and loyal sentiments which she revealed and which characterise her more truly.

As we have seen in an earlier volume [1] she opened negotiations with Voltaire soon after the battle of Kolin.   Voltaire at once set to work with an activity of which certain letters in his previously published *Correspondance* gave us a hint, and which other letters recently [1856] published have made abundantly clear. Being then in Switzerland, at Les Délices, and on intimate terms with the Tronchins of Geneva, it occurred to him to employ one of the members of that family, a banker at Lyon, and to use him as a medium of communication with the archbishop of that city, Cardinal de Tencin, formerly of the royal council, but momentarily out of office, who, nevertheless, still had friends at Versailles and gleams of hope of returning thither.

In a note dictated to Tronchin the cardinal welcomed the overture, while gently putting aside the ambitious prospect of which a glimpse was offered him; he said, among other things: "I will willingly take charge of Madame la Margrave's letter, and I think that she will do well to embody in the letter which she writes me

[1] Vol. I, p. 217.

the judicious reflections set forth by M. de Voltaire in his letter concerning the aggrandisement of the House of Austria."

A letter in the sense suggested was written by the Margravine and addressed, not to the King of France, but to the cardinal; the letter to the king was not to come until after they had felt the ground at Versailles. Meanwhile overtures were also made to the Maréchal de Richelieu, then commanding the French army in Saxony; and while no definite result was obtained with respect to the main object, they succeeded, by indirect means, in abating his individual zeal.

Then followed weeks of terrible apprehension for the Margravine. Berlin was for two days in the power of the Austrian army, which held the inhabitants to ransom. Frederick, in the curious verses which he wrote at all hazards in the brief breathing-spaces between battles, and which afterwards obtained almost as much currency as his bulletins, had manifested a design more after the antique than the modern fashion: it was, after attempting one last great *coup,* to refuse to survive his ruin—to kill himself. He had said so in the *Épître* to d'Argens. He said so again to Voltaire, in the best verses that he ever wrote:

> " Pour moi, menacé du naufrage,
> Je dois, en affrontant l'orage,
> Penser, vivre, et mourir en roi."[1]

---

[1] See Vol. I, p. 219.

He repeated it to his sister at the close of the *Épître* that he addressed to her in August, 1757:

> "Ainsi, mon seul asile, et mon unique port
> Se trouve, chère sœur, dans les bras de la mort."[1]

His sister replied at once (September 15th):

> "Your letter and the one you wrote to Voltaire, my dear brother, have almost killed me. Great God! what a ghastly determination! Ah! my dear brother, you say that you love me, and you plunge a dagger into my heart. Your *Épître*, which I have just received, has made my tears flow in rivers. I am ashamed now that I was so weak. My misery would be so great that I should find in it a more dignified resource. *Your fate will be decisive of mine; I will not survive your misfortunes nor those of my family. You may depend upon it that this is my steadfast resolution.* But, after this confession, I beg you to consider the pitiable state of your enemy [Maria-Theresa] when you were before Prague. There has been a sudden change of fortune on both sides; this change may be repeated when you least expect it. Cæsar was once the slave of pirates and became the lord of the earth. A great genius like yours finds resources even when all is lost. . . ."

Voltaire wrote to Frederick in the same strain and redeemed all his past offences by the good sense and frankness of his remonstrances. To kill one's self in order to avoid yielding would be, in Frederick's position, to commit a deed inspired by pride much more than by courage, especially the courage of a patriotic citizen.

As for the Margravine, after remonstrating to Frederick, she did not hesitate, but held herself ready to share and to imitate his fate.

[1] "And so, dear sister, my sole refuge and my only safe harbour are to be found in the arms of death."

"I am in a frightful condition," she wrote to Voltaire (August 19th), "and I shall not survive the ruin of my house and my family; that is the only consolation I have left." And on October 16th: "Our situation is still unchanged; *a tomb is our outlook.* Although all seems lost, there are some things which no one can take from us: they are steadfastness and the emotions of the heart."

Meanwhile Frederick freely discussed with her his tragic resolution, and their common destiny ; he felt the force of the arguments that were put before him and admitted them in part.

"If I followed my own inclination solely, *I should have despatched myself* instantly after the unlucky battle that I lost; but I felt that that would be rank weakness, and that it was my duty to repair the evil that had befallen. My attachment to the State reawoke; I said to myself : 'It is not in good, but in evil fortune, that one rarely finds defenders.'"

But this attachment to the State, he held, could not bind him beyond certain limits, and there were humiliations which he did not consider himself bound to undergo.

The long distances and the difficulties of communication caused breaks in their correspondence and intervals of silence which led the Margravine to fear that everything was consummated ; witness this feverish, delirious letter, which gives voice to the paroxysm of her affection and her anxiety:

"Death and ten thousand torments could offer nothing equal to my frightful state of mind. There are rumours about that make me shudder; they say that you are dangerously wounded—others say, sick. In vain have I put forth every effort to obtain news of you; I can learn nothing. O my dear brother! whatever may happen to you, I shall not survive you. If I am left in this cruel uncertainty, I shall sink un-

der it, and I shall be happy. I was on the point of sending you a
courier, but I dared not. In God's name, send me a line. I do not
know what I have written; my heart is torn asunder, and I feel as if
my mind were wandering with anxiety and terror. O my dearest,
adorable brother, have pity on me! Heaven grant that I may be mistaken and that you will scold me! but the slightest thing that con-
cerns you goes to my heart and alarms my love too keenly. May I
die a thousand deaths, if only you may live and be happy! I can say
no more,—my grief is choking me."—(October 15, 1757.)

In this extremity, while Frederick argued about his
situation like a man who had read and pondered the
twelfth chapter of the "Decline and Fall of the Roman
People," and while he assumed to usurp the most
ambitious of all privileges for a mortal,—that of "end-
ing the play" in which he was an actor "at whatever point he chose,"—the aspect of affairs suddenly
changed, and a slight puff of fortune's breath rendered of no account all his exalted reminiscences of
Cato. Every one knows the unforeseen incidents of
the battle of Rossbach: a prolonged false march, before a strongly posted enemy, who had had time to
draw up in order of battle, brought about an easy and
speedy defeat, the moral effect of which, however,
was enormous. "It was a *bataille en douceur,*"
said Frederick, announcing his victory to the Margravine (November 5th). "Thank God! I had less
than a hundred men killed." And he was justified in
adding: "Now I shall go down into the tomb in
peace, since the reputation and honour of my nation
are saved. We may be unfortunate, but we shall not
be dishonoured."

In her great joy, the Margravine wrote Voltaire a detailed bulletin; she added an assurance that their sincere desire for peace was unchanged. She drew heavily on her strength in writing these long letters; her health was wrecked, a dry cough racked her body, and she was about to enter upon the last days of her mortal suffering.

Letters between the Margravine and her brother in the early months of 1758 are rare, whether because a goodly number have been lost or suppressed, or because the Margravine's ill health made them less frequent. Frederick tries to save his sister's territory from the horrors of war, and to lead the enemy in another direction by frequent diversions. In every letter, and in the most heartfelt tone, he expresses his sympathy with her suffering and all that she is in his life.

"What! ill and weak as you are, you dwell upon my embarrassments! Upon my word, that is too much. Think rather—think and be fully convinced—that without you there is no more happiness in life for me, that my life hangs upon yours, and that it rests with you to cut short or prolong my career. If you love me, give me some hope of your recovery. No,—life would be intolerable to me without you. This is not mere empty talk, it is true. My heart and my soul are at Baireuth, with you, and my frail body vegetates here, on the highroads and in camp."

And she, when she had reached the final period of her illness and the last stage of consumption, wrote to him (August 10, 1758):

"You wish, my dear brother, to know about my condition. I have been in bed six months, like a poor Lazarus. For the last week

I have been placed on a wheeled chair to give me a little change of
position.  I have a dry cough which is very violent, and which they
cannot control; my legs, as well as my hands and face, are swollen as
big as a bushel measure.  .  .  .  I am resigned to my fate; I shall live
and die content, provided that you are happy."

She died on the 14th of October in that year (1758),
at the age of forty-nine,—the same day that her brother
was beaten at Hochkirch by the Austrians.  When
he learned of that too-long-expected death, he was
plunged in gloom and mourning.  " I never saw such
profound affliction," says his reader, Herr von Catt, in
his unpublished memoirs; " shutters closed, his room
barely lighted by a faint gleam of daylight; reading
serious works: Bossuet's *Oraisons Funèbres,* Fléchier,
Mascaron, and a volume of Young, for which he
asked me."  He consecrated to her memory a noble
passage in his " History of the Seven Years' War."
Of various passages in his poetry I say nothing; he
fully realised that not in that way would he give her
immortality.

I have no purpose to belittle the eminent qualities of
the Margravine, after striving so carefully to assemble
them and lay them before the reader's eyes.  She was
evidently a person of the greatest distinction, intellectual, unaffected, piquant, capable of satire, even more
capable of affection, tenderly devoted to her brother,
and at need measuring up to him in firmness of character and stoic determination.  In one of the most
critical emergencies which persons of their rank have
ever had to face, she conducted herself with exceeding

vigour and a self-sacrificing spirit; if Frederick had come to a violent end at that time, she would unquestionably have died with him; she had the soul of a Portia or a Roland. But why is it that her whole life, and that countenance, so animated and so brave, always lack a certain charm, a certain ideal beauty, which neither poet nor painter can bestow upon them without being unfaithful to the truth? In less distant times there was another sister of a king, who would fain have shared her brother's fate and have died with him; this other king was far from being a great man, or even superior to other men; he was simply an honourable man, and his sister was a pure, sweet, simple, pious woman, especially rich in treasures of the heart. To die with her brother, but not to kill herself with him,—that is what that angelic creature had meditated upon in her patient and tranquil heroism, at the foot of the crucifix. Let us give them their names: Louis XVI.'s sister, Madame Élisabeth, who had so many opportunities to escape and to leave France, chose to remain where danger was, and resigned herself to suffer everything and to die. The sacrifice was consummated; and thanks to the victim's simplicity of heart, thanks to the sublimity of the springs of faith whence she drew her inspiration, there descended upon her, in that supreme immolation of self, a divine ray which never leaves her, and which illumines that spotless brow and that celestial glance with the serene purity of one of Raphael's faces.

This said, let us be content to recognise in the Margravine one of the original women of the eighteenth century,—a lively wit, a rare pride, a character, and a profile which have their well-defined place, not only in anecdote, but also in the history of her time; and which will always be distinguishable in the background of the picture, beside the king, her brother. She has her name and her title in the book of the future; her *Correspondance* cloaks and redeems her *Mémoires;* and whenever she is mentioned, people will say first of all: "She was a king's sister."

# Beaumarchais.

1732–1799.

## Beaumarchais.

THE eighteenth century is no more complete
without Beaumarchais than without Diderot,
Voltaire, or Mirabeau; he is one of its most
original, most characteristic, most revolutionary personages. When he is revolutionary, it is from impulse, from precipitancy, and with no fixed purpose
to go so far as one might think. In this regard he
strongly resembles Voltaire, with whom he shares
the honour of being perhaps the wittiest man of his
time. But Voltaire had more taste than Beaumarchais; Beaumarchais followed his wit wherever it
chose to go, abandoned himself to it, and never mastered it. In speaking of him, we must take care not
to be systematic, for he himself was nothing of the
kind; he was simply a man of great natural parts,
tossed about and sometimes submerged in the waves
of his epoch, and swimming in many currents.

Pierre-Augustin-Caron, who later assumed the name
of Beaumarchais, was born in Paris, January 24, 1732,
in the parish of Saint-Jacques-la-Boucherie. His family,
originally of Normandie, had afterwards settled in
Brie; it was of the Protestant faith. Beaumarchais'

father, a watchmaker by trade, who brought up his son in the same handicraft, seems to have been a worthy, good-hearted man, who had retained, of his Protestant habits, a goodly store of religious conviction and affection. When, at a later period, during his famous lawsuits, he was sneered at because of his middle-class extraction, Beaumarchais spoke of this father of his in a charming way, which reminds one of Horace:

" You begin this masterpiece of yours," he said to Madame Goëzman (his adversary), " by reproaching me with my ancestors' trade. Alas! madame, it is too true that the last of them all combined with several branches of trade quite a reputation in the art of watchmaking. Being obliged to plead guilty to this charge, I confess with sorrow that nothing can acquit me of the just accusation which you make against me—of being the son of my father. But I pause,—for I feel him behind me, looking at what I am writing, and laughing as he embraces me. Oh! you who throw my father at my head, you have no conception of his noble heart. In truth, leaving the watchmaking out of the question, I know no other father for whom I would care to exchange him."

This sensitive, honourable, virtuous father wrote one day to his son, who was then in Spain, having gone thither to avenge one of his sisters (1764), a letter which has been published, and which would be worthy of Diderot's father, or of Diderot himself speaking through the mouth of a father in one of his dramas:

" You urge me modestly to love you a little. That is not possible, my dear boy : a son like you is not of the sort to be loved only a little by a father who thinks and feels as I do. The tears of affection which fall from my eyes on this paper are abundant proof of it. The

BEAUMARCHAIS
*From a portrait by Nattier*

excellent qualities of your heart, the strength and nobility of your mind, fill me with the most devoted love. Oh! my son, my dear son, the honour of my grey hairs, how have I deserved from my God the favours with which He overwhelms me in my dear son? To my mind, a son like you is the greatest favour that He can bestow upon an honourable, sensitive father. My great suffering has ceased since yesterday, as I am able to write to you. I was five days and four nights without eating or sleeping, and groaning constantly. In the intervals when my suffering abated a little, I read *Grandison*, and in how many places I found a striking resemblance between Grandison and my son! Father of your sisters, and friend and benefactor of your father! If England, I said to myself, has its Grandisons, France has its Beaumarchais."

To understand the enthusiasm and the tone of this letter, it should be said that Beaumarchais, about this time, had signalised himself by an energetic proof of devotion to his family. We see in it, however, the ordinary style of the family in the rare moments when they are not joking. One of Beaumarchais' sisters also compared him to Grandison. Evidently he was the hero and the hope of the family; the only son among five sisters, only three of whom had remained in France, and all of whom adored and admired him, whether for his wit, or for the qualities of his heart. Endowed with physical attractions, and with an inventive mind, overflowing with audacity and gaiety, there was in his acts and in his whole personality something which prepossessed people in his favour; and he himself was prepossessed first of all. When he made his début in letters, rather late in life, all those who spoke of him commented at the outset upon this air of self-assurance and conceit. The self-assurance, which was simply unbounded confidence in his wit and in his talents, he always retained; but the conceit was on the surface only, for all those who saw him at close quarters, people of all sorts, have acknowledged that he was an excellent fellow.

I leave it for his biographer to describe his first essays in verse, in rhymed prose. I have seen a letter that he wrote from Spain, to one of his sisters, when he was thirteen years old, in which one may detect, through the schoolboy, something of Cherubino and of the libertine, a ready pen, and abundant gaiety. This gaiety is the essential thing in Beaumarchais, and it was destined never to betray him when he gave himself up to it, whereas his sensibility sometimes impelled him toward pathos.

He continued for quite a long while in watchmaking, and his vanity did not suffer for it. He exhibited his creative talent by an escapement which he invented, and which one Lepante contested his right to. The cause was carried to the Académie des Sciences, and Beaumarchais won it. This first title of honour never ceased to be dear to him, and he kept the parchment in a casket beside the manuscript of *Figaro*. However, after spending thus a large part of his youth between four show-windows, as he says, he tired of it and took his flight. It is at this point that it would be interesting to follow in detail what he called "the philosophical romance of his life." We will simply call attention to a few heads of chapters. He was fond of music, he sang, and wrote songs; he could play the guitar, and above all the harp, then a great novelty, and he carried into these amusements that spirit of invention which he displayed in everything. What a delightful musician, what a fascinating and insinuating Lindor, Beaumarchais must have been at twenty-four years!

He became acquainted with the wife of a man who held a subordinate office at Court; she loved him, and, her husband having died, he secured the office by marrying, on November 27, 1756, the widow, whose name was Marie-Madeleine Aubertin. He was unfortunate enough to lose her shortly after, and was left a widower on September 29, 1757. However, he had this little office at Court, which gave him a foothold in the houses of the greatest courtiers. As a musician, as an agreeable young man, of no consequence, he was introduced, about 1760, into the circle of Mesdames Royales, the daughters of Louis XV.

"I passed four years," he said, "earning their goodwill by the most assiduous and most unselfish attention to various details of their amusements."

The great financier, Paris-Duverney, who had become in his old age superintendent of the École Militaire, of which he had first suggested the idea to Madame de Pompadour, and the organisation of which he had directed, ardently desired that the royal family should honour with a visit that patriotic establishment to which he was devoting his last thoughts. He had not as yet succeeded in obtaining this supreme testimony of regard when Beaumarchais undertook to arouse in Mesdames the desire to make the visit, and to communicate it through them to the dauphin, and if possible to the king himself. He succeeded. Duverney, in his gratitude, loudly declared that he would make the young man's fortune.

He kept his word. After various promising offers which did not turn out as he wished, "it occurred to him to fulfil his promise at a single stroke," says Beaumarchais, "by lending me five hundred thousand francs to purchase an office, which I was to repay at my leisure from the proceeds of the interests which he promised me in various great undertakings." This office, which was, I believe, in the Department of Forests and Public Lands, although purchased by Beaumarchais, he was unable to retain; he found an insurmountable obstacle in the united arrogant pretensions of the society which he sought to enter, and which deemed him unworthy by reason of his watchmaking antecedents. He indulged in divers philosophical reflections upon human folly, did not lose his temper, and turned in another direction. Shortly after, we find him in possession of another office at Court, his titles being equerry, counsellor-secretary to the king, and lieutenant-general of the chase in the bailiwick of the Louvre, of which the Duc de la Vallière was captain. In this capacity of lieutenant-general of the chase, he had cognisance of certain offences, and was invested with a judicial office the functions of which he performed without too much hilarity.

In 1764 (he was then thirty-two years old), one of the most dramatic episodes of his life takes place, which he himself has described in one of his memorials: I refer to the episode of Clavico, upon which dramas have been written; but the only real drama is in Beaumarchais. To confine ourselves to a simple summary: Beaumarchais was informed that, of his two sisters who had long been settled in Spain, the younger, who was not married, had been twice on the point of marrying a man of talent, one of the higher government clerks in Madrid, named Clavico, who had twice broken his word. This young sister, dying of her love and of the insult, appeals for a defender and an avenger. Beaumarchais sets out, supplied with letters from Paris-Duverney (including many letters of exchange), and with all sorts of recommendations to the ambassador. He arrives at Madrid, calls upon Clavico without giving his name, invents a pretext, tests him in conversation, talks to him about literature, flatters him, attacks him through his self-esteem, and then suddenly turns about, broaches the delicate subject, holds the sword over his head for some time, the better to thrust with it;—and his narrative of all this dialogue, with the pantomime of the victim, is a masterpiece of strategy and of shrewd management, which constantly borders on the tragic and the comic at the same time. But the end of the adventure is not at all in keeping with the beginning, and Beaumarchais is very near becoming the dupe of the knave whom he has unmasked and pressed so close.

This family affair concluded, and Beaumarchais having escaped the danger in which it had involved him, he remained another whole year in Spain, trying to engage in business and to carry through certain important enterprises in the name of a French company. So far as we can discover, it was a matter of contracting to supply various American provinces with negro slaves for ten years. Although he did not succeed, Beaumarchais impressed all those persons with whom he came in contact in Spain with a favourable idea of his capacity and his talents.

Thus far, that is to say, at the time of his return from Spain (1765), he had written nothing for the public; he was about to make his bow, and his early attempts were not happy. His drama *Eugénie,* given at the Comédie-Française in February, 1767, is in the vein of the serious, decent, domestic drama, which Diderot tried to bring into fashion. In *Eugénie,* and in *Les Deux Amis,* which followed (January, 1770), Beaumarchais is as yet simply a sentimental, bourgeois dramatist, tearful and solemn, of the type of La Chaussée and of Diderot. Even the latter did not avow him as a pupil and a son, and Collé, who knew what humour was, was very far from detecting

in him a confrère and a master. "M. de Beaumarchais," says Collé, "has proved beyond any question, by his drama, that he has neither genius, nor
talent, nor wit." This sentence Collé apologises for
in a note overflowing with admiration and repent-
ance, written after the *Barbier de Séville.*

Let us leave once for all this Beaumarchais-Grandi-
son, who is headed in the wrong direction, and let
us come at once, through the various incidents of his
life, to the real Beaumarchais, whose veritable comic
strain was destined to manifest itself unexpectedly, and
all the more naturally, even before he became the
Beaumarchais of *Figaro.* He had always had this
vein of gaiety, but it did not occur to him until late,
and only under the spur of necessity, to introduce it
into his works. His life as a private individual was at
this time most agreeable and almost opulent. He had
married a second time, April 11, 1768, a widow,
Geneviève-Madeleine Wattebled, Madame Lévesque,
but evil fortune decreed that he should lose her in
November, 1770. Paris-Duverney, who had died in
the meantime, had left for Beaumarchais a statement
of account, in which he acknowledged that he owed
him some fifteen thousand francs. It is at this point
that the famous series of lawsuits begins. Paris-Duverney's heir, the Comte de La Blache, chose to
deny the debt of fifteen thousand francs, and to argue
that the account was a forgery. Hence a lawsuit,
won in the court of first instance by Beaumarchais.

He, hunting more than one hare at once, and always confident and imprudent, had, while this lawsuit was pending in the Parliament, a violent altercation with the Duc de Chaulnes about a mistress, one Mademoiselle Mesnard. The result was that, after each of them had been in custody several days in his own house, the duke was confined in a citadel and Beaumarchais imprisoned at For-l'Évêque. His adversary, the Comte de La Blache, took advantage of the opportunity to push the affair of the fifteen thousand francs before the Parliament; he represented Beaumarchais as an abandoned person, a scoundrel who had abused the confidence of everybody with whom he came in contact. Forged letters from him or against him were circulated; it was insinuated that he had rid himself by poison of his two wives, the two widows whom he had married in succession. In brief, the Comte de La Blache resorted to all sorts of expedients, won his suit, caused the prisoner's furniture to be taken on execution, and ruined him with the costs; so that Beaumarchais found himself, within two months, "hurled down from the most agreeable condition that a private individual could enjoy, into misfortune and destitution. I was an object of shame and compassion to myself," he said.

It was at this time, in this desperate plight, that he exhibited rare energy and serenity. A curious and apparently most trivial incident gave him an opening, which he seized, to recover his advantage, and to re-

trieve, by adroitness and talent, all that he had lost.
This was the decisive moment in Beaumarchais'
destiny (June, 1773). He was then a man of forty
years, everything about whom, even his wit, had
seemed questionable up to that time. He was driven
to the wall, beaten, crushed; it was for him to display, on the instant, energy, wit, and genius; and he
did it.

The incident which served him as a battle-field when
everything seemed lost was this: being a prisoner at
For-l'Évêque, and having occasion, according to custom, to solicit his judges, he had obtained permission
to go out for three or four days, accompanied by an
officer. In that brief time, he made several useless
attempts to obtain access to Counsellor Goëzman, to
whom his cause was referred, and who was prejudiced and unfavourable to him. Then it was, in his
distress and despair, that he was told that there was
one infallible way of penetrating to this magistrate's
study, and that was to make a present to his wife. A
hundred *louis d'or,* a lovely repeating-watch set with
diamonds, and, in addition, fifteen louis *in silver,* supposed to be intended for a secretary,—all these things
were presented one after another to the wife, in order
to obtain an audience of her husband, and with a
promise on her part that they should all be returned
if the suit were lost. It was lost, and the lady, honourably enough, returned the one hundred louis and
the watch; but by a singular freak, she persisted in

keeping the fifteen wretched louis which were given in addition; hence a great outcry, complaints, and much loud talk from Counsellor Goëzman, who knew or did not know all these details, and who had the audacity to accuse Beaumarchais, on the ground that he had endeavoured to bribe his judge.

It was, I say, from this depth of oppression and prostration that Beaumarchais rose again and took the field, pen in hand, addressing himself this time, in four consecutive memorials, to public opinion, and to the public itself, whom he had the knack of impressing and exciting. To understand how he was able thus to reverse public opinion, we must not forget that this Parliament with which he had to deal was that which Chancellor Maupeou had substituted for the former Parliament, which was exiled and finally abolished. The art of Beaumarchais consisted in imperceptibly confounding his cause with the insult inflicted upon the whole nation, and in making himself, by his exacerbated pleasantries, the universal avenger. All the scenes in which he introduces Madame Goëzman—a light-headed, rather pretty woman, whose head was turned by a compliment, who was totally confused by the truth, and who offered in her whole behaviour a mixture of knavery, impudence, and innocence—are absolutely perfect scenes of comedy. The poor creature! in her cross-examination he makes her say that black is white, he makes her angry and soothes her; when he has pressed her beyond endurance, she threatens him with a slap; when he pays her a compliment, and tells her that she seems only eighteen years old instead of thirty, she smiles in spite of herself, ceases to think him so impertinent, and goes so far as to ask his hand to escort her to her carriage. It is all delicious in its gaiety, its shrewdness, and its irony. And so it is with all those whom he introduces on his stage: we recognise them, and we never forget them.

Public opinion at once declared itself, and in a few months Beaumarchais had more than regained public esteem, he possessed popularity,—that universal favour, at that time sovereign and triumphant, which did not as yet realise its limits. In the new circumstances in which he found himself thenceforth, the sentence of the Parliament was of very little importance. The judgment, which was awaited by people of all classes with indescribable curiosity, was peculiar and double-edged: by decree of February 26, 1774, Madame Goëzman was sentenced to be summoned to the Chamber, "there to be rebuked on her knees"; and Beaumarchais to undergo the same penalty; furthermore, his memorials were sentenced to be burned by the hangman, as insulting, scandalous, and defamatory. To arrive at this superb decision, the Parliament remained in session from five in the morning until almost nine at night.

On the very evening of the sentence, Beaumarchais was to take supper in the most exalted society, at Monsieur de Monaco's, where he had promised to read the *Barbier de Séville,* the performance of which was postponed, but which the dauphiness (Marie Antoinette) had openly taken under her patronage. The amiable dauphiness had hoisted the flag of Beaumarchais, so to speak, by a head-dress called the *Quesaco,* which was so named from one of the jests in the memorials. On that evening the Prince de Conti inscribed his name at Beaumarchais' house, and invited him to pass the next day with him. "I want you to come to-morrow," he said in his note; "we are of sufficiently good family to set the example to France of the way in which a great citizen like you should be treated."

The whole Court followed the prince's example and wrote their names at the condemned man's door. And so he who, at the beginning of his rejoinder, was still nothing more than "the brilliant scapegrace," as Voltaire called him, had suddenly become a "great citizen." Wherever Beaumarchais showed himself, he was surrounded and applauded with frenzy. The lieutenant of police, Monsieur de Sartine, advised him not to appear in public. "To be rebuked," he said, "is not the whole thing; you must be modest too." Shortly after, in order to preserve a position which was more brilliant than safe, and was hazardous in spite of everything, Beaumarchais went to England, on a secret mission from the king, relative to the Chevalier d'Éon, from whom it was desired to obtain some state papers. Meanwhile the Parliament Mau-

peou went to pieces; the *Barbier de Séville* was
performed in Paris, and Beaumarchais, his sentence
being ostentatiously remitted, seized every opportunity
to make a sensation and his fortune, became com-
missary in ordinary to the revolted American colonies,
and entered, with wind astern and all sails set, upon
that prosperous voyage which did not end until after
the *Mariage de Figaro*.

On the morrow of his rebuke by the Parliament and
his triumph in public opinion, Beaumarchais seems to
me to have entered into a condition of partial intoxication and excitement from which he never again
emerged. Such letters of his as we have of that date
(1774-1775) exhibit him to us as himself amazed at
his destiny; turning about, and looking at himself
sidewise, to see how strange and odd it all is; travelling about, to England and Germany,—doing seven
hundred and eighty leagues in six weeks, and more
than eighteen hundred in eight months, and boasting
of it; careful not to allow himself to be forgotten during his absences, and to reappear on the carpet from
time to time, with narratives of such perils and adventures as befell nobody else. All this kept Paris
society agape, and prevented it from going to sleep
over Beaumarchais until the first performance of the
*Barbier de Séville*.

The *Barbier* was written and announced long before. It had been accepted at the Comédie-Française in
1772; it was to have been given as a carnival farce, at

Mardi-Gras, 1773, when the violent quarrel between Beaumarchais and the Duc de Chaulnes occurred, in which the latter tried to stab his opponent. The jocund *Barbier* withstood this reverse, and was announced for the next carnival. Once more, in February, 1774, it was surely to be performed: the day was appointed, the dauphiness was to be present at the first performance; the whole hall was sold for six evenings. Again it was prohibited at the last moment, because of the author's lawsuit then pending before the Parliament. Again the *Barbier* made the best of it; Beaumarchais, instead of one comedy, produced another: the *Barbier* not having been given as announced on Saturday, February 12, on the following day, Sunday,—in fact, that very night, at the opera ball,—the author put on sale his famous fourth memorial, of which he disposed of six thousand copies and more before the authorities had time to intervene and to stop it. Meanwhile, from delay to delay, from carnival to carnival, the *Barbier's* hour arrived; it was performed on February 23, 1775. But then there befell another disappointment: the public, on the faith of the gossip of society, had anticipated so much laughter and fooling that at first it did not find enough. The play was originally in five acts, and it seemed tedious. Must we say it? the first day it was voted a bore. In order that it should succeed, it was necessary that the author should reduce the acts to four,—that he should cut himself in four pieces, as was said;—or, more simply, as he himself put it, that he should remove the fifth wheel from his carriage. Then it was that the *Barbier,* as we know it to-day, rose again and began to live its light-hearted and joyous life, never to die. When he subsequently printed it, Beaumarchais gave himself the pleasure of putting on the title-page : *"Le Barbier de Séville,* acted upon the stage of the Comédie-Française, where it failed."

Not in these days can a critic hope to discover anything new concerning the *Barbier de Séville.* In introducing Figaro for the first time, the author did not as yet undertake to make of him the soliloquising character, given to moral reflections, the satirical, political, and philosophical reasoner which he afterward became in his hands.

"Abandoning myself to my sportive disposition," he said, "I tried in the *Barbier de Séville* to restore to the stage the outspoken gaiety of the olden time, combining it with the light and airy tone of our present-day jesting; but as even that was a species of novelty, the play was hotly prosecuted. It seemed as if I had shaken the foundations of the State."

The novelty of the *Barbier* was very much as Beaumarchais defines it here. He was naturally overflowing with merriment; he ventured to be himself in the *Barbier;* and in the eighteenth century, that was a mark of originality. "Pray give us more plays of this sort, since you are the only one who dares to laugh in our faces," people said to him.

The *Barbier* was intended at first to be set to music. Beaumarchais intended to make it an opéra-comique; indeed, it is said that he presented it in that shape to the Théâtre des Italiens of his time. Luckily he changed his mind. He proposed to be master on the stage, and the composer also proposed to be; it was impossible to come to an understanding. Beaumarchais had false ideas concerning dramatic music: he thought that it could never be seriously employed on the stage "until people realised that there should be no singing there except as one way of speaking." He was mistaken therein, and it is a good thing that he was mistaken. He was obliged to rewrite his comedy as we have it now; and later, another genius [Rossini] took up the work from the musical standpoint, and produced his own comedy.

"He who says author says *one who dares,*" is a remark of Beaumarchais, and no one ever justified that definition better than he. By mingling with the old French wit the fashions of the moment,—a touch of Rabelais and of Voltaire; by covering it with a thin Spanish disguise, and casting upon it a ray or two of the sun of Andalusia, he succeeded in being the most entertaining and the most restless Parisian of his time, the Gil Blas of the epoch of the Encyclopédie, on the eve of the revolutionary epoch; he restored the vogue of all sorts of old-fashioned truths and old satires, by rejuvenating them. He remodelled a goodly number of proverbs which were well-nigh worn out. In the

matter of wit, he was a great *rejuvenator,* and that
was the most agreeable benefaction he could confer
upon that antiquated society, which dreaded nothing
so much as ennui, and even preferred danger and
imprudence.

In the matter of publicity and of theatrical management, he was a past-master; he perfected the art of
advertising and editorial puffing; the art of reading of
plays in society, which forces the hand of the authorities and compels them to allow public performances
sooner or later; the art of paving the way for such
performances by half-public rehearsals at which hired
applause is allowable; the art of maintaining and stim-
ulating attention, even in the midst of a tremendous
success, by means of trivial, unforeseen obstacles or
by ostentatious acts of beneficence, which opportunely break the monotony. But let us not anticipate
the machinery of *Figaro,*—let us observe simply that
the success of the *Barbier de Séville* was responsible
for a great reform in the relations between dramatic
authors and actors. Up to that time authors were at
the mercy of the actors, who, after a certain number of
performances, and when the receipts had fallen below
a certain fixed figure (which it was always easy to
bring about), considered that they had a right to con-
fiscate the plays, and to appropriate the profits thereafter. After thirty-two performances of the *Barbier,*
Beaumarchais, who did not consider that ''the literary
spirit was incompatible with the commercial spirit,''

thought best to call upon the actors for an accounting. They evaded the demand and tried to oppose the examination of their books. Beaumarchais persisted; he demanded, not a sum in cash, which they were very willing to offer him, but a full and clear account,— a legitimate demand which they politely refused; he demanded it less for himself, because he had no need of it, than for his confrères, the men of letters, who had always been oppressed and robbed. The affair lasted for years; Beaumarchais followed it through all the steps of litigation, from the gentlemen of the chamber even to the Constituent Assembly. In a word, he first succeeded in obtaining a definite decision as to what property in dramatic works really consists in, and in causing it to be recognised and respected. The society of dramatic authors, which has been instituted in our day, ought never to meet without saluting the bust of Beaumarchais.

The famous *Mariage de Figaro* had been written for a long while, but could not be produced in the light of day. It was the Prince de Conti who, after the *Barbier de Séville,* had, as it were, challenged the author to recur to his Figaro and exhibit him a second time under circumstances more fully developed. Beaumarchais accepted the challenge, and the *Mariage* was written, or sketched, about 1775 or 1776, that is to say, during the period which I look upon as that when Beaumarchais was in possession of all his wit and all his genius, and after which we find him degenerating slightly and going astray once more. There were five or six unique years (1771–1776), when, under the spur of adversity and necessity, and in the first breath of public favour, he attained full expression, and during which he felt the birth within him of almost supernatural faculties which he never again recovered to that degree.

It required even more wit, it has been said, to have the *Mariage de Figaro* acted than to write it. Beaumarchais worked at it for years. He had against him the king, the magistrates, the lieutenant of police, the keeper of the seals,—all the powers of the State. With that assurance and that audacious air which were peculiar to him, he sought aid and support even from the courtiers, that is to say, from those of whom he had made the most fun.

> FIGARO. . . . I was born to be a courtier.
> SUZANNE. They say that 't is so difficult a trade!
> FIGARO. To receive, to take, to ask,—behold the secret in three words!

It was, then, to the courtiers that he applied, directly. No one could be more of a courtier than Monsieur de Vaudreuil ; but he was arrogant and assuming in his courtiership, and prided himself upon not being one. And what more striking proof of independence could he give than to patronise *Figaro*? French society was at this time in a curious frame of mind: its members vied with one another in making sport of themselves and of their class, and in hastening its ruin. That seemed to be the noblest rôle of fashionable people. Beaumarchais saw plainly that, by means of the social circle of M. de Vaudreuil and Madame de Polignac, by means of the influence of the queen, and the Comte d'Artois, and by means of the curiosity of the women and of the courtiers, he could triumph over the resistance of Louis XVI; it was for him only a question of time.

We know his successive manœuvres, his marches and countermarches, so to speak, in this audacious undertaking, almost day by day. "The king does not choose to permit the performance of my play, therefore, it shall be performed." On June 12, 1783, he very nearly carried the day by surprise. By means of a tacit tolerance due to the patronage of the Comte d'Artois, and on the strength of a vague remark boldly interpreted, he had succeeded in having his play rehearsed on the stage of the Menus-Plaisirs, that is to say, upon the king's own stage. There had been a certain number of half-public rehearsals, and they were about to proceed and give the performance. The tickets were distributed, bearing an engraved figure of Figaro in his costume. The carriages arrived in great numbers, the Comte d'Artois had already started for Paris from Versailles, when the Duc de Villequier caused the actors to be informed that they must abstain from giving the play "on pain of incurring His Majesty's wrath."

At this order from the king, Beaumarchais, disappointed and frantic, insolently cried out before everybody: "Very good! he does not want us to play it here, messieurs, but I swear that rather than not be played at all, it shall be played if necessary in the very choir of Notre-Dame."

It was only a postponement. Monsieur de Vaudreuil, one of the author's patrons, obtained leave to have the play given at his house at Gennevilliers on September 26, 1783, by the actors from the Comédie-Française, before an audience of three hundred. The queen, not being well, could not be present; but the Comte d'Artois and the Duchesse de Polignac were there. All the flower of the old régime came to applaud the play that ridiculed and undermined it. Beaumarchais, who was present, was in the seventh heaven. "He ran about in all directions," says an eye-witness, "like a man beside himself; and when some one complained of the heat, he did not wait to have the windows opened, but broke all the panes with his cane, which led some one to say, after the play, that he had broken the windows twice."

Emboldened by all this approbation and, we might almost say, this complicity, and relying upon a vague word from Monsieur de Breteuil, upon which he had seized as an authorisation to proceed, Beaumarchais succeeded so well that he persuaded the actors to give his play in the latter part of February, 1784; the rehearsal had already taken place, and the lieutenant of police, Monsieur Le Noir, was obliged to write to the author and the actors to remind them of the king's final prohibition. Beaumarchais, although rebuffed again, did not consider himself beaten.

At last, on April 27, 1784, the explosion took place, and, the prohibition being removed, the play could be given at Paris. Nothing was lacking in the solemnity and the *éclat* of that first performance.

"More than one duchess," says Grimm, " deemed herself too fortunate that day to find in the balconies, where respectable women rarely sit, a wretched stool beside Mesdames Duthé, Carline, and company."

"Three hundred people," says La Harpe, " dined at the Comédie in the actors' dressing rooms, in order to be more certain to obtain seats ; and at the opening of the offices the crush was so great that three people were suffocated. That is one more than for Scudéry. . . . The first performance was very uproarious, as one can imagine, and *so extraordinarily long* that the audience was not dismissed until ten o'clock, although there was no short play; for Beaumarchais's comedy constituted the whole performance, which is in itself an additional novelty."

This extraordinary length was four hours, or four and a half, as the play began at half-past five.

Thus launched, after such a resistance, the play ran to more than one hundred performances, and was one of the great political and moral events of that time. Here it was no longer a question, as in the *Barbier*, of a mere merry, piquant, and amusing imbroglio; in the *Mariage* there was an armed Fronde,—everything that the public, since the play was prohibited, had fancied that they could see in it and had imported into it; all that the author himself had this time really

intended to put in it. Napoleon said of *Figaro* that
" it was the revolution already under way." Sensible
and moderate people of that time did not think differently. But when everybody is laughing, and when
excitement is rife, of what avail are the previsions and
reservations of a few minds against a contestant of the
strength and impetuosity of Beaumarchais ? There
are times when it seems that society as a whole re-
sponds to the advice of the doctor as Figaro does:
" Faith, monsieur, as men have little choice except
between stupidity and folly, where I see no profit I
propose at least to have some pleasure ; so *vive la
joie!* who knows whether the world will last three
weeks longer ? "

To depict this French audience of the first performance of *Figaro,* and its unbridled enthusiasm, two
facts suffice: when the hero of the fleets, the Bailli de
Suffren, entered the hall, he was applauded with
frenzy; when, a moment later, the charming actress,
Madame Dugazon, just recovered from a sickness of
which the cause was only too well known, appeared
in the front of her box, they applauded her no less
warmly.

Such a play, in which society was represented in
masks and in dishabille, as in a carnival of the Direc-
tory; where everything was taken apart and turned
upside down,—marriage, maternity, the magistracy,
the nobility, all the affairs of State; in which the
master-lackey held the key from one end to the other,

and in which licence served as an aid to politics, became a manifest signal of revolution. I would not assert that Beaumarchais himself realised its full bearing; as I have said, he was drawn on by the currents of his epoch, and if it did happen that he accelerated their course, he never dominated them. We see him, throughout the whole period of the vogue of *Figaro*, busied with his play, like an experienced author who knows the rubric of the profession, and who thinks of nothing but making the very utmost out of it, in the way of sensation and enjoyment alike. At the fourth performance, from the third tier of boxes there rained down into the auditorium hundreds of printed copies of a satirical ballad against the play, which some persons attributed under their breath to a great personage, a prince (the future Louis XVIII), and in which that classic and sarcastic *bel-esprit* perhaps had a hand. But the printing and distribution, so it was confidently asserted, were done by secret order of Beaumarchais himself. It was a scheme of a sort said to be familiar to him: to seize upon a slander, a malicious trick of which he was the object, and to spread it abroad in order the better to answer it, in order to profit by it and to make friends of all the indignant gossips. A few days later, it was a letter from him that was circulated, and was said to be addressed to a duke and peer who had asked him for a small curtained box from which certain ladies of the Court could see the play without being seen.

"I have no respect, monsieur le duc," said Beaumarchais in the letter which was circulated in society, " for women who permit themselves to witness a play which they deem indecent, provided that they can witness it secretly; I do not lend my aid to such whims. I have given my play to the public to entertain and not to instruct, and not to afford false prudes the pleasure of thinking well of it in a box, on condition of speaking ill of it in society. The pleasures of vice and the honours of virtue,—such is the prudery of the age. My play is not an equivocal work; one must either acknowledge it or avoid it. "I salute you, monsieur le duc, and I keep my box."

On going back to the source, it was discovered that the letter was not addressed to a duke and peer, and Beaumarchais himself acknowledged it, which took away materially from the boldness and insolence of the contents; it was addressed simply to Président Dupaty, a friend of the author, and was written "in the first heat of a slight disappointment." However, the effect was produced, and for several days it was an additional advertisment in fashionable society in favour of Figaro, who needed it so little.

It is said that, after the thirty-first performance of *Figaro*, the total receipts amounted to one hundred and fifty thousand francs. When the fiftieth was drawing near, Beaumarchais felt that some novelty was essential, in order to double that cape under full sail; and as charity was very fashionable at the time, he conceived the idea, partly sincere, of having recourse to it. The fiftieth performance therefore was given for the benefit of "poor wet-nurses"; and he wrote some new couplets with that in mind for the final vaudeville. Whereupon an epigram was circulated which ended with these wretched lines:

> " Il paye du lait aux enfants,
> Et donne du poison aux mères." [1]

The epoch is well characterised by these chapters from Sterne, if we may so describe them, these acts of sentimental beneficence *à la Geoffrin,* which served as an interlude to the *Mariage de Figaro,* and which accompanied its triumph. A lover of the drama having taken it into his head to raise a quibble in the *Journal de Paris,* and to propound a question relative to the *petite Figaro,* who is mentioned in the *Barbier de Séville* by Rosine, and having expressed his surprise that there was no trace in the second play of this little Figaro who antedated the marriage, Beaumarchais answered cavalierly that the little one in question was no other than a poor adopted child of whom Figaro, at Seville, had taken charge for humanity's sake; that she had come to France since then and had married in Paris a poor but honest youth, a porter at Port Saint-Nicolas, named L'Écluze, who had been crushed to death, amid his comrades, by the machine used to discharge vessels.

"He has left," he added, "his poor wife, twenty-five years of age, with one child of thirteen months, and one a week old, which she is nursing, although she is very ill and in want of everything. Her husband's poor companions, touched by her sad lot, have contributed to keep her alive for awhile. They appealed to me this morning by the pen of their inspector. I have collaborated with them with pleasure,

[1] He buys milk for the children and gives the mothers poison.

and I do not doubt, monsieur, that you will do as much. I have therefore sent a louis for her to Monsieur Merlet, inspector at Port Saint-Nicolas, and I send two more with this letter," etc., etc.

All this was addressed to the publisher of the *Journal de Paris.* Whereupon, *louis d'or* came in showers for the poor wet-nurse thus indicated. The unfortunate woman reaped the benefit of it, and so did Beaumarchais, who, at the same stroke, accomplished a generous act, a mischievous hoax, and, furthermore, an ingenious advertisement, of an altogether new variety, of the *Mariage de Figaro,* which had reached its seventy-first performance.

This affair, however, had strange results and more serious than one would have supposed. There appeared in the *Journal de Paris* a letter marked by cold and cutting irony, ostensibly written by an ecclesiastic, who declared that there was little of good morals in this way of conferring alms on the poor woman by describing her as what she was not, and baptising her with the name of a comedy in which there was little that was honourable, after all, and which might be prejudicial to her child.

To this somewhat pedantic lecture, which was publicly addressed to him, Beaumarchais replied as he alone knew how to reply and, it may be, in a more serious and more animated tone than the subject required. He fancied that he had to deal in this discussion with no one of more importance than Suard, publisher of the *Journal,* and his ordinary adversary. He was mistaken on one point.  A more punctilious author, Monsieur le Comte de Provence (again the future Louis XVIII), was hidden behind this ironical outburst of the abbé.  Angered by the tone of the reply, he complained of it, or some one complained for him, to Louis XVIII, who was annoyed by this constant disturbance over Beaumarchais, for whom he had little esteem.  It was decided that Beaumarchais should be at once arrested, and taken, not to the Bastile (that would have been too noble for him), but to a penitentiary, to Saint-Lazare, where they confined, not prostitutes as yet, but scandalous priests, and dissipated sons of good families.  Louis XVI, when he formed his determination, was at cards, and it was upon a card, the seven of spades, that he wrote, with the pencil with which he marked the *bêtes,*[1] that extraordinary order to arrest Beaumarchais and take him to Saint-Lazare (March 7, 1785).

The reader can judge of the sensation and amazement which this news produced in the public.  When they came to arrest him, Beaumarchais was entertaining at supper the Prince de Nassau, Abbé de Calonne, brother of the contrôleur-général, and other persons of note.  He was detained only six days, after which he was set at liberty.  On the one hand, a hundred carriages in line came to his house to congratulate him; on the other, verses were written against him, and caricatures handed about in which he was ex-

---

[1] *Bête,*—money left on the table by the winner.

hibited beaten with rods by a monk, and in a ridiculous posture. He was deeply wounded by this
affront, which fell upon him in the full tide of his
triumph; he remained in retirement in his own house
for some time, replying but rarely to the questions
and letters of curious folk and admirers. In a reply
which he did send to one of them, however, in June,
1785, we read:

" You ask me if it is true that the king has granted me essential aid
in my present distress; I have no more reason for concealing the evidences of his justice than I had for concealing the profound affliction
in which his unexpected wrath plunged me. The king, being deceived, punished me for an offence of which I was not guilty; but if
my enemies did succeed in arousing his wrath, they have been
unable to change his just disposition.

"Yes, monsieur, it is quite true that his Majesty has condescended
to sign for me, since my disgrace, an order for the payment of 2,150,-
000 francs, on account of advances made long ago, the repayment of
which I was soliciting from the king, while I was being accused of the
detestable crime of failing in respect to him."

After this adventure of Saint-Lazare, and this reverse which marked the close of his "Day of Folly,"
Beaumarchais, being fifty-three years old, still had
moments of celebrity and notoriety; but the wound
remained unhealed; his influence entered upon its
period of decline, his talent also degenerated, or at
least, began to work at random. His finest moment
had passed.

It certainly was not Beaumarchais who lost most
by that odious and absurd confinement at Saint-Lazare,
which happened so unexpectedly at the time of the

seventy-first performance of the *Mariage de Figaro*
To be sure, the mystifier was himself mystified for the
first time; the laughers were not all on one side.
"The public laughed heartily at this incident," says a
judicious witness; "more attention was paid to it
than to a battle or a treaty of peace." However,
when they saw that the prisoner was released after
five or six days, without any precise cause being assigned for that act of severity which bordered upon
ignominy, the public turned upon those who had
ordered it. The executive power, ashamed of what
had been done in a moment of irritation, retreated.
Reparation was the order of the day. The performances of *Figaro* resumed their course; the seventy-
second attracted no less numerous an audience than
the first. It was observed that almost all the ministers
were present. A letter from the contrôleur-général,
Monsieur de Calonne, to Beaumarchais was quoted,
in which that minister informed him that the king
accepted his justification. With a delicacy which
equalled and surpassed all possible apologies, the *Barbier de Séville* was acted at the Petit-Trianon by the
queen's intimate circle, on August 19, 1785, and the
actors were the queen herself, in the rôle of Rosine,
the Comte d'Artois as Figaro, Monsieur de Vaudreuil
playing Almaviva, etc. The author had the honour of
being present at this exquisite performance. Finally,
if Beaumarchais did recover a part of his funds as a
trader, and did receive by way of arrears more than

two millions, he declined as a man of letters to accept
a pension of more than a hundred francs upon the
privy purse. They offered him much more; he
deemed it his duty to reduce the amount himself to
that modest figure, not choosing to see or to acknowledge therein anything more than the slight bond
of a favour conferred.

But Beaumarchais was about to have to deal with
adversaries more dangerous than the executive power
itself. Like all men who have attained great renown
and are much feared, but who do not govern themselves prudently, he was about to find himself face to
face with men of talent, who were younger than he,
and bold, enthusiastic, and eager for celebrity; who
had their reputations to make, and for whom he was
likely to become, if he did not look to it, a very ap-
petising victim. Mirabeau, already well known by
reason of tremendous scandals, and very little known
as yet for any honourable reason, heaping pamphlets
upon pamphlets, wrote one against the company called
the *Compagnie des Eaux de Paris*. The Perrier
brothers had undertaken to supply Paris with an
abundance of healthful water, and at a lower price
than had ever hitherto been reached; each house
which subscribed was to receive through pipes all the
water that it needed, all of which was very advan-
tageous and most worthy of encouragement. The
shares of the company had been carried to a very high
figure, it may be by artificial means. Mirabeau, urged

on by his friend, the banker Clavière, fought the enterprise in order to depress the value of the shares. Beaumarchais entered the lists, defending the company and its manager; in my opinion, on the merits he was entirely right. But he chose to laugh at Mirabeau and his objections; recalling the criticisms which new undertakings had always had to undergo, "When they were very bitter," he said, "they were called 'Philippics'; perhaps some day some wretched joker will christen these with the pretty name of 'Mirabelles,' derived from the Comte de Mirabeau, *qui mirabilia fecit.*"—The maker of puns forgot whom he was playing against. After a long and outspoken discussion, which he concluded by wondering what motive could have induced a man of so great talent as the Comte de Mirabeau to "surrender his vigorous pen to factional interests which were not even his own," Beaumarchais was careful to close with a qualifying expression:

"Our esteem for his person," he said, "has frequently held in check the indignation which grew upon us while writing. But if, despite the moderation which we have imposed upon ourselves, any expression which he does not like has escaped us, we beg him to forgive us for it. We have combated his ideas, without ceasing to admire his style."

Mirabeau was hit; perhaps he desired to be; he rushed to the fray. Setting forth the motives, genuine or not, which had led him to enter the discussion, he marched straight for his adversary, and striking

him in the face with his sword, according to Cæsar's
advice, he sneered at that assumption of patriotism,
of disinterestedness, and of zeal for the public welfare
with which Beaumarchais loved (and sincerely enough
I think) to cover his own affairs and his financial
speculations.

" Such were my motives," he cried, already in the tone of an ora-
tor, of a master powerful in retort and invective, " and it may be
that they are not worthy of the age in which everything is done for
honour, for glory, and *nothing for money;* in which *chevaliers
d'industrie,* charlatans, merry-Andrews and panders have never had
any other ambition than glory, *without the slightest thought of
profit;* in which traffic in the city, speculation at Court, intriguing
which lives upon exactions and upon prodigality, have no other aim
than honour *without any selfish view ;* in which a person despatches
to America thirty ships loaded with rotten provisions, with useless
ammunition, with old muskets which are sold for new, all for the
glory of contributing to make a world free, and *in nowise for the
possible profits of this unselfish expedition;* in which the masterpieces of a great man [an allusion to Beaumarchais' edition of Vol-
taire] are profaned by associating with them all his *juvenilia* and his
*senilia,* all the musings which have escaped him in his long career,
wholly for the glory, and *in nowise for the profit,* of being the editor
of this monstrous collection ; in which, to make a little sensation,
and consequently, from love of glory and detestation of profit, the
Théâtre-Français is changed into a puppet show, and the comic stage
into a school of bad morals ; in which all the orders of the State, all
classes of citizens, all laws, all rules, all the proprieties, are torn
asunder, insulted, and outraged."

Behold therefore Mirabeau become the avenger of
the proprieties and of good morals against Beaumarchais, and Figaro passing his time unhappily in the
hands of the mighty athelete who whirls him about
and lifts him from the earth in the first round.   Then

he asks Beaumarchais what he thinks now of his
*Mirabelles.*   Never was pun more roughly paid for.
The peroration with which Mirabeau brought his
pamphlet to a close is still famous in the world of
invective:

"Do you, monsieur, who by misrepresenting my meaning and my
motives have compelled me to treat you with a severity which nature
has placed neither in my mind nor in my heart; you, whom I never
provoked, and with whom war could be neither profitable nor honourable,—take my advice, profit by the bitter lesson which you
have compelled me to administer to you.   Withdraw your gratuitous
eulogy; for I am unable to return it, from any point of view; withdraw the pitiful pardon for which you have asked me ; take back
even the impudent esteem which you have the hardihood to express
for me."

And he concludes with this terrible advice, the
most withering imaginable between men who are
greedy of popularity before everything: "Think
henceforward of nothing except deserving to be
forgotten."

Beaumarchais held his peace under the insult; he
had fallen in with a wrestler even more daring than
himself, and with a sturdier frame; he was outclassed
and beaten.   His reign in public opinion really came
to an end at that moment (1785–1786).

The Revolution of '89, at the outset, taught Beaumarchais how powerless he was before that vast flood
which he had been among the first to set in motion,
and which threatened him in its onward rush.   Beyond
question *Figaro* had paved the way for and presaged
that Revolution; but, when the success of the tragedy

of *Charles IX*, by Marie-Joseph Chénier, gave the signal for it, and as it were, sounded the tocsin, Beaumarchais took fright. He addressed to the actors of the Comédie-Française some most judicious and far-sighted observations on this subject (November 9, 1786), in which he dwells upon the inconveniences and perils of the performance of such a play, which are so manifest under the circumstances. We see that it is with Beaumarchais as with all of us: we become prudent and sagacious the moment that our passions subside, that our selfish interests (including the interests of our talents and of our most cherished faculties) are out of danger; the man who brought Figaro into the world, who pushed him forward in spite of, and in opposition to all men, and who now had nothing of importance to add to his work, would fain cry "Halt!" to *Charles IX*.

In a word, there was in his case infinitely less of revolutionary *design* than in the case of Mirabeau, Chamfort, and many others. When his force of impulsion was exhausted, he had reached the age at which everything would have seemed well enough to him, provided that he could have his plays performed and be joyous and happy in his garden.

During these years great changes had taken place both in Beaumarchais' mode of life and in his sentiments. He had grown old rather early; he was still in good health, but quite deaf,—an excellent man, by the way, and more and more ingenuous as he withdrew more and more into the intimate circle of his friends and his family. His life had become regular to a certain point. A son by his second marriage did not live; but he had a daughter whom he loved dearly, named Eugénie, and everything indicates that she was a charming girl. He was married a third time, March 8, 1786, to Marie-Thérèse-Émilie *Willermawla*.

In '89 he still lived on Vieille-Rue-du-Temple; but in that year he built his house, with the fine garden, at the corner of the boulevard, opposite the Bastille, which all of us may have seen in our youth. He went there to live in 1790, only to go forth a fugitive, and threatened with prosecution in '92. It was miraculous, in very truth, that that house escaped the devastating flood that daily swept from the faubourg and broke against it, as against a promontory. There were incessant domiciliary visits, threats of pillage and of burning; Beaumarchais was accused of creating a monopoly in grain, of collecting concealed weapons and storing them in subterranean passages which did not exist.

From the early days of '89 Beaumarchais was constantly in an attitude of apology and on the defensive. They tried to exclude him from the first Commune of Paris, of which he was a member; he was forced to defend himself by a petition in which he spoke grandiloquently of himself and of the services rendered by him in the American war. Doubtless he forgot many details which would have cast a shadow (n the picture, but he was justified in speaking of his zeal for the public interest, and of the patriotic aspect in which he was always careful to place, and in which he himself always viewed, his private interest. He was justified above all in speaking of his readiness to oblige, and of his kindness, which had made so many ingrates.

His longing for an active life, for new undertakings, which had survived so many disappointments, led him, in March, 1792, to engage in an affair which had the colour of patriotism, and which steeped him in vexations. The project was to purchase sixty thousand, or perhaps *two hundred thousand* muskets in Holland and supply them to the French government, which, at the near approach of war, was sadly in need of them. He broached the subject to *fourteen* ministers, who succeeded one another in office in the course of a few months, and encountered nothing but inattention and constant temporising from them all, certain men in the departments being interested, not in causing the scheme to fall through, but in taking it out of Beaumarchais' hands in order to reap the profit of it themselves. In this matter Beaumarchais did not escape one of the disadvantages which men of the shrewdest intelligence are sometimes subject to in their old age. In the memorials which he addressed to the Convention on this subject, and which he divided into six "Epochs," he was unlucky enough (a strange and unexpected circumstance!) to become tedious. Beaumarchais tedious! It is evident that he was; he is so to readers of to-day; he was so then to the very ministers whom he was pursuing with his incessant petitions, and who finally were utterly at a loss to evade his persistent requests for interviews. About the Tenth of August he was in danger of being massacred and was obliged to fly. But no matter! he thought of nothing but his muskets; he made it a point of honour to persist; it was his mania. He was imprisoned in the Abbaye; a few hours before the massacres in the prisons of the Second of September, he was set at liberty by the generosity of Manuel,[1] who went to him and said: "Leave this place instantly."

"I threw my arms about him," cries Beaumarchais theatrically, "unable to utter a single word; my eyes alone depicted the emotions of my heart; I believe that they were most expressive if they depicted all that I thought! I am as steel against injustice, but my heart softens, my eyes melt in tears at the slightest mark of kindness of heart. I shall never forget that man or that moment. I went away."

He went away, but he went to the department to follow up the affair of the muskets. During a discussion in the Council, to which he was admitted, he had difficulty in hearing Danton, although he spoke quite loud.

"M. Danton was seated on the other side of the table ; he began the discussion ; but as I am almost deaf, I rose and begged to be excused if I went nearer to the minister (because I could not hear well at a distance), and making a little trumpet with my hand as usual."

---

[1 *Procureur-Général* of the Commune, and prominent in the proceedings of the 10th of August, and 2nd of September, 1792.—TR.]

This made the ministers laugh, Danton with the rest; but Beaumarchais did not laugh; he had ceased to laugh. He insisted that the nation should have its muskets,—that it should have them *in spite of itself*. It is hard to understand such obstinacy.

"I am a dismal kind of a bird," said Beaumarchais justly enough, "for I have but one song, which for five months past has consisted in saying to all the ministers in succession : 'For Heaven's sake, Monsieur, settle the matter of the muskets in Holland!' The whole world is afflicted with vertigo."

He might have added: "And I with the rest."

Deaf as he had grown, he did not seem to have formed a very accurate idea of the general situation. At London, where he fled for refuge towards the end of 1792, he received a letter from his clerk, who held his power of attorney, informing him that he had gone to the War Department and had applied to a Sieur Hassenfratz (the scholar). "I began by asking him if I had the honour of speaking to Monsieur Hassenfratz; whereupon, with haggard eye, flushed cheeks, and clenched fist, he shouted at me in a voice of thunder and with an expression of frantic rage: 'You have not the honour; I am not monsieur; my name is Hassenfratz!'" It was when things were in this state that Beaumarchais was innocent enough to return from London and put himself in the hands of the Convention, in order to argue the same old cause, and to clear himself from the denunciation of Lecointre, whose errors and injustice he made clear beyond question. At the end of his sixth "Epoch," or memorial, we read, after a quatrain worthy of Pibrac, this naïve signature: " *The citizen, always persecuted,* Caron Beaumarchais.—Finished for my judges, this 6th of March, 1793, *in the second year of the Republic.*" Wholly engrossed by his one object, he had no very clear idea what the National Convention was; the surprising thing is that he saved his head.

Having left France once more and taken refuge in Hamburg during the following years, he lived there in poverty; he was so poor (M. de Lomenie, his biographer, tells me) that he had to save half of a match to use the next day. The thought of his family and of his darling daughter sustained him. He saw her again in 1796, and soon after returned to his house, to that lovely garden which he had peopled with statues, cenotaphs, and souvenirs, and where he had had all sorts of inscriptions carved, according to the fashion of the age.

His self-love had one last moment of enjoyment when, the Théâtre Français having revived his drama *La Mère Coupable,* which he wrote in 1791, he was loudly called for and was dragged upon the stage, where he had to appear with Molé, Fleury, and Mademoiselle Contat. He keenly relished this crowning applause, and said to himself that the public must have become more moral since it greeted favourably so excellent a work. After discharging

all the fireworks of his wit, Beaumarchais had unconsciously recurred to his original Grandisonian tendencies. But paternity had led him back, instinctively
and in thought, to the moral and virtuous drama, and
he often repeated in his old age that "every man who
is not born a detestable villain always ends by becoming a good man when the age of passions has
passed, and above all when he has tasted the exquisite
joy of being a father!"

He died at Paris during the night of the 17th and
18th of May, 1799, of an apoplectic attack, it is said, of
which he had had no warning; he fell asleep for ever
during his sleep. He was only sixty-seven years old.
A few persons, of whom I will mention Esménard,
author of the article on Beaumarchais in the *Bio-
graphie Universelle*, M. Népomucène Lemercier, and
M. Beuchot, seemed thoroughly convinced that Beaumarchais delivered himself (by means of the poison
called by the name of Cabanis) from a life which had
become too burdensome because of penury, and too
painful. His family and friends have contradicted
this rumour and this belief, which, as time passed,
had obtained some credit. Those who have no other
interest than to ascertain the truth will find no difficulty in attributing his death to apoplexy, reserving
at most a very slight doubt thereupon.

# Jacques Necker.

1732-1804.

# Jacques Necker.

AMONG the illustrious foreigners who became naturalised in France during the eighteenth century, not one had more influence, or a more direct influence, on our destinies, than M. Necker. From the political standpoint everything seems to have been said about him, and both the *pro* and the *contra* are exhausted. This political aspect of the man tempts me very little; but there is a way of studying M. Necker which not only is worn less threadbare, but is less strewn with thorns: that way is, to read him as an author who, having written a good deal, has had much to say about himself, and who has painted himself in unmistakable colours. M. Necker left no less than fifteen volumes of works; I do not advise everybody to attempt to read them; it is for the critic to undertake that task, and, after reading carefully, to select those portions which may help to depict the man, whether in respect to his moral character or in respect to his literary form and spirit; for M. Necker had some literary influence among us. When we have come to know him in this aspect, we shall have sufficient light on the subject of politics, and many consequences will follow of themselves.

This distinguished man was born at Geneva, September 30, 1732; his father was a professor of law, born at Küstrin, Prussia, who had settled in Calvin's city, and who traced his own origin to an Irish family. Young Necker was destined at an early age for the banking profession. He received an excellent home education, and began the study of the classics, but, according to all appearances, he went but a little way in that direction. The studies which he was compelled to take he paid but little attention to, so it was said, and in order to arouse his interest, it was necessary that he should propose them himself. Only by dint of prolonged inward labour was he destined to reach the height that he finally attained.

He was sent to Paris, to the banking-house of a Genevese. It is said that, even in those days, he sought the latest literary works, and that he even tried his own hand at composition; he was singularly shrewd in grasping certain social shortcomings, and he wrote several little comedies which remained in his portfolio. In fact, business soon engrossed his entire attention, and he exhibited abundant capacity therefor. Having become a partner and one of the managing men in a banking-house, he gave evidence, in his various speculations, of more than ordinary sagacity, and of a genius for laying plans which was rewarded by great wealth. But with all his success in business, he had retained from childhood one peculiar characteristic which seemed in every respect

JACQUES NECKER
*From a portrait by Duplessis*

the opposite of an enterprising spirit.   Being a thinker
by nature, he was never willing to make up his mind
about anything except for sufficient reasons.

"His mind," says a person who knew him well (the same M.
Meister whom we have seen in Grimm's service), "his mind was accustomed to consider all the aspects of a matter so carefully and with
so much thought, his forethought was so sensitive and so cautious,
that, even under the most urgent circumstances, he was impressed
solely by the difficulties of any decision that he might make, and
never made up his mind except by force, so to speak, to attempt what
he did attempt."

When, later, it was a matter of guiding the chariot
of State on a steep incline, and there was not an instant to lose, we can understand that this inborn indecision was likely to be fatal; in the ordinary affairs of
life it was simply an interesting peculiarity.   He liked
to attribute in part to the obstacles that he encountered the fault that was an essential feature of his character.   The biographer whom I quoted just now, and
who had passed much time in his company, said: "I
do not think that I ever left him more thoroughly content with my praise than when I assured him that a
very determined will seemed to me almost incompatible with great breadth, great shrewdness, and
great superiority of mind."

But having thus gone straight to the heart of our
subject at the outset, we must retrace our steps.   M.
Necker, enriched by fortunate operations, and still a
young man, having married Mademoiselle Curchod,
who worshipped intellect, maintained in Paris, from

1765, an establishment which became almost immediately the meeting-place of the most illustrious *philosophes* and literary men.   His attitude in his wife's
salon was peculiar: although it was with him in mind,
and in a large measure to gratify him and to assist and
enhance his renown, that she exerted herself to collect about her that brilliant and select circle, he was
simply a silent and cold spectator.   Marmontel observes that M. Necker's silence and gravity of demeanour, which many people have attributed to a
touch of vanity, but which he (Marmontel) noticed
before his elevation, were due  principally to discretion and caution.

One of the best witnesses of that time, Madame du
Deffand, whose acquaintance the Neckers made in
1773, has described them, both wife and husband,
especially the latter, with an accent of verity which
leaves nothing to be  desired from a social point
of view.

" They desired to know me," she says, " because
people had given me the reputation of a *bel-esprit*
who does n't care for *beaux-esprits;* that seemed to
them a rarity worthy of being inquired into."

She blames herself at first for yielding to their wish;
but soon, after she comes to know M. Necker, she
ceases to regret her compliance; she sees him frequently at Paris and Saint-Ouen; at first sight, she
prefers him to all the Encyclopædists, Economists,
and the rest; she studies and strives to comprehend

by degrees his type, his originality, and his measure
of attractiveness.

There are days when M. Necker pleases her so
much in conversation,—days when he lets himself
go,—that she detects a resemblance to Horace Walpole and ventures to avow it: " Necker has much
wit; he is not far from resembling you in some respects." Walpole was not of her opinion; Monsieur
and Madame Necker went to England in the spring of
1776, and on their return Madame du Deffand writes:

" They did not please you much, I can see; they are both bright,
but especially the man.  I admit that he lacks one of the qualities
which go farthest to make a man agreeable, namely a certain facility
in conversation which imparts wit, so to speak, to those with whom
one is talking; he does not help you to develop your thoughts, and
one is more stupid with him than when alone or with other people."

This judgment of Madame du Deffand concerning
M. Necker is in some sort definitive, considering him
as a society man; he talks well when he consents to
talk, but his conversation is not helpful to others;
with him one finds in one's self no unsuspected fund
of wit.  This distinctive trait he has in common with
the distinguished men who are described by the name
" doctrinaires," and who tried, in their day, to give a
new tone, a new ply, to French wit.

Another trait which M. Necker seemed also to have
communicated to them, and which was allied to the
preceding, was the entertaining a profound respect
for, and proclaiming aloud, the rights of mankind; the

estimating the human race at more than its real worth, perhaps, and at the same time not always according to the individuals with whom he was brought in contact the degree of esteem to which they were justly entitled. Herein there was a substantial contradiction, which we may detect without difficulty in the leaders of that aristocratic family of intellects, from M. Necker to M. Royer-Collard. It was an extraordinary oversight and negligence, due to self-esteem, on the part of those superior minds: they judged mankind by themselves and they ranked it very high; they judged other individuals by themselves likewise, and when they found that they did not measure up to their standard and were not cast in the same mould, they deemed them vastly inferior and altogether insignificant.

M. Necker's face and physique were well adapted to create an impression in Parisian society by virtue of his noble, imposing, and rather unusual aspect. "His features resemble no one else's; the shape of his face is extraordinary." It was his wife who said that, and others noticed it no less. He had a large head and a long face; the forehead and chin especially were disproportionately long. His brown eyes, bright and intelligent, and at times charmingly soft or profoundly melancholy, were surmounted by very high eyebrows, which gave to his face a most peculiar expression. In a word, his face was not of a French type. He became very stout and heavy after he passed thirty, and this tendency increased with his age. There was in his temperament a substratum of passive meditation, of lofty tranquillity, and of sloth, which he could surmount only with the aid of the most exalted incentives to action, and by his passionate love of dignified praise.

At first he wrote only upon subjects connected with his regular employments. The first work which directed public attention to him was the *Éloge de Colbert,* crowned by the Académie Française in 1773. M. Necker, having made a fortune, had just retired from the banking business; he had been appointed minister of the Republic of Geneva to the Court of Versailles, and he aimed still higher; he aspired to a political career in France. His *Éloge de Colbert* was not so much an academic discourse as a programme for the ministry. To give his readers an idea of Colbert, he thought it necessary to begin by describing the character of the ideal finance minister,—such an one as Colbert may have been, but, above all, such an one as M. Necker aspired to be.

Guided by a sort of tact foreign to the French character, M. Necker was present in his own salon when his wife read a "Portrait" of him, written in 1787; a portrait wherein his praises are sung in every key, wherein the word genius is scattered broadcast, as well as the most subtle and refined comparisons; wherein, amid an incongruous medley of similes and images, M. Necker appears successively as a living picture, an angel, a chemical substance, a lion, a hunter, a vestal virgin, an Apollo, a majestic bridge, an Albanian dog, a volcanic mountain, a pillar of fire, a cloud, a mirror, a hearthstone, a mine, the insect that produces coral, one of the genii of the Arabs, etc. He listened to this portrait when his wife read it before witnesses, as if it referred to a third person, and he afterwards included it in the volume of *Mélanges* by her, which he published in 1798.

M. Necker's second work, which was successful in spite of its subject, or, rather, because of its subject, which was then the fashion, was that entitled *Sur la Législation et le Commerce des Grains,* which appeared in 1775. It was an attack upon the arbitrary theories of the Turgot ministry, and upon the Economists, who desired entire freedom of exportation. M. Necker repeated therein, in a most unpractical form, divers truths proved by experience; it was noticed afterward that he spoke of property and land-owners rather slightingly, and that he represented those who live by toil, or the proletariat, as their victims. "They are as lions and defenceless animals living side by side," he said; "we cannot increase the share of the latter except by eluding the others' vigilance and not giving them time to spring." In attacking Turgot as "one who has only the desire for greatness without the force to attain it," he seemed to point to himself clearly enough, in more than one place, as a minister much to be preferred. "If," he said, "there were always at the head of the government a man whose far-reaching genius takes account of every circumstance; whose *plastic and flexible mind* is able to bring his plans and his wishes into conformity with those circumstances; who, being endowed with an ardent soul and calm judgment," etc. If a man is not thinking of himself when he talks in this strain and describes so complacently him whom events are calling, it shows a lack of tact at least, because he makes everybody think that he has himself in mind.

I will not dwell upon this work, of which Madame du Deffand said: "I have just read a few chapters of M. Necker, and I found it brain-splitting toil"; and of which Voltaire wrote about the same time: "Have you read Necker's book, and if you have, did you understand it as you read?" The book such as it was, skilfully put together, half understood, half read, with its blending of oratorical and emotional passages with obscure theories, created the greatest impression in the then state of men's minds, and hastened the accession of M. Necker to the ministry.

His first ministry, which lasted five years, from October 22, 1776, to May 19, 1781, seems to me to have been treated with perfect justice by M. Droz, in his *Histoire de Louis XVI:* he does full justice to his noble aims, to his disinterestedness in the matter of money, to his zeal for the partial reformation of abuses, and to the various improvements, economic and humane, which he succeeded in introducing. At the

same time he points out M. Necker's weak side,—
his excessive fondness for praise, his veneration for
public opinion, which he at that time thought only
of following and of satisfying, without apparently sus-
pecting how worthless and fickle it was.  M. Necker
afterward regretted this early worship of opinion;
glancing backward after his second ministry, in 1791,
he cried, still with a sort of *naïveté:* "I do not quite
understand why public opinion is no longer what it
once was in my eyes.  The respect which I religiously
paid to it faded away when I saw how submissive it
was to the artifices of the evil-minded, when I saw it
tremble before the same men whom formerly it would
have summoned before its tribunal, to hold them up
to shame and to brand them with the stamp of its
reprobation."

But at the time of his first ministry, public opinion
in France, in the first society, seemed a spotless queen,
to whom a statesman whose aims were pure had
only to intrust himself without reserve in order to
walk in the straight path.  Therein lay M. Necker's
illusion, by virtue of which it appeared that he was
simply a man of boundless intellect, and not a really
great minister.  As a result of the excessive relaxation
of the ruling powers, of the degeneration of morals,
and of a sort of slow and universal dissolution, there
was no longer in the France of that day a substantial
and solid dike between the great mass of the nation
and the king; the various bodies and orders of the

State no longer had the strength to subsist by themselves, and to resist, on the day when their existence
should be seriously brought in question, and there
should be only a throne left standing, in the midst of a
vast, moving plain. Now, what was public opinion
in such a State? A vague breath, which, so long as
it was mild and favourable, suggested the idea of the
ocean during a calm, but which, so soon as it should
blow from a different quarter and become irritated,
would inevitably raise a tempest.

M. Necker, face to face with this public opinion
which he did not distrust, doubtless thought before
everything of doing what was right, always on condition that he should do it to his own greater honour
and glory. When, in January, 1781, he published his
famous *Compte Rendu au Roi,* and, himself a minister,
summoned the whole nation to discuss those perplex-
ing subjects, he could not resist the temptation to
glorify himself, and to congratulate himself upon his
early successes, rather than to devote his energies to
following them up in silence and strengthening their
foundations for the future. It was his pleasure to
represent himself, in the very first lines of this *Compte
Rendu,* as a man of self-abnegation and sacrifice; he
was capable of many sacrifices, it is true, always ex-
cepting that of the approbation which he hoped to
reap from them.

On leaving the ministry, to which he was not to
return for seven years, when circumstances would

prove to be too strong for him, he continued to live in society, encompassed by almost universal favour and adulation.[1] He wrote first of all upon the government, and upon political questions; but before long, seeking, in his instinct for meditation, a more exalted and vaster diversion amid the tedium of inaction, he composed his book *De l'Importance des Idées Religieuses,* and combated the false doctrines that were widespread about him. In the interval, he had conceived the idea of writing about men and their social characteristics, and, although he left only fragmentary remarks and *Pensées* upon this subject, he depicted himself perfectly in an unexpected aspect. M. Necker as a moralist is a very shrewd, very interesting, and too much neglected writer.

Kind-hearted, but inclined to be disdainful and unindulgent mentally, with very keen and discriminating powers of observation, he had reflected deeply upon the race of fools, who, according to him, swarm in this world. He thought that it was difficult for a

---

[1] The word adulation is none too strong. The enthusiasm that M. Necker aroused among his admirers resembled the fanaticism of a religious sect. Even the gentle and lovely Duchesse de Lauzun attacked in a public garden a stranger who spoke slightingly of M. Necker, shortly after his dismissal, and forgot herself so far as to insult him. The Comte de Crillon said one day : "If the universe and I should hold one opinion, and M. Necker should express a different one, I should at once be convinced that the universe and I were wrong." [Said Barnave : "Necker was the first man in our day to enjoy what is called popularity."—Tr.]

man to hold the opinion of himself which he ought
to hold.

"The men who deem themselves perfect are happy,
but ridiculous. The men who constantly find fault
with themselves are estimable but unfortunate. It is
hard to observe a just *milieu*. One should view oneself at a distance and pass judgment upon oneself
without partiality and without bitterness, as a simple
acquaintance."

But while passing judgment upon himself in this
way and in the capacity of a simple acquaintance, it
would seem that M. Necker was never dissatisfied with
himself.

The little essay which he entitled *Le Bonheur des
Sots* was extremely relished in society in the eighteenth century. Many people to-day, who are at odds
with M. Necker on account of his ministries, would
be reconciled to him if they should read this piquant
essay, wherein a man supposed to be serious-minded
proves himself as refined a satirist as ever Rulhière could
have been. They would learn there to know a Necker
who was not at all tedious. He lays it down as a
principle that "to be happy, one must be a fool."
Folly, in his judgment, is like that first garment of
skin which God bestowed upon Adam and Eve before
driving them from Paradise.

"This robe of skin, which is intended to cloak our
nudity, consists of the attractive errors, the sweet
confidences, the fearless judgment of ourselves,—

blissful gifts, to which our corrupt age has given the name of folly, and which our ingratitude seeks to misrepresent."

And he enumerates all the treasures which are contained therein. For example: the fool never learns by experience; though he should live two hundred years, nature would still be in his eyes young and fresh; there is no connection between his ideas; he rushes wildly about on the last day as on the first; to the end, he lives in the surprise and delight of childhood. Another blessing: a fool never doubts; he is never troubled by a multitude of ideas and of points of view; is never a prey to hesitation, that torment of men of intellect. The distinguishing characteristic of folly is always to take the limits of its vision for the limits of what really is. One can imagine all that an impassive, satirical pen could make of this outline. It is all done in a tone of persiflage, and with irony rather than merriment. In a clever postscript, M. Necker observes that there is a semi-folly which makes those who have inherited it very unhappy: the fools who have an idea that perhaps they are slightly foolish, the fools *who catch a glimpse of themselves,* are as unhappy as the genuine fools are happy. Despite this exception, which occurs to him as an afterthought, the general theory holds good, and there is surely one proverb lacking in the list: "Happy as a fool."

This charming paper, which resembles Fontenelle

and Marivaux even more than La Bruyère, entertained the eighteenth century immensely, and every one imagined that he recognised his neighbour therein. After reading it I still have one difficulty, and that is, how to reconcile, in the author, so shrewd and, in substance, so contemptuous a description of the folly considered by him to be almost universal since Adam, with his unbounded respect for mankind as a whole, and with his constant veneration of present opinion.

No matter what one may say, regret is inevitable upon ceasing to be a minister, especially when one has had the experience of M. Necker in his first ministry, surrounded by public approbation and applause. Marmontel was at Saint-Brice when he learned of M. Necker's disgrace; he hurried to Saint-Ouen to call upon him, and especially upon Madame Necker, to whom he had vowed unbounded regard. He passed the whole evening alone with them and a brother of M. Necker.

"Neither the husband nor the wife," he said, "concealed their profound depression from me. I tried to lessen it by speaking of the regret which they left in the public mind, and of the well-merited regard which would follow them in their retirement; wherein I did not flatter them. 'I do not regret,' said M. Necker to me, 'anything except the good that I still had to do, and that I would have done if they had given me time.'"

The various works which M. Necker composed in the following years (1781–1788) bear the stamp of that keen and tender sensibility which he takes no pains to conceal. It was to distract his thoughts, to relieve and occupy his mind, that he conceived the idea of his estimable work against the atheists, the unbelievers, and the mocking spirits of the time, which he entitled *De l'Importance des Idées Religieuses* (1788).

The striking thing about M. Necker in religious matters is his perfect sincerity, the profound and convincing sentiment which finds expression in his words, and which often replaces metaphysics by a touching moral lesson. In the fine passages there is something of the emotional preacher. At the time when Mirabeau was already stirring up his Provence, and when the signal for the States-General was ringing through the air, "What a time," cried M. Necker in conclusion, "what a time I have chosen to discourse to the world upon morality and religion! and, too, what a theatre this is for such an undertaking! Every one is busy about his harvest; every one lives in his own affairs; every one is swallowed up in the present moment."

I have mentioned the word "preacher"; that is the word which best befits the sort of talent that M. Necker displays in this class of ideas and of religious meditations. He realised it so well that, in 1800, toward the close of his life, he published a *Cours de Morale Religieuse,* divided into discourses which are supposed to be delivered by a pastor to his flock. I particularly recommend the one entitled *De l'Union Conjugale,* which overflows with sentiment and beauty. I find, in M. Necker's last thoughts, outbursts of hope which attain a sort of splendour of expression.

" There is some magnificent secret concealed behind this superb proscenium which forms the spectacle of the world."—" We will not believe that our imagination soars beyond the present time to supply us with a mere plaything ; we should not be worth the trouble of being deceived, of being deceived with such ostentation, if we were destined to enjoy only an ephemeral existence."

By these various religious works, in which he carefully avoided touching upon points which might have suggested disagreement with the Catholic Church, M. Necker, as we see, was one of the most honourable precursors of the great movement which burst forth at the beginning of the nineteenth century, and his collection of discourses antedated by only two years the *Génie du Christianisme.*[1]

Let us come now to the minister, that is to say, to the moral man in the minister, and let us scrutinise him. On re-entering politics, M. Necker retains all his honesty and his early modesty, but he recovers his sensitiveness, his "haughty judgment," his "proud heart" (it is himself who thus describes them), and the disdain which he readily forgets in solitary and placid meditation, but which reawakens in the presence of men. His political career is sharply divided into two parts. In his first ministry, which lasted five years, he struggles against the courtiers and against abuses, and he falls, he retires, because of his inflexibility and his lack of adroitness, before old Maurepas,

[1] [Chateaubriand's greatest work.—Tr.]

whom it was a question simply of wearing out and allowing to die. In his second and third ministries, which lasted two years in all, from August, 1788, to September, 1790, and which were separated by a brief exile, by a triumphant return, and by the ineffaceable date of the fourteenth of July,[1]—in these last two ministries, which really form but one, knowing what ground to take with respect to the Court and courtiers, M. Necker does not change his opinion concerning the common people and the main body of the nation; he transfers to them his illusions and his confidence; he conceives the idea of an altogether amiable, impressible nation, easy to guide and to lead back, free from corruption and from vices, and he does not abandon that idea until the last extremity. Failing again, this time before the Constituent Assembly and before Mirabeau, he cries once more, recurring to the moderate methods which he had projected to secure the salvation of France, and contrasting them to those which have prevailed:

"What methods have been preferred to mine! Whereas, with *a little* restraint in their theories, with *a little* regard for the oppressed, with *a little* consideration for the old-fashioned opinions, and above all with *a little* love and kindness, the whole of France might have been led back to happiness by bonds of silk." He wrote this at Coppet in 1791. At that date, he still believed that with all these "littles"

[1] [The Bastille fell on July 14, 1789.—TR.]

combined and accepted by all, he could have held out
against the torrent and transformed it into a placid
canal.

There is one work of M. Necker's which enables us
to study him as a man and as a politician, — I refer to
the apology for his administration, written by himself
in 1791, immediately after his retirement to Switzerland and before the Revolution had brought forth its
last excesses. This work, which is seldom read, is
equivalent to a confession. The author, still excited
by his fall and by the ingratitude of the Assembly,
and not foreseeing that, in the woes which are preparing to burst upon all heads, this premature retirement will prove to be a decided benefit to him,—in
fact, his salvation,—the author gives free rein to all his
thoughts; he lays bare his soul, all bleeding and groaning; he exhibits it in all its sensitiveness, in its amazement, in its sufferings of all sorts, in its natural,
honourable, upright, human passions.  He would not
have dared to write thus two years later, after 1793,
for he was surely one of the privileged ones of fate;
but in 1791 he believed himself to be a victim selected
out of all the rest, and he groaned in spirit.  In the
lyrical agitation of his heart, M. Necker at that moment considered no metaphor too lofty for his individual plight; amid all these reproaches of ingratitude
that he breathes forth, it still seems to him that he indulges in clemency: "Like the Prophet, having come
upon the mountain to curse, I remain only to bless."

Such a tremendous upheaval of the heart, although his situation was really bitter and painful, goes beyond what we have a right to expect from a steadfast states-man, who has measured in advance the roads over which he must travel; the fact is that M. Necker was nothing less than such a statesman, and he is the first to tell us so. Let us leave the details to the historian. Did M. Necker do well to play fast and loose as he did, as the session of the States-General drew near? to summon the Notables again, and to allow them to discuss the form of the approaching representation, instead of having a plan decided upon at the outset? Did he do well to wait so long before declaring in favour of the double representation of the Third Es-tate? to allow the Assembly to open its sessions, without compelling the king to take the initiative in the measures that were in dispute? to give the Orders time to become irritated in preliminary discussions which might have been cut short? Did he do well to repel in that first critical hour, by his scornful recep-tion of them, the sincere overtures of Mirabeau? Was he wrong or right not to be present at the royal sitting of the 23rd of June, when the king made a speech of which he did not approve? Let us lay aside all these questions and many others, which would only result in progress too slow and too indirect for us; but let us listen to himself in his apology and in his avowals.

It is very true that in the beginning of 1789 he found himself placed, as he says, between the throne and the nation, and invested with the twofold confidence of both, amid the greatest difficulties in which a minister was ever called upon to choose his course. His extraordinary claim, which condemns him at once, is that he committed no mistake.

"In such a situation," he says, "and amid the most ardent passions, in the centre of all the enmities and hatreds that were rife, there was evidently an opportunity every day to take some false step, and some false step of the utmost moment. That is a reflection which I often suggested to the king's other ministers; and although I am unfortunately inclined to be anxious; although throughout my life I have constantly cast my eyes backward in order to judge myself anew in respect to matters that have passed; although my mind is thus burdened with all the remorse in which my conscience has never had a share,—nevertheless, and to my own amazement, I seek in vain for anything to reproach myself for."

A surprising result in very truth, and one which, if I may venture to suggest as much, is well adapted to characterise the whole flock of doctrinaire minds after their fall. Though the State had crumbled after them, and partly through their instrumentality, be well assured that they never made any mistake; they had nothing to reproach themselves for, and with their hands on their hearts and their heads erect in God's sight they would swear it. In M. Necker, the first, the purest in intention, and the most innocent of them all, this fearlessness of conscience and this assurance of impeccability were combined with a strain of *bonhomie*. Many people since his day have spoken of the perfect harmony between morality and politics; he did not simply speak of it, he believed in it, and guided his conduct by it as scrupulously as possible under all circumstances; but he understood morality in the strict and special sense of the good man acting in the sphere of private life.

The moment of vertigo and of intoxication, the apogee of his life, was his return after the fourteenth of July, when he received at Bâle letters from the king and from the National Assembly, recalling him. His return to France was a triumph. The first impulse of his kind heart was to demand the cessation of violent measures, pardon and amnesty for those who were being prosecuted, and who were already being murdered as enemies of the nation. He obtained everything that he asked at the Hôtel de Ville, at the outset, and he expressed the feelings by which he was then agitated in terms which do honour to the man and which also show how readily his hopes were aroused:

"I wish that I had enough room," he says, after giving us the amnesty decree prepared at the Hôtel de Ville, "to transcribe here the names of all of those,—such a vast number,—who benefit by this memorable act. I shall never forget you, who have caused me to enjoy for a moment the ecstasy of a century,—you, my only benefactors! Ah! how happy I was that day! Each of those moments is engraved on my memory. I had obtained the return of peace, I had obtained it without other means than the language of reason and of virtue; that thought laid hold upon me through all the emotions of my heart, and I thought for a moment that I was between heaven and earth. Ah! how happy I was as I returned to Versailles! but alas! as I have said, that felicity, that too sublime joy, was of brief duration!"

After his return to France, at the end of July, 1789,

M. Necker's influence rapidly diminished and faded away; the leading spirits of the Assembly made it their business to foil him and to ruin his popularity in every way, at the same time that the Court faction was incessantly making sport of him and annoying him with the utmost bitterness. He was between two fires. He continued to render daily services for the subsistence of the capital and to provide for the needs of the treasury; but he was soon to be outstripped and made of no account in financial matters by an Assembly which decreed the seizure of the property of the clergy and the issue of *assignats*. When he left the ministry, in September, 1790, and went away from France for ever, a little more than a year after his splendid triumph, M. Necker was forgotten. It was this indifference which tore his heart more than all the rest. In the work published by him, and intended to combat this indifference, he enumerated all the claims that he had to the gratitude of the nation, and did not forget to add the money that was owed him. He had always been disinterested in such matters; he had declined during his various ministries the salary of minister of finance and the perquisites which were attached to that office; he did not hesitate to recall that fact with a pomp which certainly balanced his disinterestedness. "And so," he cried, "the National Assembly can treat me with indifference at its pleasure,—I shall none the less continue to be a creditor of the State in several ways, and never have I enjoyed that privilege so much, never have I borne myself more magnificently."

The misfortunes of others, especially those of his virtuous king, abated his own chagrin to some extent, and in the following years he recovered his moderation of thought and the control of his pen when he wrote. The works which he subsequently composed in the capacity of spectator, and whose subject was the French Revolution considered in the various phases of its development, contain a multitude of judicious, subtle, elevated ideas, and the most honourable aspirations. During the Reign of Terror, he wrote some philosophical reflections upon the false idea of equality; he set forth the sense in which, according to his opinion, we ought to understand that men are equal in God's sight; and there again we find the traces of that aristocracy of mind of which even the Christian in M. Necker could never rid himself.

"O God!" he said, "all men are equal doubtless before Thee, when they commune with thy goodness, when they address their complaints to Thee, and when their happiness engages thine attention; but if Thou hast permitted that there should be an image of Thee upon earth, if Thou hast at all events permitted finite beings to exalt themselves to the conception of thine everlasting existence, it is only to man in his perfection that Thou hast granted this precious privilege; to the man who has succeeded by degrees in developing the noble system of his moral faculties; in a word, to man, *when he shows himself in all the glory of his intellect.*"

"The glory of the intellect!" It seems to me that that is not exactly the doctrine of the Gospel; it seems to me that the apostle, and after him Saint Augustine, Bossuet, and all the great Christians, have remarked this very glory and pride of the intellect as one of the most subtle perils and most to be dreaded by lofty minds.

Once rescued from the tempest and seated upon the shore, M. Necker becomes once more a very distinguished political writer and essayist; he analyses and criticises the various Constitutions which succeeded one another in France,—those of '91, of '93, of the year III, of the year VIII; he readily picks out their vices or their defects; then it is that he suggests and perfects at leisure his ideal of a limited monarchy and a government after the English form, to which he had given very little thought in the days when he held the helm. Disappointed and spurned in the present, he concludes almost all his works by eloquent and trustful appeals to the future, which is always vast and obscure enough to give, like the ancient oracles, responses to suit everybody.

In 1802 M. Necker published his *Dernières Vues de Politique et de Finance.* He continued to render public homage to the First Consul; considering the First Consul as a brilliant exception, and the Constitution of the year VIII as transitory, he tried to establish by theory the foundations of a more durable establishment. And herein he betrays himself most delightfully in all the natural indecision of his ideas: he proposes at the same time two parallel plans,—one a perfect republic, the other a model monarchy; he constructs these two plans in turn with great skill in analysis, he balances them against each other, and having weighed them well in every point, he says to the man whom he has proclaimed to be necessary: "Take one of my plans or take the other." And if he takes neither of them, he finds consolation in the sight of his own ideal, and, like all self-satisfied theorists, he appeals to the future, and to that common sense which, in his judgment, is sooner or later "the arbiter of human life." It is interesting to observe how we always enjoin upon future generations the common sense which it is supposed that we have not.

M. Necker died at Coppet on March 30, 1894, in his seventy-second year.

# Marie=Antoinette.

## 1755–1793.

## Marie=Antoinette.

A MONG the works which are calculated to afford a just idea of Queen Marie-Antoinette and her character in the years of her youth and prosperity, I know of none which more effectively carries conviction to the reader's mind than the simple *Notice* of the Comte de la Marck, inserted by M. de Bacourt in the introduction to his recently published work upon Mirabeau. The Comte de la Marck sketches the queen's domestic life in a few pages marked by the closest observation. We see there a genuine and natural, not an exaggerated Marie-Antoinette. We foresee the errors in which her surroundings will inevitably involve her, those which will be attributed to her, and the weapons which she will unconsciously furnish to malignity. We regret that an observer so impartial and so superior has not drawn a similar portrait of the queen at the various epochs of her life, down to the hour when she became a noble victim, and when the lofty qualities of her heart manifested themselves so clearly as to impress and interest all mankind.

There is one way of viewing Marie-Antoinette

which seems to me the true way, and which I should like to define, because it seems to me that the final judgment of history should be formed from that standpoint. A person may, influenced by an exalted feeling of compassion, become imbued with an ideal interest in Marie-Antoinette, be moved to defend her upon every point, to constitute himself her advocate, her true knight, against all men, to be indignant at the bare idea of the blemishes and weaknesses which others fancy that they discover in her life; such a rôle of defender is worthy of respect if it is sincere, and it can readily be imagined in those who professed the cult of the old-time royalty, but it touches me much less in the case of new-comers in whom it can be nothing more than a deliberate *parti pris*. Such a standpoint is not mine; it can hardly be adopted by men who have not been reared in the religion of the old monarchy; and such is, as everybody must agree, the case with the immense majority of the present generation and of those which are to come. What seems to me much more to be desired, in the very interest of this affecting memory of Marie-Antoinette, is that there shall come forth, from the multitude of writings and testimonies of which she has been the subject, a lovely, noble, gracious figure, with her weaknesses, her frivolities, her fragility it may be, but with the essential qualities of a woman, a mother, and at times a queen, retained in all their integrity, with the kindness of heart of every generous epoch, and,

MARIE ANTOINETTE
*From a portrait by Le Brun*

finally, with the merits of resignation, of courage, and of gentleness, which fitly crown great misfortunes. Once historically established in this way, she will continue to interest in future ages all those who, becoming more and more indifferent to the political forms of the past, retain the refined and humane sentiments which are a part of civilisation as of nature; all those who weep over the misfortunes of Hecuba and of Andromache, and who, when they read the narrative of such and even greater misfortunes, will be touched by hers.

But there is this difference,—that poetry alone has undertaken to hand down the tradition of Andromache and Hecuba, and that we have no memoirs of the Court of Priam; whereas we have memoirs of the Court of Louis XVI, and there is no way to avoid taking them into account. What do these memoirs say of Marie-Antoinette ? I mean the real memoirs, not the libels. What does the Comte de la Marck say, who well represents the spirit of that first period ? Arrived in France at the age of fifteen, the young dauphiness was not yet nineteen when she found herself seated on the throne beside Louis XVI. That prince, fortified by a substantial education and endowed with all the moral qualities that we know, but weak, timid, abrupt, rough, and especially unattractive with women, had none of those qualities that were essential to guide his young wife. She, the daughter of an illustrious mother, had not been reared by Maria-Theresa herself,

who was too much engrossed by affairs of State, and
her early education at Vienna had been sadly neglected. No one had ever imparted to her the taste for
serious reading. Her mind, which was reasonably
judicious and quick, "grasped and understood the
things about which people spoke to her"; but it
was not of great scope, and, in a word, had none of
those qualities which atone for lack of education, or
take the place of experience. Amiable, high-spirited,
and innocently satirical, she had above all else great
kindness of heart and a persistent desire to oblige
those persons who applied to her. She had an intense longing for affection and intimacy, and she at
once sought some person with whom she could become intimate, contrary to the custom at Court.
Evidently her ideal of happiness was, on her release
from the ceremonious scenes which bored her terribly, to find a merry, laughing, devoted, select circle,
in which she seemed to forget that she was a queen,
although in reality she remembered it perfectly. She
loved, if I may so express it, to indulge herself in the
pleasure of thus forgetting, and suddenly to remind
herself what she really was, only to lavish favours
upon all about her. We have seen, in opera-comiques
and in pastoral plays, disguised queens who are the
delight and the joy of those who surround them.
Marie-Antoinette had that ideal of a happy life, which
she might have realised without inconvenience if she
had simply reigned in some kingdom like Tuscany or

Lorraine. But in France she could not even try it
with impunity, and her Petit-Trianon, with its dai-
ries, its sheepfolds, and its theatricals, was too near
Versailles. Envy prowled about those too-favoured
spots,—envy beckoning to stupidity and slander.

M. de la Marck has convincingly pointed out the
disadvantage in the queen's confining herself at first
so exclusively to the circle of the Comtesse Jules de
Polignac, in giving to her, with the rank of a friend,
the attitude of a favourite, and to all the men of that
circle, the Vaudreuils, the Besenvals, and the Adhém-
ars, pretensions and privileges which they so speedily
abused, each according to his humour and his ambition. Although she never realised the full extent of
these disadvantages, she did detect something of
them; she felt that, where she sought repose and
relaxation from her exalted rank, she still found selfish
obsession; and when her attention was called to the
fact that she often manifested too much preference for
foreigners of distinction who were travelling in France,
and that that might injure her in the minds of the
French, she would reply sadly: "You are right, but
at all events they do not ask me for anything."

Some of the men who, being admitted into this
intimate circle, and to the queen's favour, were in
honour bound to all the more gratitude and respect,
were the first to speak slightingly of her, because they
did not find her sufficiently docile to their schemes.
As she seemed at one time to draw away a little

from the Polignac circle and to frequent the salon of
Madame d'Ossun, the lady of the bedchamber, an
habitué of the Polignac salon (whom M. de la Marck
does not name, but who seems to have been one of
the most influential members of that circle) wrote a
very spiteful couplet against the queen, and this couplet, based upon an infamous lie, circulated through
Paris. Thus it was that the Court itself and the
queen's intimate circle furnished the first leaven
which became blended with the coarse insults and
infamies on the outside. For her part, she knew
nothing of all this, and had no suspicion of the things
which were arousing disaffection against her at Versailles, any more than of those things which were
alienating people's hearts from her at Paris. To this
day, when one desires to quote some testimony which
will arouse feeling against Marie-Antoinette, the testimony of some one of importance, he seeks it in the
memoirs of the Baron de Besenval.

Summoned to her presence in 1778, at the time of
the duel between the Comte d'Artois and the Duc de
Bourbon, M. de Besenval was introduced by Campan (secretary of the cabinet) into a room with which
he was not familiar, simply but conveniently furnished. "I was surprised," he adds in passing, "not
that the queen had desired so many facilities, but that
she had dared to provide herself with them." This
simple phrase, thrown in as an aside, is full of insin-
uation, and her enemies did not fail to seize upon it.

But I will deal with hidden meanings no more than I must, and will not hesitate to touch the most delicate point. There are people whose one thought it is to deny absolutely all frivolity and all aberrations of the heart on the part of Marie-Antoinette. For my own part, I make bold to think that the interest which is attached to her memory, that the compassion aroused by her unhappy fate and the noble way in which she bore it, that the execration which her judges and her executioner deserve, do not in any wise depend upon any anterior discovery relating to female frivolity, nor are at all diminished thereby. Now, in the present state of historical information concerning Marie-Antoinette, if we give due weight to genuine testimony, and at the same time remember what we have heard from the mouths of well-informed contemporaries, it is perfectly legitimate to think that that affectionate and high spirited person, governed entirely by impulse, in love with refined manners and chivalrous customs, longing simply to pour out her heart and to be understood, may very well have had some preference during these fifteen years of her youth; if the contrary were true, it would be much more extraordinary. However, many ambitious men and many coxcombs entered the lists and failed; there were overtures and assaults without number. Lauzun described his experience in his own way; the fact is that, in one way or another, he failed. The Prince de Ligne came frequently to France during those years,

and he was one of those foreigners, wholly French in
his tastes and altogether attractive, with whom the
queen was particularly pleased. He had the honour
of riding with her in the morning.

" It was," he says, " during these rides, when I was alone with the
queen, although surrounded by her gorgeous royal suite, that she told
me a thousand interesting anecdotes concerning herself, and all the
snares that had been laid for her in order to trick her into having lovers. At one time it was the Noailles family that wanted her to take
the Viscount, at another time the Choiseul clique that destined Biron
[Lauzun] for her, who, afterward!—but he was virtuous then. The
Duchesse de Duras, when she was on duty, accompanied us in our
rides; but we left her with the equerries, and that was one of the
queen's thoughtless acts and one of her greatest crimes, since she was
guilty of nothing more than negligence with respect to the bores
of both sexes, who are always unforgiving."

Here we have the complement of Lauzun's narrative
and the queen's own version thereof. I will observe,
however, that it was not at all probable that Lauzun
acted in the interest of the Choiseul clique, with
whom he was always on ill terms; but those about
the queen had an interest in presenting him in that
aspect, in order to ruin him for good and all.

It was this same Prince de Ligne who said of her
elsewhere: "Her alleged gallantry was never anything more than a profound feeling of friendship,
more marked, it may be, for one or two persons, and
the general coquettish desire of a woman and a queen
to please everybody." This impression, or conjecture,
which I find also in other shrewd observers who saw
Marie-Antoinette at close quarters, is, I think, the most

probable. These *two persons* whom she especially distinguished at different times seem to have been, first, the Duc de Coigny, a sagacious and already mature man, and, secondly, M. de Fersen, colonel of the royal Swedish regiment in the French service, a man of exalted and chivalric character, who, in the days of evil fortune, betrayed himself only by his utter devotion.

However, when we come to these intimate and secret details concerning which it is so easy to find innumerable hints and so difficult to acquire certainty, I think that it is well to remember the sensible remark which Madame de Lassay (the natural daughter of a Condé) made one day to her husband, whom she heard discussing and attacking the virtue of Madame de Maintenon; she gazed at him in amazement and said to him, with admirable sang-froid: "How does it happen, monsieur, that you are so certain of these things ?"

The queen's beauty in her youth has been enthusiastically praised. She was not a beauty, if we take her features in detail: the eyes, although expressive, were not very fine, her aquiline nose seemed too pronounced. "I am not quite sure that her nose belonged to her face," said a clever observer. Her lower lip was more prominent and thick than one expects in a pretty woman; her figure also was a little full; but the general effect was of a noble manner and sovereign dignity. Even in négligé hers was the beauty of a queen, rather than of a woman of fashion.

" No woman," said M. de Meilhan, " ever carried her head better, and it was so set upon her shoulders that every movement she made was instinct with grace and nobility. Her gait was stately, yet light, and recalled Virgil's phrase, ' *incessu patuit dea.*' And there was in her person a still rarer quality,—the union of grace and of the most imposing dignity."

Add a dazzlingly fresh complexion, beautiful arms and hands, a charming smile, and tactful speech which found its inspiration less in the mind than in the heart, in the desire to be kind and to please.

For a long while this gracious creature, full of confidence in the prestige of royalty, and with no other thought than to temper it slightly in her own circle, paid no heed to politics, or at all events only at intervals, and when she was, as it were, driven to the wall by her intimate friends. She continued her life of illusions even when hateful remarks, satirical verses, and execrable pamphlets were being circulated in Paris, imputing to her a secret and constant influence which she never had. The affair of the necklace was the first signal of her misfortunes, and the bandage which had covered her eyes up to that date was torn away. She began to emerge from her enchanted village, and to know the world as it is when it has an interest in being cruel. When she was induced to give her attention regularly to public affairs and to form an opinion upon the extraordinary measures and occurrences which daily compelled attention, she brought thereto the least politic disposition that can be imagined,—I mean, indignation against the prevailing cowardice, personal prejudices over which her manifest interest did not always enable her to triumph, a resentment of insults which was not thirst for vengeance but rather the shrinking and proud suffering of wounded dignity. If Louis XVI had been a different man, and if he had offered any opportunity for a vigorous and enthusiastic impelling force, there is no doubt that at some time or other, under the queen's inspiration, he would have attempted some enterprise which might well have been a reckless one, but which perhaps would have re-established for a while the tottering monarchical system. But nothing of the sort took place; Louis XVI's mind escaped and shrank from acting his rôle of king by reason of his very virtues; his nature, which was a mixture of piety and humanity, always inclined to sacrifice, and passing from one weakness to another, he was destined never to become great again until he became a martyr. The queen had not those qualities which she needed to triumph over such utter incapacity and inertia on the part of the king. She had flashes of energy, but there was no coherence. This is the complaint that constantly recurs under the pen of the Comte de la Marck in the secret correspondence which has just been published.

" The queen," he wrote to the Comte de Mercy-Argenteau on December 30, 1790, " the queen certainly has the intellect and strength of mind to do great things; but it must be confessed, and you have had a better opportunity than I to notice it, that, whether in business, or simply in conversation, she does not always display that degree of

attention which is indispensable to learn thoroughly what it is necessary to know in order to guard against errors and to make sure of
success."

And again, to the same correspondent, September
28, 1791:

" I must speak plainly,— the king is incapable of reigning and the
queen, if well supported, might make up for his incapacity; but even
that would not be enough: it is essential also that the queen should
realise the necessity of attending to public affairs with some method
and order; that she should make it a rule no longer to grant a sort of
half-confidence to many people, but that she should give her entire
confidence to the one man whom she may choose to support her."

And again, on October 10, 1791:

" The queen, with abundant intelligence and tried courage, nevertheless allows all the opportunities of seizing upon the reins of government and surrounding the king with faithful subjects, devoted to her
service and to serving the State with her and through her,—all these
opportunities she allows to escape her."

In truth, one does not recover in a day from so long-
continued and habitual frivolity; it would have been
none too great an exploit for the genius of a Catherine
of Russia to contend against dangers so unforeseen
by her who had never opened a volume of history in
her life, and who had dreamed of a royalty of idleness
at Trianon; it is enough that her past frivolity had in
no wise impaired or deteriorated her heart, and that
when the test came it approved itself as noble, as
proud, as regal, and as fully endowed as it could have
been when it came from the hands of nature.

I do not propose to discuss the political course

which Marie-Antoinette thought it well to adopt when she was abandoned to her own resources. We are no constitutional purists; what she desired was certainly not the Constitution of '91, but the salvation of the throne, the salvation of France as she understood it, the king's honour and her own, the honour of the nobility, and the integrity of the inheritance which she hoped to bequeath to her children; do not ask her for anything more. Those letters of hers which have already been published, and others which will be published some day, enable us to establish this portion of history with certainty. She desired the salvation of the State through her brother the emperor, through foreign powers, but not through the émigrés. She could not contain her indignation against them. "The cowards," she cried, "after deserting us, have the assurance to demand that we alone should expose ourselves to danger, and that we alone should serve their interests!"

In a very noble letter, addressed to the Comte de Mercy-Argenteau, in which these words occur, she also said, after setting forth the details of a desperate plan (August, 1791):

"I have listened, as well as I could, to people on both sides, and from all their opinions I have formed my own; I do not know whether it will be followed,—you know the person with whom I have to deal [the king]: just when I think that he is persuaded, a word, an argument, makes him change unwittingly; and that is why innumerable things cannot be undertaken. However, whatever happens, retain your friendship and your attachment to me; I need them sadly, and

be assured, that no matter what misfortune may pursue me, I may
yield to the force of circumstances, but I shall never consent to anything unworthy of me; only in misfortune does one realise what one
really is. My blood flows in my son's veins, and I hope that some
day he will show himself a worthy grandson of Maria Theresa."

The last ray of joy and of hope that she knew was
at the time of the flight to Varennes. At the moment
when this so long postponed journey was at last about
to be undertaken, toward midnight, the queen, as she
crossed the Carrousel on foot, toward the carriage
made ready for the royal family by M. de Fersen,
passed M. de Lafayette's carriage; she recognised it,
and she actually indulged a fantastic impulse to try to
touch all the wheels with a switch which she held
in her hands. It was an innocent revenge. That tap
with the switch was, as it were, her last outburst of
gaiety. Three days later, how different was the prospect! The moment that Madame Campan met her
after the return from Varennes, the queen removed
her hat and bade her see the effect which sorrow had
produced upon her hair: "In a single night it had become as white as that of a woman of seventy!" She
was thirty-six!

The queen's last two years would suffice to redeem,
a thousand times over, more errors than that refined
and charming young woman could possibly have
committed in her years of frivolity, and to sanctify
such a destiny in the compassion of future ages. A
prisoner in her own family, subject to incessant an-
guish of mind, we see her become purified beside that

saintlike sister, Madame Élisabeth, and arm herself more and more with those sentiments of domesticity which afford such entire consolation only to hearts that are naturally kind and not corrupt. On the fatal day, the day of insurrection and uprising, when every part of her abode is invaded, she is at her post; she endures insult with pride, with dignity, with clemency, at the same time that she shields her children with her own body; amid her own perils, she is entirely engrossed, in her kindness of heart, by the perils of others, and she displays the utmost anxiety to compromise no one uselessly in her cause. On the last day, the supreme day of royalty, the Tenth of August, she tries to impart to Louis XVI an enthusiasm which would have caused him to die like a king, like a descendant of Louis XIV; but it was as a Christian and as a descendant of Saint Louis that he was destined to die.

In her turn she enters upon that path of heroism all instinct with resignation and patience. Once imprisoned in the Temple, she works at her tapestry, attends to the education of her son and daughter, composes a prayer for her children, and accustoms herself to drink the bitter cup in silence. The head of the Princess of Lamballe, held against the bars of her window, caused her to feel the first shudder of death. When she left the Temple to be transferred to the Conciergerie, she struck her head against the wicket, having forgotten to stoop. Some one asked if she had hurt herself.

"Oh, no!" she replied, "nothing can hurt me now." But every moment of her agony has been described, and it is not for us to repeat it. In my opinion, it is impossible to imagine a monument of more atrocious stupidity and more ignominious to the human race than the trial of Marie-Antoinette, as it is officially reported in Volume XXIX of the *Histoire Parliamentaire de la Révolution Française.* Most of the answers which she made to the charges are mutilated or suppressed, but, as in every iniquitous prosecution, the mere text of the charges testifies against the assassins. When we reflect that an age called an age of enlightenment and of the most refined civilisation resorted to public acts of such utter barbarity, we begin to doubt human nature and to shrink from the savage beast, no less bestial than savage in very truth, which human nature holds sometimes within itself, and which asks nothing better than to come forth.

Immediately after her sentence, when she had been taken back from the Tribunal to the Conciergerie, Marie-Antoinette wrote a letter dated October 16th, at half-past four in the morning, and addressed to Madame Élisabeth. In this letter, which is marked by the utmost simplicity, we read:

"To you, my sister, I write for the last time. I have been sentenced, not to a shameful death,—for it is shameful only to criminals, —but to join your brother. Innocent like him, I hope to display the same firmness that he did in these final moments. I am calm as one is calm when conscience has no reproach to make; I profoundly regret having to abandon my poor children. You know that I have existed solely for them; and you, my dear and loving sister, you who through your love sacrificed everything to be with us,—in what a position I leave you!"

The most sincere sentiments of the mother, of the friend, of the refined Christian, breathe in this testamentary letter. We know that Marie-Antoinette gave proof, a few hours later, of that tranquillity and steadfastness which she hoped to command at the last moment; and even the report of the executioners admits that she mounted the scaffold "with reasonable courage."

I think that we have not even yet all the elements to write with befitting simplicity the life of Marie-Antoinette; there are in existence manuscript collections of letters to her brother the Emperor Joseph, and to the Emperor Leopold, and the Chancellery of Vienna must contain treasures of this description. But I venture to prophesy that the publication of these confidential documents, if it ever takes place, will simply confirm the idea that reflection and a careful perusal of the extant memoirs may well afford to-day. Marie-Antoinette's noble mother, from whom she inherited that eagle nose and that regal bearing, imprinted upon her the seal of her race; but that imperial temperament, which appeared at critical moments, was not the habitual temperament of her mind, of her education, and of her dreams; she appeared as the daughter of the Cæsars only by flashes. She was made to be the peaceful and slightly rustic heiress of the Empire, rather than to conquer her kingdom for herself ; most of all, beneath that august brow, she was made to be a lovable wife, a loyal and constant friend, a tender and devoted mother.  She had all the good qualities and the charms, and some of the weaknesses too, of woman.  Adversity supplied her with womanly virtues; elevation of the heart and dignity of character manifested themselves with the more splendour because they were not accompanied by a mind altogether equal to the circumstances of her destiny. Such as she is, a victim of the most detestable and most brutal of sacrifices, an example of the most horrible of vicissitudes, she does not need that the veneration for ancient families should still exist to arouse a feeling of sympathy and of tender compassion in all those who read the story of her brilliant years and of her last agony.  Every man who has in his heart any touch of the generosity of a Barnave will experience the same impression, and, if it must be said, the same conversion that he experienced on approaching that noble and bitterly outraged figure. As for the women, Madame de Staël long ago said to them the word best fitted to go to their hearts, in her defence of Marie-Antoinette: "I turn again to you, to you women, sacrificed one and all in so loving a mother, sacrificed one and all by so murderous an attack upon womanly weakness; it is all over with your empire if brutal ferocity is to hold sway."

In truth, Marie-Antoinette is even more mother than

queen. Every one knows the first words that fell from her, when, being as yet only dauphiness, somebody reproved in her presence a woman, who, to obtain the pardon of her son, who had been involved in a duel, had appealed to Madame Du Barry herself: "If I had been in her place, I would have done the same, and if necessary I would have thrown myself at the feet of Zamore" [Madame Du Barry's little negro page].

And we know also that last remark of Marie-Antoinette before the atrocious Tribunal, when, being questioned concerning certain shocking imputations, which assailed the innocence of her son, her only reply was to exclaim: "I appeal to all mothers!" That is the supreme outcry which dominates her life, the outcry which goes to the inmost heart, and which will echo in her behalf in ages to come.

# PORTRAITS OF THE EIGHTEENTH CENTURY

## *Collation of Texts*

For the benefit of those readers who may want to compare these translations to the original, the following table indicates the sources and dates of each essay. A detailed collation has not been included in the collection as being specialized in interest and too cumbersome to tabulate. It has, however, seemed vital to an understanding of Saint-Beuve's original articles to give the date and reference to the ones which appear here. The references are to the standard current editions of his works.

| | | |
|---|---|---|
| C.L. | *Causeries du Lundi* (1870 edition) | 15 vols. |
| P.L. | *Portraits littéraires* (1862 edition) | 3 vols. |

## *Volume II*

1. ABBÉ PRÉVOST

| | | |
|---|---|---|
| p. 3-30 | Sept. 25, 1831 | P.L. I, 265-286 |
| 30-31 | Nov. 7, 1853 | C.L. IX, 134 |
| 31-32 | Sept. 25, 1831 | P.L. I, 286-288 |
| 33 | Nov. 7, 1853 | C.L. IX, 138 |
| 33-34 | Sept. 25, 1831 | P.L. I, 288-289 |

2. MADAME DE LAMBERT and MADAME NECKER

| | | |
|---|---|---|
| | June 9,1851 | C.L. IV, 217-261 |

3. DENIS DIDEROT

| | | |
|---|---|---|
| p. 89-98 | June 26, 1831 | P.L. I, 239-246 |
| 99 | Jan. 20, 1851 | C.L. III, 294-295 |
| 99-105 | June 26, 1831 | P.L. I, 246-253 |
| 105-106 | Jan. 20, 1851 | C.L. III, 295 |
| 106 | June 26, 1831 | P.L. I, 253-254 |
| 107 | Jan. 20, 1851 | C.L. III, 296 |
| 107-109 | June 26, 1831 | P.L. I, 254-257 |
| 109-119 | Jan. 20, 1851 | C.L. III, 299-311 |
| 119-122 | June 26, 1831 | P.L. I, 258-259 |
| 122-124 | Jan. 20, 1851 | C.L. III, 311-313 |
| 124-125 | June 26, 1831 | P.L. I, 259-261 |

4. JEAN-JACQUES ROUSSEAU
p. 129-145    Apr. 29, 1850    C.L. II, 63-84
   145-168    Nov. 4, 1850     C.L. III, 78-97
   168 170    Apr. 29, 1850    C.L. II, 81-82
5. FRIEDRICH MELCHIOR GRIMM
p. 173-197    Jan. 10, 1853    C.L. VII, 287-307
   197-218    Jan. 17, 1853    C.L. VII, 308-328
6. MADAME D'EPINAY
              June 10, 1850    C.L. II, 187-207
7. BUFFON
p. 245-251    July 21, 1851    C.L. IV, 348-352
                          p. 247-l. 7–248 l. 17 in neither text
   252-261    July 21, 1851    C.L. IV, 352-363
   261-267    Apr. 10, 1854    C.L. X, 58-64
   267-272    July 21, 1851    C.L. IV, 364-368
   272-273    Apr. 10, 1854    C.L. X, 71-72
8. BERNARDIN DE SAINT-PIERRE
p. 277-278    Aug. 30, 1852    C.L. VI, 415
   278-279    Oct. 1836        P.L. II, 112-113
   279-296    Aug. 30, 1852    C.L. VI, 416-432
   296-313    Sept. 6, 1852    C.L. VI, 436-455
9. FREDERICK THE GREAT
p. 317-334    Dec. 2, 1850     C.L. III, 144-164
   334-349    Dec. 16, 1850    C.L. III, 185-205
10. WILHELMINA, MARGRAVINE OF BAIREUTH
p. 353-367    Sept. 1, 1856    C.L. XII, 395-413
   368-379    Sept. 8, 1856    C.L. XII, 414-431
11. BEAUMARCHAIS
p. 383-397    June 14, 1852    C.L. VI, 201-219
   397-413    June 21, 1852    C.L. VI, 220-241
   413-425    June 28, 1852    C.L. VI, 242-257
12. JACQUES JECKER
p. 429-443    Jan. 24, 1853    C.L. VII, 329-347
   443-454    Jan. 31, 1853    C.L. VII, 350-369
13. MARIE-ANTOINETTE
              July 14, 1851    C.L. IV, 330-346